The Spirit of the Living God

The Doctrine of the Holy Spirit

A Study in the Series on Systematic Theology
in Relation to the Holy Spirit

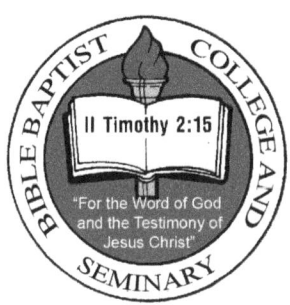

by

Pastor Michael D. McCubbins, Th.D., President
Bible Baptist College and Seminary
Arleta, California

© Copyright 2021 by Michael David McCubbins, Th.D.

ISBN: 978-1-63073-362-9

eBook ISBN: 978-1-63073-363-6

Published by Express Image Publishers
Bible Baptist College and Seminary
20422 Tuba Street
Chatsworth, California 91311

Designed & Distributed by:
Faithful Life Publishers
North Fort Myers, FL 33903
FaithfulLifePublishers.com
info@FaithfulLifePublishers.com

All Scripture quotes, unless otherwise noted, are from The Holy Bible: King James Version, (1995), electronic ed. of the 1769 edition of the 1611 Authorized Version. Bellingham WA: Logos Research Systems, Inc."

24 23 22 21   1 2 3 4 5

Contents

– Introduction to Pneumatology 1

Chapter 1 – The Deity of the Holy Spirit 33

Chapter 2 – The Personality of the Holy Spirit 72

Chapter 3 – The Ministry of the Holy Spirit between the
    Old and the New Testament 88

Chapter 4 – The Baptism and the Filling of the Holy Spirit 127

Chapter 5 – The Gifts of the Holy Spirit 158

Chapter 6 – The Relationship of the Holy Spirit
    to the Works of God 187

Chapter 7 – The Names and Symbols of the Holy Spirit 229

Acknowledgments

I want to thank Haylee Nicole and Elsie Grace Moon for
the graphic design on the front cover

I would like to thank the following people for
the many hours spent in editing this volume:

Mrs. Elaine F. McCubbins

Mrs. Lisa J. Moon

Mrs. Anita Fordyce

Introduction to Pneumatology

In today's world, there are an abundance of extremely heretical teachings about the Person, work, and attributes of the Holy Spirit. For that reason, it is very important to know what God says in the Bible about the Holy Spirit. The study of the doctrine of the Holy Spirit is called Pneumatology. There are many errors being propagated by cults that seem to control the conversation about the Holy Spirit, and there are few books being published that contradict these errors or teach the truth about the Third Person of the Trinity. The majority of books, it seems to me, either ignore Him, or overemphasize Him while ignoring the other Persons of the Godhead.

The word "Pneumatology" comes from two Greek words which are πνεῦμα [pneuma] and λόγια [logia]. Let's consider the meaning of these two words. The lexicon[1] defines the word πνεῦμα [pneuma] as:

> πνεῦμα (pneuma), ατος (atos), τό (to): a neuter noun; 1. Holy Spirit (Mk 1:12); 2. spirit, non material being (Jn 4:24; Ac 23:8); 3. evil spirit (Mt 8:16); 4. ghost (Lk 24:37, 39); 5. inner being, non material faculty that can respond to God (Ac 17:16; Eph 5:9); 6. way of thinking, attitude, disposition (Gal 6:1); 7. wind (Jn 3:8); 8. breath (2Th 2:8).

The Greek word λόγια [logia], ων, τό is defined in the lexicon[2] as:

---
1 Swanson, J. (1997). *Dictionary of Biblical Languages with Semantic Domains: Greek (New Testament)* (electronic ed.). Oak Harbor: Logos Research Systems, Inc. #4460.
2 Ibid. #3359

λόγια (*logia*), ων (*ōn*), τό (*to*): a neuter noun [served by λόγιον [(*logion*)]; (pl.) sayings, words, oracles (Ac 7:38; Ro 3:2; Heb 5:12; 1Pe 4:11)

The word "Pneumatology" therefore, means the doctrine of the Holy Spirit. The importance of this doctrine is evidenced by the fact that various aspects of the doctrine were covered in the series of essays[3] called *The Fundamentals: a Testimony to the Truth*. Many of the essays referenced the doctrine of the Holy Spirit in part, or in whole. A few of the articles that dealt with this doctrine were titled, "The Personality and Deity of the Holy Spirit" by R. A. Torrey, "The Holy Spirit and the Sons of God" by W. J. Erdman, and "Modern Spiritualism Briefly Tested by Scripture" by Algernon J. Pollock. Another testimony to the importance of this doctrine is the fact that it is in the list of doctrines that comprise the systematic theologies of every fundamental or evangelical author. But its importance in the Bible should be that which concerns us the most.

The Third Person of the Trinity is described in some detail in nearly every Christian doctrinal statement. He is certainly described in every Fundamental Baptist doctrinal statement. In the London Baptist Confession of 1689, it was stated in the section about the Trinity:

> In this divine and infinite Being there are three subsistences, the Father, the Word or Son, and Holy Spirit, of one substance, power, and eternity, each having the whole divine essence, yet the essence undivided: the Father is of none, neither begotten nor proceeding; the Son is eternally begotten of the Father; the Holy Spirit proceeding from the Father and the Son; all infinite, without beginning, therefore but one God, who is not to be divided in nature and being, but distinguished by several peculiar relative properties and personal relations; which doctrine of the Trinity is the foundation of all

---
3 Often just referred to as The Fundamentals. They were originally published as 90 essays in twelve volumes by the Testimony Publishing Company of Chicago, 1910-1915.

our communion with God, and comfortable dependence on him. (I John 5:7; Matthew 28:19; II Corinthians 13:14; Exodus 3:14; John 14:11; I Corinthians 8:6; John 1:14, 18; John 15:26; Galatians 4:6)

While there are other references to the Holy Spirit in the London Baptist Confession of 1689, for now let's consider how the doctrinal statement of Bible Baptist Church in Arleta, California deals with the Holy Spirit. In Section 2, entitled, "The True God," it says:

> We believe there is one and only one living and true God, and infinite Spirit, the Maker and Supreme Ruler of heaven and earth; inexpressibly glorious in holiness, and worthy of all possible honor, confidence, and love; and that in the unity of the Godhead there are three persons, the Father, the Son, and the Holy Spirit, equal in every divine perfection and executing distinct but harmonious offices in the great work of redemption (Exodus 20:2-3; I Corinthians 8:6; Revelation 4:11).

This is followed in Sub-Section B: The Holy Spirit:

Paragraph 1. His Person and Presence: We believe that the Holy Spirit is a divine person, equal with God the Father and God the Son and of the same essence; that He was active in the creation.

Paragraph 2. His Ministries: We believe that the Holy Spirit's relation to the unbelieving world is that He restrains the evil one until God's purpose is fulfilled; that He bears witness to the truth of the gospel in preaching and testimony; that He is the Agent in the new birth; that He indwells, seals, empowers, guides, teaches, witnesses, sanctifies, and helps the believer. Every true believer receives the indwelling of the Holy Spirit at the time of salvation (Genesis 1:1-3; Matthew 28:19; Mark 1:8; Luke 1:35; 24:49; John 1:33; 14:16-17, 26; 16:8-11; Acts 11:16;

Romans 8:14, 16, 26-27; I Corinthians 12:13; Ephesians 1:13-14; Hebrews 9:14).

Paragraph 3. His Temporary Gifts: We believe that the Holy Spirit equips believers for service by bestowing upon them spiritual gifts. The charismatic gifts (such as tongues, healing, casting out of demons, etc.) as found in I Corinthians 12:8-10 and Mark 16:17-18 were temporary signs given to the apostles and prophets for the writing of the New Testament, until the close of the canon, and are not operative today. The Holy Spirit's charismatic gifts have ceased, but we do believe that God in His goodness does still heal and deliver from demons (At the same time, we do not doubt the sincerity of some who wrongly claim to practice these things). (Romans 12:1-8; I Corinthians 12-14; Ephesians 2:20; 3:3-5; 4:4-16; II Corinthians 12:11-12; Hebrews 2:4).

Pneumatology Is a Doctrine that Is Mentioned, Taught, and Detailed Over and Over Again in the Bible

The importance of Pneumatology can be seen, in the first place, by the fact that we find the Greek word, πνεῦμα [*pneuma*], or one of its derivatives, used in 264 verses of the New Testament. The vast number of verses that speak about the Spirit should help us to see the importance of this doctrine to God.

A second way that we can see the importance of the doctrine of Pneumatology is seeing all the important sub-doctrines of Pneumatology cited in the Bible. These sub-doctrines include, but are not limited to:

1. **The deity of the Spirit of God**
2. **The attributes of the Spirit of God**
3. **The relationship between the members of the Trinity**
4. **The gifts of the Spirit of God**

5. The filling of the Spirit of God
6. The baptism by the Spirit of God
7. The baptism in the Spirit of God
8. The work of conviction by the Spirit of God
9. The work of the Spirit of God in salvation
10. The difference of the ministry of the Spirit of God between the Old and the New Testament
11. The Personality of the Spirit of God
12. The part that the Spirit of God had and has in the works of God

In addition to the above listed twelve sub-doctrines, there are many related studies that could be included, such as, healing, speaking in tongues, interpreting of tongues, prophecy, casting out of demons, lifting up serpents, word of knowledge, word of wisdom, and many more. A book that covers many of these topics is *Though I Speak - the Biblical Qualifications of a Prophet* which I wrote many years ago. Now we will look at the effects of Pneumatology on the other doctrines of Systematic Theology.

The Effect of Pneumatology on the Other Doctrines of Systematic Theology

Since all doctrine is intertwined, the effect of what we believe about the Spirit of God will naturally affect what we believe about all other doctrine. For that reason, great care must be exercised in any discussion of doctrine. For instance, the doctrine of the Holy Spirit definitely affects the doctrine of Bibliology, since Christ, in John 14:16-17, called the Spirit of God the Comforter, and the Spirit of Truth.

> And I will pray the Father, and he shall give you another Comforter, that he may abide with you for ever; Even the Spirit of truth; whom the world cannot receive, because it seeth him not, neither knoweth him: but ye know him; for he dwelleth with you, and shall be in you.

Christ again spoke of the effect of Pneumatology on Bibliology in John 15:25-27 where Christ said that the coming of the Spirit of Truth would enable the apostles to bear witness, that is, to write the New Testament.

> But this cometh to pass, that the word might be fulfilled that is written in their law, They hated me without a cause. But when the Comforter is come, whom I will send unto you from the Father, even the Spirit of truth, which proceedeth from the Father, he shall testify of me: And ye also shall bear witness, because ye have been with me from the beginning.

Christ again spoke of the effect of the Holy Spirit on Bibliology in John 16:8-15. He detailed how the Spirit would teach the apostles that which He had insufficient time to teach them, because "... ye cannot bear them now" (verse 12). He would guide them "... into all truth" (verse 13) and show them "... things to come." Everything that they wrote was inspired: the past, the truth that Christ had not yet revealed, and future events.

> And when he is come, he will reprove the world of sin, and of righteousness, and of judgment: Of sin, because they believe not on me; Of righteousness, because I go to my Father, and ye see me no more; Of judgment, because the prince of this world is judged. I have yet many things to say unto you, but ye cannot bear them now. Howbeit when he, the Spirit of truth, is come, he will guide you into all truth: for he shall not speak of himself; but whatsoever he shall hear, that shall he speak: and he will shew you things to come. He shall glorify me: for he shall receive of mine, and shall shew it unto you. All things that the Father hath are mine: therefore said I, that he shall take of mine, and shall shew it unto you.

From the point of view of Pneumatology, the doctrine of Bibliology would be viewed as the communication inspired by the Holy Spirit.

In the same way Theology Proper would be viewed in two different ways when viewed from the perspective of Pneumatology. First, Theology Proper would be considered *the deity of the Holy Spirit.* His deity was affirmed by Peter in Acts 5:3–5 where he first accused Ananias of lying to the Holy Ghost (verse 3), and then stated that lying to the Holy Ghost was the same as lying to God (verse 5).

> But Peter said, Ananias, why hath Satan filled thine heart to lie to the Holy Ghost, and to keep back part of the price of the land? Whiles it remained, was it not thine own? and after it was sold, was it not in thine own power? why hast thou conceived this thing in thine heart? thou hast not lied unto men, but unto God. And Ananias hearing these words fell down, and gave up the ghost: and great fear came on all them that heard these things.

Secondly, the doctrine of Theology Proper is affected by Pneumatology when we see the relationship of the Father and the Son to the Spirit of God as described in John 15:26.

> But when the Comforter is come, whom I will send unto you from the Father, even the Spirit of truth, which proceedeth from the Father, he shall testify of me:

The doctrine of Christology is affected by Pneumatology to the extent that Christology is seen as the Savior conceived by the Holy Spirit.

> But while he thought on these things, behold, the angel of the Lord appeared unto him in a dream, saying, Joseph, thou son of David, fear not to take unto thee Mary thy wife: for that which is conceived in her is of the Holy Ghost (Matthew 1:20).

This was also stated in Luke 1:35 where the angel said to Mary:

> And the angel answered and said unto her, The Holy Ghost shall come upon thee, and the power of the Highest shall overshadow thee: therefore also that holy thing which shall be born of thee shall be called the Son of God.

Even the words of Christ were considered "Spirit" according to John 6:63.

> It is the spirit that quickeneth; the flesh profiteth nothing: the words that I speak unto you, they are spirit, and they are life.

If we were to consider the doctrine of Angelology from the point of view of Pneumatology, we would describe the angels as the celestial messengers of the Holy Spirit. We can easily see this in Matthew 1:20 where the angel Gabriel told Joseph that Christ was conceived by the Holy Ghost.

> But while he thought on these things, behold, the angel of the Lord appeared unto him in a dream, saying, Joseph, thou son of David, fear not to take unto thee Mary thy wife: for that which is conceived in her is of the Holy Ghost.

Again, as stated in Luke 1:26-35, the angel Gabriel was sent to tell Mary of the work of the Holy Spirit in the conception of Jesus Christ.

> And in the sixth month the angel Gabriel was sent from God unto a city of Galilee, named Nazareth, To a virgin espoused to a man whose name was Joseph, of the house of David; and the virgin's name was Mary. And the angel came in unto her, and said, Hail, thou that art highly favoured, the Lord is with thee: blessed art thou among women. And when she saw him, she was troubled at his saying, and cast in her mind what manner of salutation this should be. And the angel said unto her, Fear not,

> Mary: for thou hast found favour with God. And, behold, thou shalt conceive in thy womb, and bring forth a son, and shalt call his name JESUS. He shall be great, and shall be called the Son of the Highest: and the Lord God shall give unto him the throne of his father David: And he shall reign over the house of Jacob for ever; and of his kingdom there shall be no end. Then said Mary unto the angel, How shall this be, seeing I know not a man? And the angel answered and said unto her, The Holy Ghost shall come upon thee, and the power of the Highest shall overshadow thee: therefore also that holy thing which shall be born of thee shall be called the Son of God.

The doctrine of Soteriology, viewed from the point of view of Pneumatology, is defined as the salvation brought about by the Holy Spirit. In that way, Soteriology is spoken of as the work of the Spirit of God. This is certainly the viewpoint of John 3:3–8 where the new birth is viewed as a work of the Spirit of God.

> Jesus answered and said unto him, Verily, verily, I say unto thee, Except a man be born again, he cannot see the kingdom of God. Nicodemus saith unto him, How can a man be born when he is old? can he enter the second time into his mother's womb, and be born? Jesus answered, Verily, verily, I say unto thee, Except a man be born of water and of the Spirit, he cannot enter into the kingdom of God. That which is born of the flesh is flesh; and that which is born of the Spirit is spirit. Marvel not that I said unto thee, Ye must be born again. The wind bloweth where it listeth, and thou hearest the sound thereof, but canst not tell whence it cometh, and whither it goeth: so is every one that is born of the Spirit.

The doctrine of Hamartialogy, which is the doctrine of sin, would be defined as disobedience to the will of the Holy Spirit. In John 16:7-11, Jesus laid the groundwork for an understanding of the relationship of Pneumatology and Hamartialogy.

> Nevertheless I tell you the truth; It is expedient for you that I go away: for if I go not away, the Comforter will not come unto you; but if I depart, I will send him unto you. And when he is come, he will reprove the world of sin, and of righteousness, and of judgment: Of sin, because they believe not on me; Of righteousness, because I go to my Father, and ye see me no more; Of judgment, because the prince of this world is judged.

The present ministry of the Holy Spirit toward the lost is to convict or reprove the world of the sin of unbelief. The ministry of the Holy Spirit in the life of the believer, according to Romans 8:2-6, is to set "... me free from the law of sin and death." To accomplish that, the Spirit of God needs for the believer to be "... spiritually minded."

> For the law of the Spirit of life in Christ Jesus hath made me free from the law of sin and death. For what the law could not do, in that it was weak through the flesh, God sending his own Son in the likeness of sinful flesh, and for sin, condemned sin in the flesh: That the righteousness of the law might be fulfilled in us, who walk not after the flesh, but after the Spirit. For they that are after the flesh do mind the things of the flesh; but they that are after the Spirit the things of the Spirit. For to be carnally minded is death; but to be spiritually minded is life and peace.

The doctrine of Anthropology, when viewed from Pneumatology, sees man as the one who was given life by the Holy Spirit. Genesis chapter 1, certainly views the soul and spirit of man as the product of creation by the Triune God. The Holy Spirit had a part in that creation. Specifically, Genesis chapter 2, states that man was given life by the Spirit of God. In Genesis 2:7, God states that "...

the breath[4] of life," which means "the Spirit of lives," entered into man, and he "... became a living soul."

> And the LORD God formed man of the dust of the ground, and breathed into his nostrils the breath of life; and man became a living soul.

The doctrine of Ecclesiology would be viewed from Pneumatology as the company of those saved by the work of the Holy Spirit. Many look at I Corinthians 3:16-17 as if it were talking to individual Christians, but this stern warning was given to the church. That can be easily seen in the use of the plural "ye" in the passage instead of the singular "thou" or you.

> Know ye not that ye are the temple of God, and that the Spirit of God dwelleth in you? If any man defile the temple of God, him shall God destroy; for the temple of God is holy, which temple ye are.

The same thing is true in I Corinthians 6:19-20 where all the pronouns again are plural. "Your body" is σῶμα ὑμῶν [soma humon], which means, "your (plural) body."

> What? know ye not that your body is the temple of the Holy Ghost which is in you, which ye have of God, and ye are not your own? For ye are bought with a price: therefore glorify God in your body, and in your spirit, which are God's.

The church is not only viewed as "the body of Christ," but also as "the temple of the Holy Ghost."

The last doctrine that we will consider from the list of Systematic Theology is the doctrine of future things, which is called Eschatology. The doctrine of Eschatology then would be viewed as the future works of the Holy Spirit.

---

4 נְשָׁמָה [nâshamah], according to the *Enhanced Strong's Lexicon*, Hebrew #5397, means: "1 breath, spirit. 1A breath (of God). 1B breath (of man). 1C every breathing thing. 1D spirit (of man)."

Seeing how our understanding of Pneumatology affects every other doctrine of Systematic Theology makes us all the more cognizant of how careful we must be in every detail of this study. In its article on Pneumatology, Wikipedia[5] says:

> Pneumatology in Christianity refers to a particular discipline within Christian theology that focuses on the study of the Holy Spirit. The term is essentially derived from the Greek word Pneuma (πνεῦμα), which designates "breath" or "spirit" and metaphorically describes a non-material being or influence. The English term pneumatology comes from two Greek words: πνεῦμα (pneuma, spirit) and λόγος (logos, teaching about). Pneumatology includes study of the person of the Holy Spirit, and the works of the Holy Spirit. This latter category also includes Christian teachings on new birth, spiritual gifts (charismata), Spirit-baptism, sanctification, the inspiration of prophets (sic), and the indwelling of the Holy Trinity (which in itself covers many different aspects). Different Christian denominations have different theological approaches on various pneumatological questions.

The Objections to the Study of Pneumatology

Some people say that doctrine divides while love unifies. These people resist those who are dogmatic about any doctrine while accepting those who unify, though they may disagree with them about nearly everything. They argue that there is strength in numbers, but I believe there is strength in God Alone Who, John said, "… is light, and in Him is no darkness at all" (I John 1:5).

While the unity of the Godhead is important, and the unity of the believer with Christ and the other Persons of the Godhead is likewise important, I do not find any instruction in the Bible for the uniting of believers and unbelievers. To the contrary, I do

---
5 https://en.wikipedia.org/wiki/Pneumatology

Introduction to Pneumatology

find instructions for believers to separate from unbelievers in II Corinthians 6:14–18.

> Be ye not unequally yoked together with unbelievers: for what fellowship hath righteousness with unrighteousness? and what communion hath light with darkness? And what concord hath Christ with Belial? or what part hath he that believeth with an infidel? And what agreement hath the temple of God with idols? for ye are the temple of the living God; as God hath said, I will dwell in them, and walk in them; and I will be their God, and they shall be my people. Wherefore come out from among them, and be ye separate, saith the Lord, and touch not the unclean thing; and I will receive you, And will be a Father unto you, and ye shall be my sons and daughters, saith the Lord Almighty.

I have often heard the Lord's High Priestly prayer quoted as if it were a plea for unity among all believers, but the unity of which Christ spoke was a unity between the Father and the Son, as well as the unity of the true believer with the Trinity as can be seen in John 17:11.

> And now I am no more in the world, but these are in the world, and I come to thee. Holy Father, **keep through thine own name those whom thou hast given me, that they may be one, as we are.**

The entire prayer recorded in John 17:1–26 is a plea for the believer to be perfectly united with Christ forever, and nothing about a unity with the unbelievers or any sort of benefit in numbers that could be achieved.

> These words spake Jesus, and lifted up his eyes to heaven, and said, Father, the hour is come; glorify thy Son, that thy Son also may glorify thee: As thou hast given him power over all flesh, that he should give eternal life to as many as thou hast given him. And this is life eternal, that

they might know thee the only true God, and Jesus Christ, whom thou hast sent. I have glorified thee on the earth: I have finished the work which thou gavest me to do. And now, O Father, glorify thou me with thine own self with the glory which I had with thee before the world was. I have manifested thy name unto the men which thou gavest me out of the world: thine they were, and thou gavest them me; and they have kept thy word. Now they have known that all things whatsoever thou hast given me are of thee. For I have given unto them the words which thou gavest me; and they have received them, and have known surely that I came out from thee, and they have believed that thou didst send me. I pray for them: I pray not for the world, but for them which thou hast given me; for they are thine. And all mine are thine, and thine are mine; and I am glorified in them. And now I am no more in the world, but these are in the world, and I come to thee. Holy Father, keep through thine own name those whom thou hast given me, that they may be one, as we are. While I was with them in the world, I kept them in thy name: those that thou gavest me I have kept, and none of them is lost, but the son of perdition; that the scripture might be fulfilled. And now come I to thee; and these things I speak in the world, that they might have my joy fulfilled in themselves. I have given them thy word; and the world hath hated them, because they are not of the world, even as I am not of the world. I pray not that thou shouldest take them out of the world, but that thou shouldest keep them from the evil. They are not of the world, even as I am not of the world. Sanctify them through thy truth: thy word is truth. As thou hast sent me into the world, even so have I also sent them into the world. And for their sakes I sanctify myself, that they also might be sanctified through the truth. Neither pray I for these alone, but for them also which shall believe on me through their word; That they all may be one; as thou,

> Father, art in me, and I in thee, that they also may be one in us: that the world may believe that thou hast sent me. And the glory which thou gavest me I have given them; that they may be one, even as we are one: I in them, and thou in me, that they may be made perfect in one; and that the world may know that thou hast sent me, and hast loved them, as thou hast loved me. Father, I will that they also, whom thou hast given me, be with me where I am; that they may behold my glory, which thou hast given me: for thou lovedst me before the foundation of the world. O righteous Father, the world hath not known thee: but I have known thee, and these have known that thou hast sent me. And I have declared unto them thy name, and will declare it: that the love wherewith thou hast loved me may be in them, and I in them.

Often times John 13:34–35 will be quoted saying that what we need is love, not doctrine. The doctrine of Pneumatology divides the true believer from the false cults of Pentecostalism and Mormonism. It divides the Theist from the Deist. It divides the true worshiper from the idolater. But it also makes the true believer love his fellow believer more, which is the real meaning of John 13:34–35.

> A new commandment I give unto you, That ye love one another; as I have loved you, that ye also love one another. By this shall all men know that ye are my disciples, if ye have love one to another.

While love is important, and the doctrine of love should be taught, so should the doctrine of separation. Our love for God must be such that we are willing to be set-apart wholly unto God. Our love for our fellow believer ought to be so genuine that we would not want to compromise his wellbeing before the Lord by leading him into compromise with darkness, sin, or the devil. We find that truth expressed in I John 1:3–2:29.

That which we have seen and heard declare we unto you, that ye also may have fellowship with us: and truly our fellowship is with the Father, and with his Son Jesus Christ. And these things write we unto you, that your joy may be full. This then is the message which we have heard of him, and declare unto you, that God is light, and in him is no darkness at all. If we say that we have fellowship with him, and walk in darkness, we lie, and do not the truth: But if we walk in the light, as he is in the light, we have fellowship one with another, and the blood of Jesus Christ his Son cleanseth us from all sin. If we say that we have no sin, we deceive ourselves, and the truth is not in us. If we confess our sins, he is faithful and just to forgive us our sins, and to cleanse us from all unrighteousness. If we say that we have not sinned, we make him a liar, and his word is not in us. My little children, these things write I unto you, that ye sin not. And if any man sin, we have an advocate with the Father, Jesus Christ the righteous: And he is the propitiation for our sins: and not for ours only, but also for the sins of the whole world. And hereby we do know that we know him, if we keep his commandments. He that saith, I know him, and keepeth not his commandments, is a liar, and the truth is not in him. But whoso keepeth his word, in him verily is the love of God perfected: hereby know we that we are in him. He that saith he abideth in him ought himself also so to walk, even as he walked. Brethren, I write no new commandment unto you, but an old commandment which ye had from the beginning. The old commandment is the word which ye have heard from the beginning. Again, a new commandment I write unto you, which thing is true in him and in you: because the darkness is past, and the true light now shineth. He that saith he is in the light, and hateth his brother, is in darkness even until now. He that loveth his brother abideth in the light, and there is none occasion of stumbling in him. But he that hateth his brother is in darkness, and walketh in darkness, and knoweth not whither he goeth, because that darkness hath blinded his eyes. I write unto you, little children, because your sins are forgiven you for his name's sake. I write unto you, fathers, because ye have known him that is from the beginning. I write unto you, young men, because ye have overcome the wicked one. I write unto you, little children, because ye have known the Father. I have written unto you, fathers, because ye have known him that is from the beginning. I have written unto you, young men, because ye are strong, and the word of God abideth in you, and ye have overcome the wicked one. Love not the world, neither the things that are in the world. If any man love the world, the love of the Father is not in him. For all that is in the world, the lust of the flesh, and the lust of the eyes, and the pride of life, is not of the Father, but is of the world. And the world passeth away, and the lust thereof: but he that doeth the will of God abideth for ever. Little children, it is the last time: and as ye have heard that antichrist shall come, even now are there many antichrists; whereby we know that it is the last time. They went out from us, but they were not of us; for if they had been of us, they would no doubt have continued with us: but they went out, that they might be made manifest that they were not all of us. But ye have an unction from the Holy One, and ye know all things. I have not written unto you because ye know not the truth, but because ye know it, and that no lie is of the truth. Who is a liar but he that denieth that Jesus is the Christ? He is antichrist, that denieth the Father and the Son. Whosoever denieth the Son, the same hath not the Father: (but) he that acknowledgeth the Son hath the Father also. Let that therefore abide in you, which ye have heard from the beginning. If that which ye have heard from the beginning shall remain in you, ye also shall continue in the Son, and in the Father. And this is the promise that he hath promised us, even eternal life. These things have I written unto you concerning them that seduce you. But the anointing which ye have received of him abideth in you, and ye need not that any man teach you: but as the same anointing teacheth you of all things, and is truth, and is no lie, and even as it hath taught you, ye shall abide in him. And now, little children, abide in him; that, when he shall appear, we may have confidence, and not be ashamed before him at his coming. If ye know that he is righteous, ye know that every one that doeth righteousness is born of him.

The Substitution of Emotion and Experience for Doctrine

One of the major flaws of Pentecostalism and the Charismatic movement is its doctrinal shallowness and dependence on experience. I have heard some Charismatics criticize Baptists as well as Protestants by saying that an emphasis on doctrine seems sterile and cold. But the true worship of God is built on knowledge and truth, not on experience and emotion. Jesus criticized the Samaritan worship as ignorant (ye know not what) and said that "... we know what we worship" and that true worship had to be both "... in spirit and in truth" in John 4:22-24.

Ye worship ye know not what: we know what we worship: for salvation is of the Jews. But the hour cometh, and now is, when the true worshippers shall worship the Father in spirit and in truth: for the Father seeketh such to worship him. God is a Spirit: and they that worship him must worship him in spirit and in truth.

Emotion and experience are no substitute for being taught sound doctrine through the Holy Spirit's ministry of illumination. In John 6:63-64, Jesus spoke of the value of His Words, calling them both Spirit and life. He said that real spiritual worship in truth was brought about by His Word, not experience or emotion. That is called doctrine.

It is the spirit that quickeneth; the flesh profiteth nothing: the words that I speak unto you, they are spirit, and they are life. But there are some of you that believe not. For Jesus knew from the beginning who they were that believed not, and who should betray him.

Prejudices and Suppositions

We can try very hard to avoid prejudices and suppositions about any given doctrine, but the honest truth is that as we approach this study on Pneumatology, we all have some prejudices and presuppositions. I have suppositions also. I believe that God exists based on the facts, but I cannot prove that God exists to an atheist any more than the atheist can prove to me that He does not exist. I have the supposition that the Bible is true and must be believed since it was inspired and preserved. These suppositions could be called prejudices since I take them with me in any discussion of any doctrine. Those that oppose sound doctrine also have prejudices and suppositions.

As we get into this study we will refer to the presuppositions and prejudices that others have about the doctrine of Pneumatology, but right now I will admit to my own presuppositions that I make. First, I believe that the Bible is the inspired and preserved Word of God. I believe that every jot and tittle was inspired and preserved. I can defend my reason for believing in plenary-verbal inspiration, but that is not my purpose here. In the second place, I believe that truth is whatever God says that it is. Truth is reality and therefore it is not relative. Truth is not based on human reasoning or on human judgment. Third, I freely admit to being prejudiced in favor of Biblical authority. I am convinced that the Bible is the only authority in all matters of which it speaks and in all matters to which it addresses itself.

Biblical Hermeneutics

This is not a study of the rules and principles of Biblical Hermeneutics, that is, Biblical interpretation. However, out of necessity, as in any Biblical study, our study of Pneumatology will follow the rules of Hermeneutics. These rules are generally defined as the normal, grammatical, historical method of interpretation. What I mean by that is that I will follow the seven rules of Biblical interpretation that I have delineated in my book on Bibliology entitled, *A More Sure Word of Prophecy*.

A. Literal interpretation

I believe in interpreting the Bible literally. That does not mean that we ignore or misinterpret figurative language as can be seen in the third rule below. It means that we literally interpret figurative language, such as parables as parables, metaphors as metaphors, similes as similes, etc. But the dominant rule that I follow in this study is that of literal interpretation as described in II Peter 1:20-21.

> Knowing this first, that no prophecy of the scripture is of any private interpretation. For the prophecy came not in old time by the will of man: but holy men of God spake as they were moved by the Holy Ghost.

Why does Peter condemn private interpretation? He condemns it because there is no such thing as "private prophecy" since the prophecy was given through "... holy men of God" who wrote as they were carried by the Holy Spirit.

B. Contextual interpretation

We will interpret the Bible according to the context of the verses that we quote. We will consider the universal context in that way, using the principles of first mention, continuous mention and full mention. As an example, we could not give a thorough study about the devil without beginning with the first mention of the serpent in Genesis 3:1 and tracing the existence of this malevolent being through the Bible to the full mention in Revelation 20:2. A verse that seemed to say that salvation is by works would need to be interpreted in the light of more than six hundred verses that say that man is saved by faith or believing in Jesus Christ.

> And they said, Believe on the Lord Jesus Christ, and thou shalt be saved, and thy house (Acts 16:31). ... Therefore being justified by faith, we have peace with God through our Lord Jesus Christ (Romans 5:1).

When we talk about contextual interpretation, we are principally speaking of the immediate context. In order to properly interpret John 3:16 we must at least examine John 3:14-18. We need to see the context here of the comparison to Moses and the bronze serpent in the wilderness and how God saved the Jewish people from their sin of rebellion symbolically with the serpent being nailed on a pole, and truly through Christ being nailed on the cross. This love of God, displayed in verse sixteen, was that God gave His Only Begotten Son to die in our place on Calvary that we would have eternal life through faith in Him. The man who believes God's promise of eternal life that can never perish will never face the condemnation of God either. That is a very brief contextual interpretation of John 3:16.

> And as Moses lifted up the serpent in the wilderness, even so must the Son of man be lifted up: That whosoever believeth in him should not perish, but have eternal life. For God so loved the world, that he gave his only begotten Son, that whosoever believeth in him should not perish, but have everlasting life. For God sent not his Son into the world to condemn the world; but that the world through him might be saved. He that believeth on him is not condemned: but he that believeth not is condemned already, because he hath not believed in the name of the only begotten Son of God.

C. Grammatical interpretation

When considering the interpretation of a passage we must first properly define the tense, conjugation, and mood of the verbs. One of the examples of first century misinterpretation is easily seen in John 21:23. Jesus here made a statement that is found in a clause that is contrary to fact, and John found it necessary to correct this misinterpretation. John wrote:

> Then went this saying abroad among the brethren, that that disciple should not die: yet Jesus said not unto him, He shall not die; but, If I will that he tarry till I come, what is that to thee?

A careful reading of what Jesus said would have led them to properly interpret what had been said.

In the second place we must interpret a verse while maintaining the agreement between nouns and adjectives, and between verbs and adverbs. This was the kind of agreement that Paul maintained while interpreting the Old Testament prophecies about Christ in Galatians 3:16. His whole argument here is based on the absence of an "s" ("im" in Hebrew) on the word seed. That is grammatical interpretation.

> Now to Abraham and his seed were the promises made. He saith not, And to seeds, as of many; but as of one, And to thy seed, which is Christ.

In the third place we interpret grammatically by interpreting according to the usage of figurative forms. What are figurative forms? An example of figurative forms is a parable: a comparison which uses a story to compare. Jesus often used parables to teach truth, as we can see in Mark 4:34.

> But without a parable spake he not unto them: and when they were alone, he expounded all things to his disciples.

Introduction to Pneumatology

Parables are always literally interpreted as parables, and they are grammatically interpreted as parables also. That is the case with the parable found in Matthew 13:3-9. Its interpretation given by our Lord in Matthew 13:18-23 as well.

> And he spake many things unto them in parables, saying, Behold, a sower went forth to sow; And when he sowed, some seeds fell by the way side, and the fowls came and devoured them up: Some fell upon stony places, where they had not much earth: and forthwith they sprung up, because they had no deepness of earth: And when the sun was up, they were scorched; and because they had no root, they withered away. And some fell among thorns; and the thorns sprung up, and choked them: But other fell into good ground, and brought forth fruit, some an hundredfold, some sixtyfold, some thirtyfold. Who hath ears to hear, let him hear. … Hear ye therefore the parable of the sower. When any one heareth the word of the kingdom, and understandeth it not, then cometh the wicked one, and catcheth away that which was sown in his heart. This is he which received seed by the way side. But he that received the seed into stony places, the same is he that heareth the word, and anon with joy receiveth it; Yet hath he not root in himself, but dureth for a while: for when tribulation or persecution ariseth because of the word, by and by he is offended. He also that received seed among the thorns is he that heareth the word; and the care of this world, and the deceitfulness of riches, choke the word, and he becometh unfruitful. But he that received seed into the good ground is he that heareth the word, and understandeth it; which also beareth fruit, and bringeth forth, some an hundredfold, some sixty, some thirty.

We have considered one type of figurative language which is the parable. Another kind of figurative language is the metaphor. Metaphors are a comparison using a figure that normally speaks of another thing, such as "an anchor of the soul" in Hebrews 6:19, and it will literally and grammatically be interpreted as a metaphor.

> Which hope we have as an anchor of the soul, both sure and stedfast, and which entereth into that within the veil;

A third type of figurative language is the simile. Similes are a comparison between two unlike things and are frequently expressed by introducing the simile with either the word "like" or the word "as." This can be seen in Psalm 1:3-4 where it says that the godly man is "... like a tree." It does not call him a tree, which would be a metaphor.

> And he shall be like a tree planted by the rivers of water, that bringeth forth his fruit in his season; his leaf also shall not wither; and whatsoever he doeth shall prosper. The ungodly are not so: but are like the chaff which the wind driveth away.

Of course, there are other grammatical forms that must be considered, such as the differences between prepositions, pronouns, and syntax. There are also other literary devices such as the metonymy, the synecdoche, the personification and the anti-personification, the apostrophe, the hyperbole, and sarcasm. All of these are used in the Bible as figurative language and are literally and grammatically interpreted as such. This book will use these rules of Hermeneutics, but a greater and deeper study of Hermeneutics is not within the scope of this book.

D. Dispensational interpretation

I use a dispensational hermeneutic in my interpretation. That means that I will interpret a verse or passage according to the dispensation about which it was written. This is in general agreement with the admonition that Paul gave to Timothy in II Timothy 2:15. He was warned that, as a workman in order to not face shame, he needed to cut the Word of God straight.

Study to shew thyself approved unto God, a workman that needeth not to be ashamed, rightly dividing the word of truth.

As a dispensationalist, I give a priority to the New Testament which is also a recognition of progressive revelation and the full, complete revelation of every doctrine in the New Testament.

E. Directional interpretation

By directional interpretation we are saying that to determine the correct interpretation of the Scripture we must first determine to whom it was directed, and by and for whom it was stated. Misinterpretations of the Bible often occur when someone does not pay close attention to these details. This happened even at the time of the writing of the Bible when Peter turned and saw John and questioned if the message about his own suffering and death also applied to John. We read this in John 21:20-22.

> Then Peter, turning about, seeth the disciple whom Jesus loved following; which also leaned on his breast at supper, and said, Lord, which is he that betrayeth thee? Peter seeing him saith to Jesus, Lord, and what shall this man do? Jesus saith unto him, If I will that he tarry till I come, what is that to thee? follow thou me.

Another example of directional interpretation can be seen in Exodus 31:13-18. God emphasized repeatedly that the Sabbath was not given to the church, but to the "Children of Israel." A proper interpretation of this passage would never have produced a heresy such as the Seventh Day Adventism. Notice carefully the highlighted words in the passage.

> Speak thou also unto **the children of Israel**, saying, Verily my sabbaths *ye* shall keep: for it is a sign between me and *you* throughout *your* generations; that ye may know that I am the LORD that doth sanctify *you*. *Ye shall keep the sabbath* therefore; for *it is holy unto you*: every one that defileth it shall surely be put to death: for whosoever

doeth any work therein, that soul **shall be cut off from among his people.** Six days may work be done; but in the seventh is the sabbath of rest, holy to the LORD: whosoever doeth any work in the sabbath day, he shall surely be put to death. Wherefore **the children of Israel shall keep the sabbath,** to observe the sabbath **throughout their generations**, for a perpetual covenant. **It is a sign** between me and **the children of Israel for ever**: for in six days the LORD made heaven and earth, and on the seventh day he rested, and was refreshed. And he gave unto Moses, when he had made an end of communing with him upon mount Sinai, two tables of testimony, tables of stone, written with the finger of God.

The Ten Commandments and the Sabbath, in particular, were given as a sign to the Children of Israel. Like circumcision, it was never intended as a sign or command for Gentiles.

F. Cultural interpretation

When we talk about cultural interpretation, we are not talking about interpreting the Bible according to the culture of the reader, but according to the culture of the writer. Cultural interpretation must take into account the culture of the Jewish people generally, but also the educational culture of such writers as Moses, Paul, and Luke. In any given culture there is a difference between the culture of the uneducated, such as Peter, and the educated, such as Paul. We can see references in the Bible to the culture of the Jewish people in John 19:40 as an example.

> Then took they the body of Jesus, and wound it in linen clothes with the spices, as the manner of the Jews is to bury.

We can easily see how the first burial by Joseph of Arimathea was unacceptable according to Matthew 27:59.

> And when Joseph had taken the body, he wrapped it in a clean linen cloth,

Introduction to Pneumatology

Mark 15:46 also speaks of the shameful way in which our Lord's body was buried at His death.

> And he bought fine linen, and took him down, and wrapped him in the linen, and laid him in a sepulchre which was hewn out of a rock, and rolled a stone unto the door of the sepulchre.

Luke 23:53-56 tells us that the women planned on re-burying the body of our Lord because they saw the way that His body was laid.

> And he took it down, and wrapped it in linen, and laid it in a sepulchre that was hewn in stone, wherein never man before was laid. And that day was the preparation, and the sabbath drew on. And the women also, which came with him from Galilee, followed after, and beheld the sepulchre, and how his body was laid. And they returned, and prepared spices and ointments; and rested the sabbath day according to the commandment.

G. Interpretation that is without personal prejudice

Often times a person can be heard beginning his interpretation of a passage saying, "To me this passage means ..." That is automatically a private interpretation. It admits it saying, "To me." The Bible does not say something to me that it says to no one else. God says what He means, and means what He says. II Peter 1:20–21 clearly states that in saying "... that no prophecy of the Scripture is of any private interpretation."

> Knowing this first, that no prophecy of the scripture is of any private interpretation. For the prophecy came not in old time by the will of man: but holy men of God spake as they were moved by the Holy Ghost.

An interpretation that is without prejudice also means that I must not have a personal agenda, or look for a desired outcome when I interpret the Bible. This is the problem with the Adventist interpretation of Exodus 31:13-18, where they leave the purpose of the sign to Israel out of their interpretation and make it a sign of obedience to the church. Read Exodus 31:13-18 carefully again, this time without prejudice, seeking no outcome except a faithfulness to God in the interpretation.

> Speak thou also unto **the children of Israel**, saying, Verily my sabbaths **ye** shall keep: for it is a sign between me and **you** throughout **your** generations; that ye may know that I am the LORD that doth sanctify **you. Ye shall keep the sabbath** therefore; for **it is holy unto you**: every one that defileth it shall surely be put to death: for whosoever doeth any work therein, that soul **shall be cut off from among his people**. Six days may work be done; but in the seventh is the sabbath of rest, holy to the LORD: whosoever doeth any work in the sabbath day, he shall surely be put to death. Wherefore **the children of Israel shall keep the sabbath**, to observe the sabbath **throughout their generations**, for a perpetual covenant. **It is a sign** between me and **the children of Israel for ever**: for in six days the LORD made heaven and earth, and on the seventh day he rested, and was refreshed. And he gave unto Moses, when he had made an end of communing with him upon mount Sinai, two tables of testimony, tables of stone, written with the finger of God.

Why the Doctrine of the Holy Spirit Is Important

The doctrine of the Spirit of God is important for many reasons. One of those reasons is that there are modern issues that are resolved by the doctrine of Pneumatology. All doctrine is highly practical, and that includes Pneumatology. As we have stated from the beginning, all doctrine is intertwined and therefore, we must be sure that our doctrine is Biblical. The practical effects of Pneumatology, as with all doctrine, were stated by the Apostle Paul in II Timothy 3:16-17. The effects are fourfold: doctrine, reproof, correction, and instruction in righteousness. The desired outcome is always the same: "That the man of God may be perfect, throughly furnished unto all good works."

> All scripture is given by inspiration of God, and is profitable for doctrine, for reproof, for correction, for instruction in righteousness: That the man of God may be perfect, throughly furnished unto all good works.

Antibiblical perspectives and misinterpretations of verses that deal with the doctrine of Pneumatology will automatically produce doctrinal errors, and cause the end result to be an imperfect man who is unequipped to serve God in every good work. If we want to have mature Christians in the church, we need to teach Pneumatology.

One such error has been the growth of psychology and so-called "Christian psychology." The result of this amalgamation of "Christian" with "psychology" has produced a philosophy that has no need for salvation for man. When we believe that the Spirit of God has the answer for man's every problem and say, "The Holy Spirit, through the use of His Word, has the answer" they retort, "What was the question?" Christian psychology presents the elevated view of man that says he has no need of individual guilt, and replaces it with a call for "self-esteem." It calls sin a disease or a disorder, such as multiple personality disorder, or as it is now known, dissociative identity disorder.

The Bible clearly teaches that the Holy Spirit is the Creator of all things, bringing light and life to the entire creation. He is God, and as such He brought all things into existence and gave life to man.

> And God said, Let us make man in our image, after our likeness: and let them have dominion over the fish of the sea, and over the fowl of the air, and over the cattle, and over all the earth, and over every creeping thing that creepeth upon the earth. So God created man in his own image, in the image of God created he him; male and female created he them (Genesis 1:26–27). ... And

the LORD God formed man of the dust of the ground, and breathed into his nostrils the breath of life; and man became a living soul (Genesis 2:7).

In Psalm 104:29-30, the Bible speaks of the work of the Holy Spirit in the creation and the preservation of the universe.

Thou hidest thy face, they are troubled: thou takest away their breath, they die, and return to their dust. Thou sendest forth thy spirit, they are created: and thou renewest the face of the earth.

As the Creator and sustainer of the universe, the Holy Spirit is also the Agent of Salvation and the regeneration, as it says in Titus 3:5.

Not by works of righteousness which we have done, but according to his mercy he saved us, by the washing of regeneration, and renewing of the Holy Ghost;

Titus 3:5 in the Scrivener's Greek Textus Receptus (1881) says:
οὐκ ἐξ ἔργων τῶν ἐν δικαιοσύνῃ ὧν ἐποιήσαμεν ἡμεῖς, ἀλλὰ κατὰ τὸν αὐτοῦ ἔλεον ἔσωσεν ἡμᾶς, διὰ λουτροῦ παλιγγενεσίας καὶ ἀνακαινώσεως Πνεύματος Ἁγίου,

Notice the Greek word παλιγγενεσίας [*palingenesias*], which is translated "regeneration." This Greek word literally means a new Genesis or a new beginning. The Holy Spirit was there creating the first beginning and is therefore present to create the new beginning. He is the One Who gives life and light to the new beginning as well.

In attacking the creation, the evolutionist is attacking the fact that the Spirit of God is the Creator of mankind and all things. As the Creator, He is also the One Who regenerates. If the Spirit of God is not the Creator and regenerator of mankind, then mankind cannot be made subject to Him, and furthermore man is reduced to being nothing more than a different species of animal. It is not murder, in that case, to kill a man since he has no more rights than any other animal. Abortion and euthanasia naturally become viable solutions to problems and should not be considered murder. That is the logical outcome of not having a firm Biblical stand on the doctrine of Pneumatology. But, in a multitude of verses, the Bible tells us otherwise.

> Thou shalt not kill (Exodus 20:13). ... Whoso sheddeth man's blood, by man shall his blood be shed: for in the image of God made he man (Genesis 9:6). ... But thou art he that took me out of the womb: thou didst make me hope when I was upon my mother's breasts. I was cast upon thee from the womb: thou art my God from my mother's belly (Psalm 22:9-10). ... The wicked are estranged from the womb: they go astray as soon as they be born, speaking lies (Psalm 58:3). ... By thee have I been holden up from the womb: thou art he that took me out of my mother's bowels: my praise shall be continually of thee (Psalm 71:6). ... Lo, children are an heritage of the LORD: and the fruit of the womb is his reward (Psalm 127:3). ... For thou hast possessed my reins: thou hast covered me in my mother's womb (Psalm 139:13). ... Thus saith the LORD that made thee, and formed thee from the womb, which will help thee; Fear not, O Jacob, my servant; and thou, Jesurun, whom I have chosen. ... Thus saith the LORD, thy redeemer, and he that formed thee from the womb, I am the LORD that maketh all things; that stretcheth forth the heavens alone; that spreadeth abroad the earth by myself (Isaiah 44:2, 24). ... Listen, O isles, unto me; and hearken, ye people, from far; The LORD hath called me from the womb; from the bowels of my mother hath he made mention of my name. ... And now, saith the LORD that formed me from the womb to be his servant, to bring Jacob again to him, Though Israel be not gathered, yet shall I be glorious in the eyes of the LORD, and my God shall be my strength. ... Can a woman forget her sucking child, that she should not have compassion on the son of her womb? yea, they may

> forget, yet will I not forget thee (Isaiah 49:1, 5, 15). ... Before I formed thee in the belly I knew thee; and before thou camest forth out of the womb I sanctified thee, and I ordained thee a prophet unto the nations (Jeremiah 1:5). ... Give them, O LORD: what wilt thou give? give them a miscarrying womb and dry breasts (Hosea 9:14). ... But when it pleased God, who separated me from my mother's womb, and called me by his grace (Galatians 1:15).

If man is the product of evolution then he has no Creator and can have no relationship with a Creator. If man evolved, then he has no relationship with God and could not have disobeyed God, which ultimately means he is not fallen. If he did not fall, then he does not need salvation. What we said about evolution is true for Theistic evolution as well. A further problem of evolution is that it creates a powerless God. It leaves us wondering, if God could not create man without the help of evolution, could he save man without man's help?

An errant view of Pneumatology can lead to many different heresies. Catholicism errs in its understanding of the Holy Spirit being the Third Person of the Trinity and concludes that Mary is higher than the Holy Spirit since she is the "Mother of God." Mormonism errs and ends up concluding that Adam, who is identified by them as God the Father, had sexual relations with Mary, one of his celestial wives, and thus Jesus was born. Because they leave the Holy Spirit out of the conception of Christ, Jesus was not conceived of a virgin, but the wife of Adam. The many heresies of Mormonism find their roots in an errant view of Pneumatology. The same could be said of Seventh Day Adventism, Russellism, and many more false cults. It behooves us to have this doctrine firmly established in our hearts and minds.

Pentecostalism and the Charismatic movement today are also firmly rooted in erroneous beliefs about the Holy Spirit. That is why we need to study this doctrine thoroughly and stand firm on the truth with the aid of the Spirit of God.

Chapter One

THE DEITY OF THE HOLY SPIRIT

As I begin writing this chapter, I am very aware that many have formed an opinion about the deity of the Holy Spirit. Some people find it very difficult to change their minds, even when proven wrong. Thomas Jefferson recognized this tendency when writing the Declaration of Independence and said: *"... all experience hath shewn that mankind are more disposed to suffer, while evils are sufferable than to right themselves by abolishing the forms to which they are accustomed."* There are several reasons that people have given me for continuing to hold to an error, rather than accepting correction of their doctrine.

A. Agreeing with the Word of God

Changing what you believe in order to be in agreement with the Bible also affects other things that you believe. What you believe about the Holy Spirit may also change what you believe about the doctrines of Theology, Christology, Bibliology, Eschatology, etc. All doctrine is interrelated and tied together. For that reason, some find it difficult to change what they believe.

B. The Existence of Spiritual Pride

Some people oppose any change in doctrine because they are already known to hold a certain viewpoint, and do not want to be embarrassed before others when they admit that they were wrong.

This tendency is known as pride, and every one of us has to contend with this. It would be more shameful, however, to stand before the Lord someday and have to admit that pride kept us from believing the truth.

C. The Existence of Spiritual Laziness

In the third place, some oppose changes in doctrine because it is easier for them to continue in error than thoroughly study the Bible. I know college students who only study enough to pass their exams and graduate, and then never want to study again. But a person who looks for an end to study will never grow. The easy way is not necessarily the right way. There are three basic motives that are behind the desire to take the easy path.

First, some people foster within themselves a lazy spiritual life. These people do not take the initiative. They want someone else to feed them. If they don't get fed, they simply don't eat. Often, they are willing to listen to someone else on the radio, television, or the internet rather than develop good study habits of their own. It appears that their favorite verse is Ecclesiastes 12:12 where King Solomon wrote:

> And further, by these, my son, be admonished: of making many books there is no end; and much study is a weariness of the flesh.

But the motive for studying should not only be to know the truth, but also to transmit the truth to others. In II Timothy 2:15, Paul admonished Timothy to rightly divide the Word of Truth. To rightly divide the Word of Truth, you must do the hard work of studying. Laziness in study is a deadly character flaw in the child of God.

> Study to shew thyself approved unto God, a workman that needeth not to be ashamed, rightly dividing the word of truth.

Second there are those who think that we must not talk about doctrine, since it divides, because loving our "brother" is more important for them. This can be another form of false spirituality, or spiritual pride. It is neither love of my brother, nor love of God. The lordship of Christ demands that I believe and teach only what He says.

> But in vain they do worship me, teaching for doctrines the commandments of men (Matthew 15:9).

Third, there are those who believe that their experience is more important than the truth. These people, in reality, reject the fact that truth is absolute. They may not define their idea as being "relative truth," but that is, in reality, what they believe. Truth is what it is to them. It is what matches their experience and not what the Bible says. They feel more comfortable saying, "It seems to me ..." rather than saying "Thus saith the Lord."

I had the opportunity to teach a group of Pentecostal pastors the doctrine of the Holy Spirit. At the conclusion of the study one of the pastors said to me, "I know that you are right. The Bible says exactly what you are saying, but I have experienced speaking in tongues, and I cannot deny the truth of my experience." The desire to cling to experience as the revelation of truth often leaves a person teaching error in order to maintain his experience. Paul charged Timothy in I Timothy 1:3, and 9-10, to teach absolute truth as given to us in the Word of God.

> As I besought thee to abide still at Ephesus, when I went into Macedonia, that thou mightest charge some that they teach no other doctrine. ... Knowing this, that the law is not made for a righteous man, but for the lawless and disobedient, for the ungodly and for sinners, for unholy and profane, for murderers of fathers and murderers of mothers, for manslayers, For whoremongers, for them that defile themselves with mankind, for menstealers, for liars, for perjured persons, and if there be any other thing that is contrary to sound doctrine;

The seduction of following experience rather than the Word of God was rejected by the apostles. The Apostle Paul told Timothy in I Timothy 4:1, 6, and 16 that these experiences could be used by "seducing spirits" or "devils." The true servant of God follows the Scriptures and the Biblical doctrines that come out of them, wherever that doctrine leads us.

> Now the Spirit speaketh expressly, that in the latter times some shall depart from the faith, giving heed to seducing spirits, and doctrines of devils ... If thou put the brethren in remembrance of these things, thou shalt be a good minister of Jesus Christ, nourished up in the words of faith and of good doctrine, whereunto thou hast attained. ... Take heed unto thyself, and unto the doctrine; continue in them: for in doing this thou shalt both save thyself, and them that hear thee.

In I Timothy 6:3-5, Paul again warned Timothy against those that put experience, or their own words, above the Word of God.

> If any man teach otherwise, and consent not to wholesome words, even the words of our Lord Jesus Christ, and to the doctrine which is according to godliness; He is proud, knowing nothing, but doting about questions and strifes of words, whereof cometh envy, strife, railings, evil surmisings, Perverse disputings of men of corrupt minds, and destitute of the truth, supposing that gain is godliness: from such withdraw thyself.

Paul commanded Timothy to stay true to the Word of God and its doctrine. This is absolutely necessary, and we must not abandon this principle. We are not judged by what others around us do, but by our own faithfulness to teaching doctrine as it is given in the Word of God. Paul warned Timothy that the day would come when men, with itching ears, would desire to hear something that would satisfy "... their own lusts" rather than hearing the Word. Certainly,

II Timothy 4:2-3 warns of that day, but it probably began during Paul's lifetime.

> Preach the word; be instant in season, out of season; reprove, rebuke, exhort with all longsuffering and doctrine. For the time will come when they will not endure sound doctrine; but after their own lusts shall they heap to themselves teachers, having itching ears;

We can see from these Scriptures, in the first place, that teaching experience in the place of doctrine is condemned. In the second place, it is easy to discern from the Word of God that putting your own word or your own experience higher than the Word of God is also condemned.

D. The Existence of Presuppositions and Prejudices

We are not ignorant, however, that everyone has presuppositions. We also have them. We discussed this a little bit in the introduction. Therefore, we will begin this study with a basic presupposition: we believe that the Bible is the Word of God, inspired and preserved, and for that reason it is authoritative in everything that it says. Paul stated clearly that very thing in II Timothy 3:16-17.

> All scripture is given by inspiration of God, and is profitable for doctrine, for reproof, for correction, for instruction in righteousness: That the man of God may be perfect, throughly furnished unto all good works.

The second prejudice or presupposition that I will confess to having is that my Hermeneutic (that is my method of Biblical interpretation) will follow the normal rules of Biblical Hermeneutics. I will follow the rule of literal and contextual interpretation as given by Peter in II Peter 1:19-21.

> We have also a more sure word of prophecy; whereunto ye do well that ye take heed, as unto a light that shineth in a dark place, until the day dawn, and the day star arise

in your hearts: Knowing this first, that no prophecy of the scripture is of any private interpretation. For the prophecy came not in old time by the will of man: but holy men of God spake as they were moved by the Holy Ghost.

In being literal and contextual in our Hermeneutic, we will emphasize the teachings of the New Testament because revelation is progressive. The progressive nature of the revelation of truth in the Bible gives us a more comprehensive picture of a doctrine when seen in the fullness of its development in the New Testament.

We need to use proof-texts to prove things, but we need to be careful about their usage. We should never use a proof-text without fully understanding its context. A second caution about the use of proof-texts is that we must not think that there must be a verse that *exactly* says what we want to prove. For example, the word "Trinity" cannot be found in any verse that would be quoted as a proof-text for the existence of the Trinity. The words "rapture," "Christology," and even the word "deity" or "Pneumatology" are nowhere found in the Holy Scriptures. That does not mean that these words cannot be legitimately used, nor does it mean that there are no proof-texts that can be quoted.

E. The Personal Qualifications of the Student

To really benefit from this study the student must have certain qualifications and develop certain others. The first qualification is that **he must be a believer**. What I mean by this is that he must be saved in order to understand the Scriptures fully, as Paul wrote in I Corinthians 2:10–16.

> But God hath revealed them unto us by his Spirit: for the Spirit searcheth all things, yea, the deep things of God. For what man knoweth the things of a man, save the spirit of man which is in him? even so the things of God knoweth no man, but the Spirit of God. Now we have received, not the spirit of the world, but the spirit which

is of God; that we might know the things that are freely given to us of God. Which things also we speak, not in the words which man's wisdom teacheth, but which the Holy Ghost teacheth; comparing spiritual things with spiritual. **But the natural man receiveth not the things of the Spirit of God:** for they are foolishness unto him: neither can he know them, because they are spiritually discerned. But **he that is spiritual judgeth all things,** yet he himself is judged of no man. For who hath known the mind of the Lord, that he may instruct him? But we have the mind of Christ.

A second necessary qualification that the Bible student must possess is the ability to think and study. The greatest benefit to this study on the deity of the Holy Spirit is that which can be earned by doing your own research and thinking through each of the elements of the study on your own, like the Bereans who "... with all readiness of mind" did the hard work of searching the Scriptures daily, according to Acts 17:10–12.

And the brethren immediately sent away Paul and Silas by night unto Berea: who coming thither went into the synagogue of the Jews. These were more noble than those in Thessalonica, in that they received the word with all readiness of mind, and searched the scriptures daily, whether those things were so. Therefore many of them believed; also of honourable women which were Greeks, and of men, not a few.

A third qualification that the student needs is to depend on God with the assurance that He will teach him His Word. In this, the student needs true faith that does not waver in its conviction so that if we lack wisdom, God will give it to us, as He promised in James 1:5–8.

If any of you lack wisdom, let him ask of God, that giveth to all men liberally, and upbraideth not; and it shall be given him. But let him ask in faith, nothing wavering. For he that wavereth is like a wave of the sea driven with the wind and tossed. For let not that man think that he shall receive any thing of the Lord. A double minded man is unstable in all his ways.

To the student who lacks faith to depend on God to teach him, let me remind you that God wants you to learn more than you want to learn. In I Corinthians 2:10-16, Paul informed the Corinthians that God revealed truth to the Apostles and prophets so that they could write that truth into the Holy Scripture for the purpose of illuminating us as we read that truth.

But God hath revealed them unto us by his Spirit: for the Spirit searcheth all things, yea, the deep things of God. For what man knoweth the things of a man, save the spirit of man which is in him? even so the things of God knoweth no man, but the Spirit of God. Now we have received, not the spirit of the world, but the spirit which is of God; that we might know the things that are freely given to us of God. Which things also we speak, not in the words which man's wisdom teacheth, but which the Holy Ghost teacheth; comparing spiritual things with spiritual. But the natural man receiveth not the things of the Spirit of God: for they are foolishness unto him: neither can he know them, because they are spiritually discerned. But he that is spiritual judgeth all things, yet he himself is judged of no man. For who hath known the mind of the Lord, that he may instruct him? But we have the mind of Christ.

In the fourth place, to be a good student of the Word of God, all of us must surrender to God, allowing Him to form and conform our lives and our doctrine. In Romans 12:1-2, Paul pleads with us for that kind of conformity, that we might be transformed by the renewing of our minds.

> I beseech you therefore, brethren, by the mercies of God, that ye present your bodies a living sacrifice, holy, acceptable unto God, which is your reasonable service. And be not conformed to this world: but be ye transformed by the renewing of your mind, that ye may prove what is that good, and acceptable, and perfect, will of God.

In order to study the deity of the Holy Spirit, it is necessary to conduct a brief review of Theology Proper, which is the Doctrine of God.

A Short Review of the Doctrine of God

It would be best to take the class, "Theology Proper" before taking "Pneumatology," or at least study my book "*The Only True God*" before entering this study. I will, however, provide a short summary of Theology Proper.

When we speak of deity, we are referencing God's nature, which includes that which is His essence. The essence of God is what makes God Who He is; it is His basic nature. In John 4:24 Jesus described God's essence:

> God is a Spirit: and they that worship him must worship him in spirit and in truth.

From a reading of John 4:24, we learn several things about God. The first thing is that God is Immaterial. Another way of expressing that is that God is not composed of matter. He created all things including matter, according to Genesis 1:1.

> In the beginning God created the heaven and the earth.

That God is the Creator of all matter is confirmed in Hebrews 11:3, as well.

> Through faith we understand that the worlds were framed by the word of God, so that things which are seen were not made of things which do appear.

In Colossians 1:16-17, Paul clearly stated that God not only created the visible, but also the invisible creation.

> For by him were all things created, that are in heaven, and that are in earth, visible and invisible, whether they be thrones, or dominions, or principalities, or powers: all things were created by him, and for him: And he is before all things, and by him all things consist.

We can also understand from Jesus' proclamation that God is Spirit which means that God is incorporeal. He has no body; He is Spirit.

We also know that since God is Spirit, that automatically means that He is Invisible. The divine essence is invisible. In at least three places in the New Testament, the Apostle Paul stated clearly that God is invisible.

> Who is the image of **the invisible God**, the firstborn of every creature (Colossians 1:15). ... Now unto the King eternal, immortal, **invisible**, the only wise God, be honour and glory for ever and ever. Amen (I Timothy 1:17). ... By faith he forsook Egypt, not fearing the wrath of the king: for he endured, as seeing him who is **invisible** (Hebrews 11:27).

Again, the fact that God is Spirit gives us a fourth thing that we can say about God: He is alive. In Joshua 3:10, He is called "... the living God."

> And Joshua said, Hereby ye shall know that the living God is among you, and that he will without fail drive out from before you the Canaanites, and the Hittites, and the Hivites, and the Perizzites, and the Girgashites, and the Amorites, and the Jebusites.

David also referred to God as "... the living God" in I Samuel 17:26.

> And David spake to the men that stood by him, saying, What shall be done to the man that killeth this Philistine, and taketh away the reproach from Israel? for who is this uncircumcised Philistine, that he should defy the armies of the living God?

Paul referred to God as "... the living and true God" in I Thessalonians 1:9.

> For they themselves shew of us what manner of entering in we had unto you, and how ye turned to God from idols to serve the living and true God;

When we talk about the essence of God we have to talk about His Personality. What we mean by the Personality of God is that God is a Person. He is not a force, even though He is strong. Another way to describe Personality is to say that He has the power of self-consciousness. By self-consciousness we are stating the fact or the state of being conscious of His Own existence. Furthermore, God's Personality means that He has self-determination. This means that by an act of freewill God determines his actions in, and by Himself. These two things are true with God and therefore, God is a Person. The Bible affirms the Personality of God many times. Let's look first at what God said to Moses in Exodus 3:14.

> And God said unto Moses, I AM THAT I AM: and he said, Thus shalt thou say unto the children of Israel, I AM hath sent me unto you.

We can certainly see that God is a Person in the creation of man in the image and likeness of God. If man is a person, and created in the image and likeness of God, then God must also be a Person, as it states in Genesis 1:26.

> And God said, Let us make man in our image, after our likeness: and let them have dominion over the fish of the sea, and over the fowl of the air, and over the cattle, and

over all the earth, and over every creeping thing that creepeth upon the earth.

Because God is a Person, He also has the attribute of intellect. God is intelligent. God has knowledge and wisdom, as it says in Psalm 147:5.

> Great is our Lord, and of great power: his understanding is infinite.

In referring to Personality, we are also affirming that God has sensibility. The attribute of sensibility means that God has emotions such as love and delight, as it states in Jeremiah 9:24 and Jeremiah 31:3.

> But let him that glorieth glory in this, that he understandeth and knoweth me, that I am the LORD which exercise lovingkindness, judgment, and righteousness, in the earth: for in these things I delight, saith the LORD. ... The LORD hath appeared of old unto me, saying, Yea, I have loved thee with an everlasting love: therefore with lovingkindness have I drawn thee.

The third aspect of the Personhood of God is what we call volition. This means that God has freewill; God can, and does decide things by, and for Himself. According to Ephesians 1:5, the freewill of God allowed Him to decide to save the believer,

> Having predestinated us unto the adoption of children by Jesus Christ to himself, according to the good pleasure of his will,

The opponents of the doctrine of the Trinity will often point to the fact that the word "Trinity" is never found in the Bible. While it is true that the word "Trinity" was not used in the Bible, there exists a lot of Biblical teaching on this matter. Let's begin with the Old Testament development of the doctrine of the Trinity.

The Deity of the Holy Spirit

God revealed truth in what we call "progressive revelation of the truth." In the Old Testament we find the first mention of the Holy Spirit and then the progressive mentions, until we get to the full mention, which is generally in the New Testament. The Old Testament presents the unity of God. In Deuteronomy 6:4, we see the existence of the Trinity in the statement of the unity of God.

> Hear, O Israel: The LORD our God is one LORD:

The Trinity here is known by both LORD and God, yet this is not two different gods, for He is identified as "one LORD." There is only one God. Exodus 20:3 also makes that clear, saying:

> Thou shalt have no other gods before me.

There are, nonetheless, indications in the Old Testament of the existence of a plurality in the unity of God. The doctrine of the Trinity in no way teaches any concept of three gods. That would be a grave error. We can see, however, in the usage of plural words to speak of the unity of God, that there is more than one Person in the Godhead. Plural verbs and pronouns were used in Genesis 1:26 in speaking of God in the creation of man.

> And God said, *Let us make* man in our image, after *our* likeness: and let them have dominion over the fish of the sea, and over the fowl of the air, and over the cattle, and over all the earth, and over every creeping thing that creepeth upon the earth.

Plural verbs and pronouns were also used in Genesis 3:22 at the fall of man.

> And the LORD God said, Behold, the man is become as *one of us*, to know good and evil: and now, lest he put forth his hand, and take also of the tree of life, and eat, and live for ever:

Plural verbs and pronouns were again used in Genesis 11:7 at the tower of Babel.

> Go to, *let us go down*, and there confound their language, that they may not understand one another's speech.

Plural verbs and nouns were also used in Isaiah 6:8 at the call of Isaiah.

> Also I heard the voice of the Lord, saying, Whom shall I send, and who will go for *us*? Then said I, Here am I; send me.

There are also multiple mentions of angels in the Old Testament that have nothing to do with the existence of the Trinity. The references to the Angel of the LORD, however, seem to be indications of the appearances of the pre-incarnate Jesus Christ. One such instance is found in Genesis 16:7-13.

> And the angel of the LORD found her by a fountain of water in the wilderness, by the fountain in the way to Shur. And he said, Hagar, Sarai's maid, whence camest thou? and whither wilt thou go? And she said, I flee from the face of my mistress Sarai. And the angel of the LORD said unto her, Return to thy mistress, and submit thyself under her hands. And the angel of the LORD said unto her, I will multiply thy seed exceedingly, that it shall not be numbered for multitude. And the angel of the LORD said unto her, Behold, thou art with child, and shalt bear a son, and shalt call his name Ishmael; because the LORD hath heard thy affliction. And he will be a wild man; his hand will be against every man, and every man's hand against him; and he shall dwell in the presence of all his brethren. And she called the name of the LORD that spake unto her, Thou God seest me: for she said, Have I also here looked after him that seeth me?

Hagar gives every indication that she knew the deity of the Angel of the LORD that spoke with her. "She called the name of the LORD that spake unto her, Thou God seest me." The Bible confirms that the Angel of the LORD was the LORD and God. We can find

The Deity of the Holy Spirit

another illustration of this with Abraham at the sacrifice of Isaac in Genesis 22:11-17.

> And the angel of the LORD called unto him out of heaven, and said, Abraham, Abraham: and he said, Here am I. And he said, Lay not thine hand upon the lad, neither do thou any thing unto him: for now I know that thou fearest God, seeing thou hast not withheld thy son, thine only son from me. And Abraham lifted up his eyes, and looked, and behold behind him a ram caught in a thicket by his horns: and Abraham went and took the ram, and offered him up for a burnt offering in the stead of his son. And Abraham called the name of that place Jehovahjireh: as it is said to this day, In the mount of the LORD it shall be seen. And the angel of the LORD called unto Abraham out of heaven the second time, And said, By myself have I sworn, saith the LORD, for because thou hast done this thing, and hast not withheld thy son, thine only son: That in blessing I will bless thee, and in multiplying I will multiply thy seed as the stars of the heaven, and as the sand which is upon the sea shore; and thy seed shall possess the gate of his enemies;

Abraham called the place "Jehovahjireh." He did not call it, "The Angel of Jehovahjireh." He knew that the Angel of the LORD was the LORD.

Another pre-incarnate appearance of the Lord Jesus Christ as the Angel of the LORD is seen in the experience of Moses with the burning bush which was recorded in Exodus 3:1-6. The Angel of the LORD is first identified as the Angel of the LORD (verse 2) and then as the LORD and later as God (verse 4). In verse 6, He identified Himself as "… the God of thy father, the God of Abraham, the God of Isaac, and the God of Jacob."

> Now Moses kept the flock of Jethro his father in law, the priest of Midian: and he led the flock to the backside of the desert, and came to the mountain of God, even to

Horeb. And the angel of the LORD appeared unto him in a flame of fire out of the midst of a bush: and he looked, and, behold, the bush burned with fire, and the bush was not consumed. And Moses said, I will now turn aside, and see this great sight, why the bush is not burnt. And when the LORD saw that he turned aside to see, God called unto him out of the midst of the bush, and said, Moses, Moses. And he said, Here am I. And he said, Draw not nigh hither: put off thy shoes from off thy feet, for the place whereon thou standest is holy ground. Moreover he said, I am the God of thy father, the God of Abraham, the God of Isaac, and the God of Jacob. And Moses hid his face; for he was afraid to look upon God.

In Malachi 3:1, we find another reference to this Angel of the LORD. He was first called "me" and then "the Lord." At the end of the verse He is called "… the LORD of hosts."

Behold, I will send my messenger, and he shall prepare the way before me: and the Lord, whom ye seek, shall suddenly come to his temple, even the messenger of the covenant, whom ye delight in: behold, he shall come, saith the LORD of hosts.

In all of these verses that we have seen, and those that follow, there exists a distinction in the Persons of the Trinity. In that respect, there exists a difference between Lord, LORD and God. Notice how Genesis 19:24 speaks about the LORD.

Then the LORD rained upon Sodom and upon Gomorrah brimstone and fire from the LORD out of heaven;

In Hosea 1:7, the LORD is also referred to as "the God."

But I will have mercy upon the house of Judah, and will save them by the LORD their God, and will not save them by bow, nor by sword, nor by battle, by horses, nor by horsemen.

In Isaiah 59:20, the Redeemer that had to be human, as well as deity, is distinguished from God.

> And the Redeemer shall come to Zion, and unto them that turn from transgression in Jacob, saith the LORD.

The Spirit is distinguished from God in Isaiah 48:16, which also distinguishes Lord (אֲדֹנָי ['*Adonay*]) and GOD (יהוה [*Yâhweh*]).

> Come ye near unto me, hear ye this; I have not spoken in secret from the beginning; from the time that it was, there am I: and now the Lord GOD, and his Spirit, hath sent me.

A distinction is made again between LORD (יהוה [*Yâhweh*]) and "My Spirit" in Isaiah 59:21.

> As for me, this is my covenant with them, saith the LORD; My spirit that is upon thee, and my words which I have put in thy mouth, shall not depart out of thy mouth, nor out of the mouth of thy seed, nor out of the mouth of thy seed's seed, saith the LORD, from henceforth and for ever.

In Isaiah 63:9-10, the Bible makes a distinction between "... the Angel of His Presence" that saved them, loved them, had pity on them, redeemed them, bare them, and carried them, and the Holy Spirit.

> In all their affliction he was afflicted, and the angel of his presence saved them: in his love and in his pity he redeemed them; and he bare them, and carried them all the days of old. But they rebelled, and vexed his holy Spirit: therefore he was turned to be their enemy, and he fought against them.

The distinctions made between the members of the Trinity show the existence of the Trinity in the Old Testament, but are not to be considered as absolute proofs of the existence of the Trinity.

These references, though, certainly indicate the existence of the three Persons of the Godhead.

Let's turn our attention, now, to the New Testament, which provides ample evidence of the unity of the Triune God. In James 2:19, the Bible says that a man does "well" to believe "... that there is one God." Belief in the unity of God is insufficient for salvation, but a man does well to at least believe that. But even "... the devils" believe in the unity of God.

> Thou believest that there is one God; thou doest well: the devils also believe, and tremble.

But we must go further than the unity of God to look at the New Testament evidence of the existence of the Trinity. To do so, we will begin with John 6:27, where the "Son of man" is distinguished from "God the Father."

> Labour not for the meat which perisheth, but for that meat which endureth unto everlasting life, which the Son of man shall give unto you: for him hath God the Father sealed.

The Word, while being identified as God, was said to be "... with God" in John 1:1. He is God, and yet distinguished from God.

> In the beginning was the Word, and the Word was with God, and the Word was God.

In Acts 5:3-4, the Holy Ghost (verse 3) is identified as God (verse 4).

> But Peter said, Ananias, why hath Satan filled thine heart to lie to the Holy Ghost, and to keep back part of the price of the land? Whiles it remained, was it not thine own? and after it was sold, was it not in thine own power? why hast thou conceived this thing in thine heart? thou hast not lied unto men, but unto God.

If you have not done so already, take a moment and memorize this definition of God:

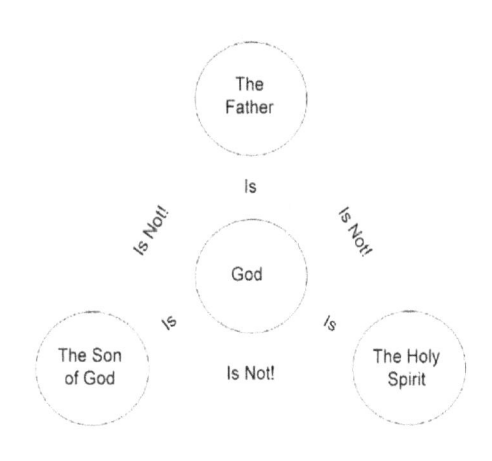

God is the Infinite and Supreme Being, the Creator and Sustainer of the universe; He is the personal, eternal, unique, immutable, true, holy, loving and perfect Spirit. The essence of God, which is indivisible, eternally exists in three Persons.

The diagram is accurate in displaying that the Father is not the Son of God and He is not the Holy Spirit. But the Father is God and the Son of God is God, as is the Holy Spirit. Almost every perversion of the doctrine of the Trinity gets that wrong. Let's consider a few of the perversions of the doctrine of the Trinity.

Sabellianism is a very old heresy about the existence of the Trinity. Sabellianism is the belief that there is only one Divine Person with three different spheres of activity. This viewpoint was developed by the heretic Sabellius, in the third century A.D.

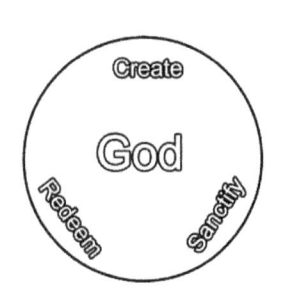

The essence of this heresy is represented in the diagram on the left. Sabellius denied the distinction between the three Persons of the Trinity. He maintained the idea that there is just one Divine Person that created, redeemed and sanctified man; that these are merely three spheres of activity of just One Divine Person.

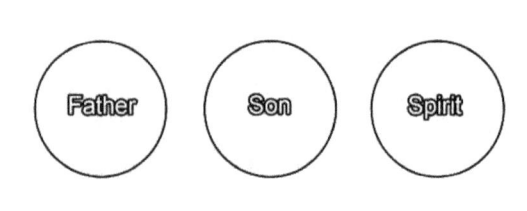

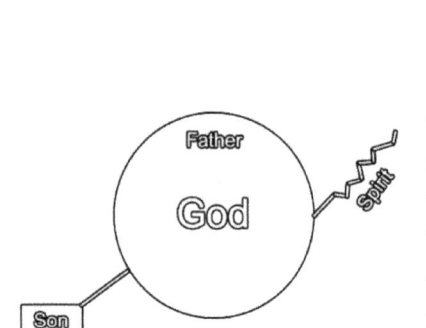

The next perversion of the doctrine of the Trinity is called Tritheism. This heresy is the belief that each of the three Persons is a different God. We could represent this heresy by the diagram on the left.

This diagram represents the last perversion of the doctrine of the Trinity that we will consider. It is called Unitarianism. Unitarians believe that there is only one Divine Person, which is God the Father. The Unitarian believes that the Son of God was created by God. He believes that the Spirit of God is an influence that proceeds from the Father. The Jehovah's Witnesses are Unitarians in their beliefs about the Trinity.

Proofs of the Deity of the Holy Spirit

Let's now consider the six proofs of the deity of the Holy Spirit.

A. The Bible gives Him divine titles

When the Bible speaks of the existence of a man, it speaks of his spirit. In like manner, when the Bible speaks of God, it speaks of the Spirit of God, such as in I Corinthians 2:11.

> For what man knoweth the things of a man, save the spirit of man which is in him? even so the things of God knoweth no man, but the Spirit of God.

The Deity of the Holy Spirit

No one doubts that a man has a spirit. In the same way God speaks of His Spirit with divine titles. In Romans 8:9-11, He was given names that are associated with all the members of the Trinity. He is called "the Spirit," "the Spirit of God," "the Spirit of Christ" and "His Spirit."

> But ye are not in the flesh, but in the Spirit, if so be that the Spirit of God dwell in you. Now if any man have not the Spirit of Christ, he is none of his. And if Christ be in you, the body is dead because of sin; but the Spirit is life because of righteousness. But if the Spirit of him that raised up Jesus from the dead dwell in you, he that raised up Christ from the dead shall also quicken your mortal bodies by his Spirit that dwelleth in you.

He was called the "Spirit of God" in I Corinthians 2:11.

> For what man knoweth the things of a man, save the spirit of man which is in him? even so the things of God knoweth no man, but the Spirit of God.

He was also identified as the "Spirit of God" in Romans 8:13-14.

> For if ye live after the flesh, ye shall die: but if ye through the Spirit do mortify the deeds of the body, ye shall live. For as many as are led by the Spirit of God, they are the sons of God.

He was called the "Spirit of Jehovah" (The LORD) in Isaiah 11:2.

> And the spirit of the LORD shall rest upon him, the spirit of wisdom and understanding, the spirit of counsel and might, the spirit of knowledge and of the fear of the LORD;

Isaiah 61:1 calls Him "... the Spirit of the Lord GOD" and calls Him "... the LORD."

> The Spirit of the Lord GOD is upon me; because the LORD hath anointed me to preach good tidings unto the meek; he hath sent me to bind up the brokenhearted, to proclaim liberty to the captives, and the opening of the prison to them that are bound;

He was called "the Spirit, "the Spirit of God, and "the Spirit of Christ" in Romans 8:9.

> But ye are not in the flesh, but in the Spirit, if so be that the Spirit of God dwell in you. Now if any man have not the Spirit of Christ, he is none of his.

The Holy Spirit was identified with "... the Spirit of Christ" in I Peter 1:11.

> Searching what, or what manner of time the Spirit of Christ which was in them did signify, when it testified beforehand the sufferings of Christ, and the glory that should follow.

When speaking of Jehovah God, as the LORD, Moses referred to the Spirit as His Spirit in Numbers 11:29.

> And Moses said unto him, Enviest thou for my sake? would God that all the LORD'S people were prophets, and that the LORD would put his spirit upon them!

When referring to God, both Nehemiah 9:30 and Psalm 143:10 refer to the Spirit as "Thy Spirit."

> Yet many years didst thou forbear them, and testifiedst against them by thy spirit in thy prophets: yet would they not give ear: therefore gavest thou them into the hand of the people of the lands. ... Teach me to do thy will; for thou art my God: thy spirit is good; lead me into the land of uprightness.

He is called "... the Spirit of the Lord" in II Corinthians 3:18.

> But we all, with open face beholding as in a glass the glory of the Lord, are changed into the same image from glory to glory, even as by the Spirit of the Lord.

We have considered the first proof of the deity of the Holy Spirit in that the Bible gives Him divine titles. Now let's consider the second proof of the deity of the Holy Spirit.

B. The Bible directly calls Him God

The Bible directly calls the Holy Spirit "God" in Acts 5:3-4. Peter accused Ananias of lying to the Holy Spirit in verse 3, and then turned around and defined that as lying to God in verse 4.

> But Peter said, Ananias, why hath Satan filled thine heart to lie to the Holy Ghost, and to keep back part of the price of the land? Whiles it remained, was it not thine own? and after it was sold, was it not in thine own power? why hast thou conceived this thing in thine heart? thou hast not lied unto men, but unto God.

In Acts 16:7, the Holy Spirit is spoken of as being a Person of the Godhead in saying that He would not allow the Apostle Paul and his group "... to go into Bithynia." A force cannot have a will; only a Person can have a will.

> After they were come to Mysia, they assayed to go into Bithynia: but the Spirit suffered them not.

Just like the Lord Jesus Christ, "... the Spirit of our God" is not only called God, but is stated to be the One Who washed, sanctified, and justified us according to I Corinthians 6:11.

> And such were some of you: but ye are washed, but ye are sanctified, but ye are justified in the name of the Lord Jesus, and by the Spirit of our God.

In Romans 8:15, the Holy Spirit is called "... the Spirit of Adoption" as the Person of the Trinity Who makes us adult sons to God the Father.

> For ye have not received the spirit of bondage again to fear; but ye have received the Spirit of adoption, whereby we cry, Abba, Father.

He is given as the "Comforter" by God the Father according to John 14:16.

> And I will pray the Father, and he shall give you another Comforter, that he may abide with you for ever;

We have seen the first two proofs of the deity of the Holy Spirit in that the Bible gives Him divine titles, and directly calls Him God. Now let's consider the third proof of the deity of the Holy Spirit.

C. The Bible Directly Says that He Has the Attributes of God

The first attribute that we will consider is that of Spirituality. It should be obvious to say that the Spirit of God is Spirit. I Corinthians 2:10-12 gives this attribute to the Spirit of God.

> But God hath revealed them unto us by his Spirit: for the Spirit searcheth all things, yea, the deep things of God. For what man knoweth the things of a man, save the spirit of man which is in him? even so the things of God knoweth no man, but the Spirit of God. Now we have received, not the spirit of the world, but the spirit which is of God; that we might know the things that are freely given to us of God.

The Lord, after His resurrection, clearly stated, in Luke 24:39, that being a spirit means that the Holy Spirit does not have a corporal body.

> Behold my hands and my feet, that it is I myself: handle me, and see; for a spirit hath not flesh and bones, as ye see me have.

A second attribute of God is life. In Romans 8:2, the Scriptures affirm that the Spirit of God has the attribute of life.

> For the law of the Spirit of life in Christ Jesus hath made me free from the law of sin and death.

God has the attribute of Personality. By Personality we are saying that God is a Person. A necessary component of Personality is, in the first place, Intellect. God is intelligent. To prove that the Holy Spirit is a divine Person, He must have intellect. Isaiah 40:13–15 demonstrates that the Spirit of the LORD has intellect.

> Who hath directed the Spirit of the LORD, or being his counsellor hath taught him? With whom took he counsel, and who instructed him, and taught him in the path of judgment, and taught him knowledge, and shewed to him the way of understanding? Behold, the nations are as a drop of a bucket, and are counted as the small dust of the balance: behold, he taketh up the isles as a very little thing.

The Apostle Paul also spoke of the intellect of the Holy Spirit in I Corinthians 2:10–11.

> But God hath revealed them unto us by his Spirit: for the Spirit searcheth all things, yea, the deep things of God. For what man knoweth the things of a man, save the spirit of man which is in him? even so the things of God knoweth no man, but the Spirit of God.

Another attribute that is a component of Personality is sensibility, or feelings, in other words. Ephesians 4:30 says that He can be grieved.

> And grieve not the holy Spirit of God, whereby ye are sealed unto the day of redemption.

The Holy Spirit can have joy, according to I Thessalonians 1:6.

> And ye became followers of us, and of the Lord, having received the word in much affliction, with joy of the Holy Ghost:

James 4:5 says that the Holy Spirit can be jealous of us.

> Do ye think that the scripture saith in vain, The spirit that dwelleth in us lusteth to envy?

The third thing that must be present to be a Person is volition. Volition means that God has a will, as seen in Romans 8:27.

> And he that searcheth the hearts knoweth what is the mind of the Spirit, because he maketh intercession for the saints according to the will of God.

Likewise, Hebrews 2:4 affirms that the Holy Spirit has a free will.

> God also bearing them witness, both with signs and wonders, and with divers miracles, and gifts of the Holy Ghost, according to his own will?

Another attribute of God that the Scriptures assign to the Holy Spirit is that of love. According to Galatians 5:22, the Spirit of God produces love.

> But the fruit of the Spirit is love, joy, peace, longsuffering, gentleness, goodness, faith,

The fifth attribute that we can find in the Holy Spirit is that of infinity. By infinity we mean that God has no boundaries or limits. Man's existence has a limit because God created him. But God's existence has no boundaries or limits. The Holy Spirit does not depend on anyone for His existence. He has self-existence, which is indicated in Genesis 1:2.

> And the earth was without form, and void; and darkness was upon the face of the deep. And the Spirit of God moved upon the face of the waters.

The Spirit of God is infinite in His unity. He is One, and is indivisible, according to Ephesians 4:4.

The Deity of the Holy Spirit

> There is one body, and one Spirit, even as ye are called in one hope of your calling;

The Spirit of God is infinite in regards to time. That is what eternality means. The Holy Spirit has neither a beginning, nor end. Hebrews 9:14 calls Him the Eternal Spirit.

> How much more shall the blood of Christ, who through the eternal Spirit offered himself without spot to God, purge your conscience from dead works to serve the living God?

The Holy Spirit is infinite in His knowledge. That is what we call the attribute of omniscience, which means that He knows everything. Isaiah 40:13-15 says that no one ever taught Him, and yet He has perfect understanding.

> Who hath directed the Spirit of the LORD, or being his counsellor hath taught him? With whom took he counsel, and who instructed him, and taught him in the path of judgment, and taught him knowledge, and shewed to him the way of understanding? Behold, the nations are as a drop of a bucket, and are counted as the small dust of the balance: behold, he taketh up the isles as a very little thing.

I Corinthians 2:10-12 says that the Spirit even knows "... the deep things of God" which no man knows.

> But God hath revealed them unto us by his Spirit: for the Spirit searcheth all things, yea, the deep things of God. For what man knoweth the things of a man, save the spirit of man which is in him? even so the things of God knoweth no man, but the Spirit of God. Now we have received, not the spirit of the world, but the spirit which is of God; that we might know the things that are freely given to us of God.

According to Romans 11:33, the Holy Spirit's wisdom and knowledge are infinite and unsearchable.

> O the depth of the riches both of the wisdom and knowledge of God! how unsearchable are his judgments, and his ways past finding out!

The Holy Spirit was called "... the Spirit of wisdom" in Exodus 28:3.

> And thou shalt speak unto all that are wise hearted, whom I have filled with the spirit of wisdom, that they may make Aaron's garments to consecrate him, that he may minister unto me in the priest's office.

The omniscience of the Spirit can be seen in Isaiah 11:2, where He is called "the Spirit of wisdom," "the Spirit of understanding," "the Spirit of counsel," and the "Spirit of knowledge."

> And the spirit of the LORD shall rest upon him, the spirit of wisdom and understanding, the spirit of counsel and might, the spirit of knowledge and of the fear of the LORD;

Omnipotence means that the Spirit of God is not limited in power. Isaiah 11:2 lists the Spirit of might as one of His attributes.

> And the spirit of the LORD shall rest upon him, the spirit of wisdom and understanding, the spirit of counsel and might, the spirit of knowledge and of the fear of the LORD;

The Spirit of God is directly called "... the Almighty" in Job 33:4.

> The Spirit of God hath made me, and the breath of the Almighty hath given me life.

Paul attributed power to the Spirit of God in Romans 15:19.

> Through mighty signs and wonders, by the power of the Spirit of God; so that from Jerusalem, and round about unto Illyricum, I have fully preached the gospel of Christ.

Another of the attributes of the Holy Spirit that shows His infinity is the attribute of omnipresence. The Spirit of God is not limited by space. He is omnipresent. According to Psalm 139:7–10, there is no place where you cannot find the presence of the Holy Spirit.

> Whither shall I go from thy spirit? or whither shall I flee from thy presence? If I ascend up into heaven, thou art there: if I make my bed in hell, behold, thou art there. If I take the wings of the morning, and dwell in the uttermost parts of the sea; Even there shall thy hand lead me, and thy right hand shall hold me.

The Holy Spirit is not only omnipresent, but in a special way is present in the lives of those that believe Him, as it says in John 14:17.

> Even the Spirit of truth; whom the world cannot receive, because it seeth him not, neither knoweth him: but ye know him; for he dwelleth with you, and shall be in you.

The Holy Spirit has the attribute of truth, as the Scriptures affirm in John 14:17, John 15:26, and I John 5:6.

> Even the Spirit of truth; whom the world cannot receive, because it seeth him not, neither knoweth him: but ye know him; for he dwelleth with you, and shall be in you. ... But when the Comforter is come, whom I will send unto you from the Father, even the Spirit of truth, which proceedeth from the Father, he shall testify of me ... This is he that came by water and blood, even Jesus Christ; not by water only, but by water and blood. And it is the Spirit that beareth witness, because the Spirit is truth.

The attribute of holiness is one of the attributes of God that the Holy Spirit possesses, according to Romans 1:4.

> And declared to be the Son of God with power, according to the spirit of holiness, by the resurrection from the dead:

The attribute of holiness is seen in His name, "the Holy Ghost," in Matthew 1:20.

> But while he thought on these things, behold, the angel of the Lord appeared unto him in a dream, saying, Joseph, thou son of David, fear not to take unto thee Mary thy wife: for that which is conceived in her is of the Holy Ghost.

He is called the Holy One in I John 2:20.

> But ye have an unction from the Holy One, and ye know all things.

He was again called the Holy Ghost according to Matthew 12:32.

> And whosoever speaketh a word against the Son of man, it shall be forgiven him: but whosoever speaketh against the Holy Ghost, it shall not be forgiven him, neither in this world, neither in the world to come.

God's attribute of simplicity means that God is indivisible. God cannot be divided, and neither can the Holy Spirit. The Spirit of God is simple as we read in Ephesians 2:18.

> For through him we both have access by one Spirit unto the Father.

According to I Corinthians 12:4, there are diversities of gifts, but the Spirit Himself is indivisible.

> Now there are diversities of gifts, but the same Spirit.

The attribute of simplicity is stated as belonging to the Spirit, according to I Corinthians 12:11.

> But all these worketh that one and the selfsame Spirit, dividing to every man severally as he will.

The last attribute of God that we will consider that shows the Holy Spirit's infinity is that of perfection. Perfection means that God is complete or mature. The Holy Spirit is complete and lacking nothing to be God. Revelation 1:4 calls Him the Seven Spirits to emphasize how complete He is.

> John to the seven churches which are in Asia: Grace be unto you, and peace, from him which is, and which was, and which is to come; and from the seven Spirits which are before his throne;

Likewise, Revelation 3:1 addresses the Spirit of God as the Seven Spirits of God.

> And unto the angel of the church in Sardis write; These things saith he that hath the seven Spirits of God, and the seven stars; I know thy works, that thou hast a name that thou livest, and art dead.

We have seen the first three proofs of the deity of the Holy Spirit in that the Bible gives Him divine titles, calls Him God, and says that He has all the attributes of God. The fourth proof of the deity of the Holy Spirit is:

D. The Bible Directly Declares that the Holy Spirit Did the Works of God

According to Genesis 1:2, the Holy Spirit was active with the Father and the Son in the work of the creation of the universe.

> And the earth was without form, and void; and darkness was upon the face of the deep. And the Spirit of God moved upon the face of the waters.

Psalm 104:24–30 states that the Spirit of God made everything and that He gave life to everything.

> O LORD, how manifold are thy works! in wisdom hast thou made them all: the earth is full of thy riches. So is this great and wide sea, wherein are things creeping innumerable, both small and great beasts. There go the ships: there is that leviathan, whom thou hast made to play therein. These wait all upon thee; that thou mayest give them their meat in due season. That thou givest them they gather: thou openest thine hand, they are filled with good. Thou hidest thy face, they are troubled: thou takest away their breath, they die, and return to their dust. Thou sendest forth thy spirit, they are created: and thou renewest the face of the earth.

The Holy Spirit was also active in the inspiration of the Scriptures. He moved, that is, carried the prophets and the apostles to produce the inspired Word of God, according to II Peter 1:21.

> For the prophecy came not in old time by the will of man: but holy men of God spake as they were moved by the Holy Ghost.

Both Gospel accounts that talk about the conception of Christ in Mary, a virgin, talk about this being a work of the Holy Spirit. The angel Gabriel told Mary that the conception of Christ would be the special work of the Holy Spirit in Luke 1:35.

> And the angel answered and said unto her, The Holy Ghost shall come upon thee, and the power of the Highest shall overshadow thee: therefore also that holy thing which shall be born of thee shall be called the Son of God.

In Matthew 1:20, the angel told Joseph the same thing, that is, that the Lord Jesus Christ was conceived by the Holy Spirit.

> But while he thought on these things, behold, the angel of the Lord appeared unto him in a dream, saying, Joseph,

> thou son of David, fear not to take unto thee Mary thy wife: for that which is conceived in her is of the Holy Ghost.

A fourth work of God that is performed by the Holy Spirit is the conviction of sin. According to John 16:8-11, Jesus told the apostles that the coming of the Holy Spirit was necessary because He would do the ministry of the conviction "... of sin, and of righteousness, and of judgment."

> And when he is come, he will reprove the world of sin, and of righteousness, and of judgment: Of sin, because they believe not on me; Of righteousness, because I go to my Father, and ye see me no more; Of judgment, because the prince of this world is judged.

The Greek word that is translated "reprove" is the word ἐλέγχω [*elegcho*]. The lexicon[1] defines this word as:

> Verb. Of uncertain affinity; 17 occurrences; 1 to convict, refute, confute. 1A generally with a suggestion of shame of the person convicted. 1B by conviction to bring to the light, to expose. 2 to find fault with, correct. 2A by word. 2A1 to reprehend severely, chide, admonish, reprove. 2A2 to call to account, show one his fault, demand an explanation. 2B by deed. 2B1 to chasten, to punish.

The Holy Spirit's work of conviction is "to bring to light, (and) to expose." His work is "to find fault with, (and) correct."

The fifth work of God, which is performed by the Holy Spirit, is that of giving life. In the Garden of Eden, He gave life to man so that man would become "a living soul" (Genesis 2:7). According to what Jesus said in John 3:6, the new birth gives life through the work of the Spirit of God.

> That which is born of the flesh is flesh; and that which is born of the Spirit is spirit.

---
1 Strong, J. (1995). *Enhanced Strong's Lexicon*. Woodside Bible Fellowship, #1651.

This leads us to the sixth work of God that the Holy Spirit performs, which is the work of regeneration. According to Titus 3:5, the Holy Spirit washes, regenerates, and renews.

> Not by works of righteousness which we have done, but according to his mercy he saved us, by the washing of regeneration, and renewing of the Holy Ghost;

In John 14:16, we see the seventh work of the Holy Spirit, which is consolation.

> And I will pray the Father, and he shall give you another Comforter, that he may abide with you for ever;

The word "Comforter" is the translation of the Greek word παράκλητος [parakletos], which the lexicon[2] defines as:

> 1 summoned, called to one's side, esp. called to one's aid. 1A one who pleads another's cause before a judge, a pleader, counsel for defense, legal assistant, an advocate. 1B one who pleads another's cause with one, an intercessor.

While the Holy Spirit is called to our side to aid us and to comfort or console us, His work is also that of intercession. This is the eighth work of the Holy Spirit. According to Romans 8:26-27, the Holy Spirit makes intercession on behalf of the will of God.

> Likewise the Spirit also helpeth our infirmities: for we know not what we should pray for as we ought: but the Spirit itself maketh intercession for us with groanings which cannot be uttered. And he that searcheth the hearts knoweth what is the mind of the Spirit, because he maketh intercession for the saints according to the will of God.

While the Holy Spirit is making intercession for us, according to the will of God, His intercession will always be with the desire to

---

2 Ibid. #3875.

produce our sanctification. Sanctification is the ninth work of the Holy Spirit. The Apostle Paul listed it in II Thessalonians 2:13.

> But we are bound to give thanks alway to God for you, brethren beloved of the Lord, because God hath from the beginning chosen you to salvation through sanctification of the Spirit and belief of the truth:

We have seen four proofs of the deity of the Holy Spirit. We have proven that He is God since the Bible gives Him divine titles, and the Bible directly calls Him God. Furthermore, the Bible directly says that He has all the attributes of God, and the Bible directly states that He performed the works of God. It is now time to see a fifth proof of the deity of the Holy Spirit.

E. The Bible Directly Declares that the Holy Spirit Is Worshipped as God

Only God is to be worshipped by man or any created being. Idols, men, and angels are not to be worshipped. The Bible clearly and directly states that the Spirit is to be worshipped in John 4:23-24.

> But the hour cometh, and now is, when the true worshippers shall worship the Father in spirit and in truth: for the Father seeketh such to worship him. God is a Spirit: and they that worship him must worship him in spirit and in truth.

In Philippians 3:3, Paul also wrote that the Spirit is worshipped as God.

> For we are the circumcision, which worship God in the spirit, and rejoice in Christ Jesus, and have no confidence in the flesh.

We have proven the deity of the Holy Spirit in five different ways. It would be to our advantage to memorize this list with at least one verse for each proof. First, the Bible gives Him divine titles.

Second, the Bible directly calls Him God. Third, the Bible directly says that He has all the attributes of God. Fourth, the Bible directly states that He performed the works of God. Fifth, the Bible directly declares that the Holy Spirit is worshipped as God. Now we come to the sixth proof of the deity of the Holy Spirit, which should also be memorized.

F. Grammatically the Holy Spirit Is Associated with the Other Persons of the Trinity

The Bible often speaks of the Holy Spirit in the same context with God the Father and the Son of God. An understanding of grammar would lead us to understand that there is an equality between them. That is what we see in Matthew 28:19. There is only one Name for God listed here. The verse says, "... in the name," not in the names. The Father, the Son, and the Holy Ghost are in the genitive case[3] (τὸ ὄνομα τοῦ Πατρὸς καὶ τοῦ Υἱοῦ καὶ τοῦ Ἁγίου Πνεύματος·)[4], which displays an equality between them.

> Go ye therefore, and teach all nations, baptizing them in the name of the Father, and of the Son, and of the Holy Ghost:

Paul also wrote of the equality of the Holy Spirit with the other Persons of the Trinity in the grammar of II Corinthians 13:14. Here the ministry of Each Person of the Trinity is mentioned.

> The grace of the Lord Jesus Christ, and the love of God, and the communion of the Holy Ghost, be with you all. Amen.

We can again see the equality of the Persons of the Trinity in the grammar of Matthew 3:16-17 where the Holy Spirit is mentioned equally with Jesus and the Father at the baptism of Jesus Christ.

> And Jesus, when he was baptized, went up straightway out of the water: and, lo, the heavens were opened unto him,

---

[3] The Greek genitive case shows possession, meaning that Each of the Persons of the Trinity equally possesses the Name.

[4] *Scrivener's 1881 Textus Receptus.* (1995). (electronic ed., Mt 28:19). Oak Harbor: Logos Research Systems.

The Deity of the Holy Spirit

and he saw the Spirit of God descending like a dove, and lighting upon him: And lo a voice from heaven, saying, This is my beloved Son, in whom I am well pleased.

The Procession of the Holy Spirit – His Eternal Relationship with the Father and the Son

The relationship of the Holy Spirit to the Father and the Son of God is defined in John 15:26 as that of a voluntary submission by the usage of the word "... proceedeth." This relationship is both eternal and continuous. Let's look at John 15:26, first in English and then in Greek.

> But when the Comforter is come, whom I will send unto you from the Father, even the Spirit of truth, which proceedeth from the Father, he shall testify of me:

> ὅταν δὲ ἔλθῃ ὁ παράκλητος, ὃν ἐγὼ πέμψω ὑμῖν παρὰ τοῦ πατρός, τὸ πνεῦμα τῆς ἀληθείας, ὃ παρὰ τοῦ πατρὸς ἐκπορεύεται, ἐκεῖνος μαρτυρήσει περὶ ἐμοῦ·

The Greek word that is translated proceedeth is ἐκπορεύεται. It is a verb and means "to proceed from, to leave from, or to go out from." In John 15:26, Jesus established that the Holy Spirit had this relationship with Him (Whom I will send) and with the Father (which proceedeth from the Father). Furthermore, the Greek word ἐκπορεύεται is written in present tense, which indicates that the action of proceeding is both eternal and continuous. This means that the Spirit has eternally taken the position of voluntary submission to the Father and the Son and that He will take this position forever. Jesus spoke of this relationship in John 14:26 also. He said that the Comforter would be sent by "... the Father," "... in my name." The ministry of the Comforter would be to "... teach you all things, and bring all things to your remembrance, whatsoever I have said unto you." According to John 14:26, the ministry of the Comforter was eternally one of voluntary submission to the Father and the Son.

> But the Comforter, which is the Holy Ghost, whom the Father will send in my name, he shall teach you all things, and bring all things to your remembrance, whatsoever I have said unto you.

This continuous and eternal submission was also described in John 15:26.

> But when the Comforter is come, whom I will send unto you from the Father, even the Spirit of truth, which proceedeth from the Father, he shall testify of me:

In John 16:7 we can see the relationship of the Holy Spirit in submission to Christ defined as Christ sending the Spirit of God.

> Nevertheless I tell you the truth; It is expedient for you that I go away: for if I go not away, the Comforter will not come unto you; but if I depart, I will send him unto you.

In Psalm 104:30, the Father sends the Spirit to do His work. The word "sendest" also indicates that the voluntary submission of the Spirit is both continuous and eternal.

> Thou sendest forth thy spirit, they are created: and thou renewest the face of the earth.

Galatians 4:6 also speaks of the procession of the Holy Spirit. God the Father "... hath sent forth the Spirit of His Son." The Spirit continuously and eternally submits to the Father and the Son.

> And because ye are sons, God hath sent forth the Spirit of his Son into your hearts, crying, Abba, Father.

Romans 8:9 denotes the voluntary submission of the Holy Spirit. In this verse the Spirit is called the Spirit of God, and then the Spirit of Christ.

> But ye are not in the flesh, but in the Spirit, if so be that the Spirit of God dwell in you. Now if any man have not the Spirit of Christ, he is none of his.

The procession of the Spirit can again be seen I Corinthians 2:11-12. There are several key phrases that indicate the voluntary submission of the Spirit to the Father and the Son. He is called "the Spirit of God" and then He is called "... the Spirit which is of God." Then I Corinthians 2:11-12 refers to Him as He that causes us to "know the things that are freely given to us of God."

> For what man knoweth the things of a man, save the spirit of man which is in him? even so the things of God knoweth no man, but the Spirit of God. Now we have received, not the spirit of the world, but the spirit which is of God; that we might know the things that are freely given to us of God.

Unitarians and Jehovah's Witnesses often speak of the "Procession of the Holy Spirit" as proof of the inferiority of the Spirit of God. They reason that voluntary, continuous, and eternal submission to the Father and the Son means that the Spirit is not equal to the other Persons of the Godhead. They reason that the "Procession of the Holy Spirit" renders Him inferior to God. But voluntary submission neither indicates inferiority nor does it indicate that He is not God.

Allow me to illustrate voluntary submission in human terms. My wife "voluntarily" submits to me, her husband. That does not mean that she is inferior to me at all. She is equally human and intelligent as I. She is equally saved as I, and equally has the same Holy Spirit as I. She didn't become less of a human through voluntary submission to her husband; she simply defined the relationship between us.

The Holy Spirit's relationship to the Father and the Son is continuous. It is the same today as it was before the creation of the world, and it will continue to be the same for all eternity. He is the eternal God, the Spirit. He has an eternal relationship of submission to the other Members of the Triune God.

Chapter Two

THE PERSONALITY OF THE HOLY SPIRIT

The question of "Personality" is not a discussion of whether the Spirit of God is sanguine or choleric, but rather, is He a Person or an influence. The theological usage of "Personality" speaks of personhood, not temperament.

There are several ways that we define personality. The first way is to say that by personality, someone has the power of self-consciousness and self-determination. Self-consciousness is the act or state of being aware of oneself, while self-determination is an act of one's own freewill whereby a person determines his actions from within. Both of these things are true of God; God has self-consciousness and self-determination. God is aware of His Own existence, and no one decides what God must do; He makes His Own decisions. We see this in Exodus 3:14.

> And God said unto Moses, I AM THAT I AM: and he said, Thus shalt thou say unto the children of Israel, I AM hath sent me unto you.

Furthermore, we can see in Genesis 1:26 that God has Self-determination, since He decided things, when as yet, there was no other being in existence that could have told Him what to do.

> And God said, Let us make man in our image, after our likeness: and let them have dominion over the fish of the

sea, and over the fowl of the air, and over the cattle, and over all the earth, and over every creeping thing that creepeth upon the earth.

Another way that we define personality is by showing the components of personality. To be a person, one must possess the attributes of personhood, which are intellect, sensibility, and volition. For the Holy Spirit to be a Person, He must be shown to have the attributes of Personality. One of the things that false cults often say is that the Holy Spirit is an influence or the power of God in an attempt to deny His Personality. For that reason, and many more, it is important to prove that the Holy Spirit, just like the Father and the Son, has the attributes of Personality.

The Spirit Has All the Attributes of Personality

A. Intellect

The Bible is full of verses that attribute intelligence to the Spirit of God. The Holy Spirit has a mind that is known to God the Father, according to Romans 8:27 where the Greek says, οἶδε τί τὸ φρόνημα τοῦ Πνεύματος[1] [*oide ti to fronema tou Pneumatos*], which literally means, "He knows what the mind (or thinking) of the Spirit is."

> And he that searcheth the hearts knoweth what is the mind of the Spirit, because he maketh intercession for the saints according to the will of God.

If God the Father knows what the thinking of the Spirit is, then the Spirit has to be thinking things. He has intellect. He can think and reason. This is not true of a force or influence. As it says in I Corinthians 2:10–11, the Spirit of God is a Person. He knows even the deep things of God.

> But God hath revealed them unto us by his Spirit: for the Spirit searcheth all things, yea, the deep things of God.

---

[1] *Scrivener's 1881 Textus Receptus.* (1995). (electronic ed., Ro 8:27). Oak Harbor: Logos Research Systems.

> For what man knoweth the things of a man, save the spirit of man which is in him? even so the things of God knoweth no man, but the Spirit of God.

Continuing on to I Corinthians 2:13, we can see that the Holy Spirit takes the knowledge that He has and teaches wisdom.

> Which things also we speak, not in the words which man's wisdom teacheth, but which the Holy Ghost teacheth; comparing spiritual things with spiritual.

We have looked at the first part of Personality, which is Intellect. Now it's time to look at the second part of Personality.

B. Sensibility

We could examine all the different emotions that the Holy Spirit possesses as proof of sensibility, but let's just examine two for right now. In Romans 15:30, the Bible confirms that the Holy Spirit is a Person by saying that He loves.

> Now I beseech you, brethren, for the Lord Jesus Christ's sake, and for the love of the Spirit, that ye strive together with me in your prayers to God for me;

In Ephesians 4:30, the Apostle Paul wrote that He has another emotion, and that is that He can be grieved.

> And grieve not the holy Spirit of God, whereby ye are sealed unto the day of redemption.

C. Volition

The third component of Personality is volition. By the word volition we are saying that the Holy Spirit has a freewill. I Corinthians 12:11 confirms that the Holy Spirit has a will when it says that He divides "... to every man severally as He will."

> But all these worketh that one and the selfsame Spirit, dividing to every man severally as he will.

The Personality of the Holy Spirit

Again, in Acts 16:6–10, the Bible uses several key words and phrases to indicate that the Holy Spirit has a will. It says that those accompanying the Apostle Paul "... were forbidden of the Holy Ghost to preach the word in Asia" (verse 6). When they tried to go into Bithynia, the "... Spirit suffered them not" (verse 7). While at Troas they endeavored to go into Macedonia being assured that "... the Lord had called" them "... to preach the Gospel unto them" (verse 10).

> Now when they had gone throughout Phrygia and the region of Galatia, and were forbidden of the Holy Ghost to preach the word in Asia, After they were come to Mysia, they assayed to go into Bithynia: but the Spirit suffered them not. And they passing by Mysia came down to Troas. And a vision appeared to Paul in the night; There stood a man of Macedonia, and prayed him, saying, Come over into Macedonia, and help us. And after he had seen the vision, immediately we endeavoured to go into Macedonia, assuredly gathering that the Lord had called us for to preach the gospel unto them.

We have seen that the Holy Spirit is a Person because He has the power of self-consciousness and of self-determination. He knows that He exists and determines things by Himself. No one else determines His course of action. Furthermore, the Holy Spirit has the attributes of personality. He has intellect, sensibility, and volition. Let's now consider another way that we can prove that He is a Person and not a force or an influence.

He Did and Does That Which Only a Person Could Do

The following twelve things that the Bible says about the Holy Spirit are things that only a Person could do. A force or an influence could do none of these twelve things. Let's consider them one-by-one.

A. He spoke and revealed

In I Timothy 4:1, Paul wrote to Timothy saying that the Spirit spoke in express words, revealing what the latter times would be like. Only a Person can speak and reveal things.

> Now the Spirit speaketh expressly, that in the latter times some shall depart from the faith, giving heed to seducing spirits, and doctrines of devils;

B. He teaches

C. He caused the apostles to remember

In John 14:26, it says that the Holy Spirit taught the apostles whatever they needed to know, and He brought "... all things to (their) remembrance" that Christ had said to them. These are two more things that only a Person could have done.

> But the Comforter, which is the Holy Ghost, whom the Father will send in my name, he shall teach you all things, and bring all things to your remembrance, whatsoever I have said unto you.

D. He testifies

According to John 15:26, the Holy Spirit testifies, that is, He provides an "eyewitness" account about Jesus Christ. An influence or a force cannot do so. Jesus declared, in John 15:26, "... He shall testify of me."

> But when the Comforter is come, whom I will send unto you from the Father, even the Spirit of truth, which proceedeth from the Father, he shall testify of me:

This word "testify" is the translation of the Greek word μαρτυρέω [martureo], which the lexicon[2] defines as:

---

2 Strong, J. (1995). *Enhanced Strong's Lexicon*. Woodside Bible Fellowship, #3140.

Verb. From μάρτυς [*martus*]. 79 occurrences. 1 to be a witness, to bear witness, i.e. to affirm that one has seen or heard or experienced something... 1A to give (not to keep back) testimony. 1B to utter honourable testimony, give a good report. 1C conjure, implore.

The Holy Spirit is called into a court of law "... to be a witness, to bear witness, i.e. to affirm that (He) has seen or heard or experienced something." This is not the action of a force or influence; this is the action of a Person. The same word is used of the Holy Spirit in Romans 8:16.

> The Spirit itself beareth witness with our spirit, that we are the children of God:

E. He guides

The next thing that the Holy Spirit does that demonstrates that He is a Person is that He leads or guides the sons of God according to Romans 8:14.

> For as many as are led by the Spirit of God, they are the sons of God.

F. He convicts

In John 16:7-8, we see another thing that is done by the Holy Spirit that no force or influence could perform. He reproves or convicts of sin.

> Nevertheless I tell you the truth; It is expedient for you that I go away: for if I go not away, the Comforter will not come unto you; but if I depart, I will send him unto you. And when he is come, he will reprove the world of sin, and of righteousness, and of judgment:

G. He strives

The Spirit of the LORD "strives" with man. The Hebrew word that is translated "strive" in Genesis 6:3 means "to contend" or "to plead." God's Spirit "pleads a cause" with man. Only a Person can strive or plead a cause. This is also another proof of the Personality of the Holy Spirit.

> And the LORD said, My spirit shall not always strive with man, for that he also is flesh: yet his days shall be an hundred and twenty years.

H. He commands and directs

In Acts 8:29, the Spirit commanded Philip to join the Ethiopian eunuch who was in his chariot. Philip was directed to this spot by the Spirit so that he could "... go near" and speak to the Ethiopian.

> Then the Spirit said unto Philip, Go near, and join thyself to this chariot.

I. He performs miracles

After baptizing the eunuch, the Spirit of the Lord "... caught away Philip" (Acts 8:39). This Greek verb that is translated "caught away" is the verb ἁρπάζω [harpazo] which the lexicon[3] defines as:

> 1 to seize, carry off by force. 2 to seize on, claim for one's self eagerly. 3 to snatch out or away.

The action that this verb describes could not be done by a force or influence. Acts 8:39 clearly demonstrates through the performance of this miracle that the Holy Spirit is a Person.

> And when they were come up out of the water, the Spirit of the Lord caught away Philip, that the eunuch saw him no more: and he went on his way rejoicing.

J. He calls to the ministry

His Personality can again be seen in Acts 13:2 where He called Barnabas and Saul to the work.

---

3 Ibid. #726.

The Personality of the Holy Spirit

> As they ministered to the Lord, and fasted, the Holy Ghost said, Separate me Barnabas and Saul for the work whereunto I have called them.

K. He sends laborers

The Holy Spirit sends forth laborers as can be seen in Acts 13:4. A force or influence cannot send forth laborers. That requires a Person.

> So they, being sent forth by the Holy Ghost, departed unto Seleucia; and from thence they sailed to Cyprus.

L. He helps our infirmities

M. He intercedes

Romans 8:26 states two things that the Third Person of the Trinity performs: He helps and He intercedes.

> Likewise the Spirit also helpeth our infirmities: for we know not what we should pray for as we ought: but the Spirit itself maketh intercession for us with groanings which cannot be uttered.

It is very interesting to note what the Spirit is doing when it says that He "… also helpeth our infirmities." The Textus Receptus[4] here says, συναντιλαμβάνεται ταῖς ἀσθενείαις ἡμῶν· [sunantilambanetai tais astheneiais hemon]. συναντιλαμβάνεται [sunantilambanetai] is the present tense, middle voice, indicative mood, third person singular conjugation of the verb συναντιλαμβάνομαι [sunantilambanomai] which means[5]:

> 1 to lay hold along with, to strive to obtain with others, help in obtaining. 2 to take hold with another.

The word συναντιλαμβάνομαι [sunantilambanomai] is an interesting combination of Greek words and really explains what

---
4 *Scrivener's 1881 Textus Receptus.*
5 Strong, J., #4878.

Romans 8:26 is stating when it says that the Spirit "helpeth." The word begins with the preposition σύν [sun] which means "together with." This preposition denotes union. He does not do all the work for us. Together with us He does the work. σύν [sun] lets us know that the Holy Spirit helps us, but we have to do our part as well.

The next part of the verb is ἀντιλαμβάνομαι [antilambanomai] which combines ἀντί [anti], which means "over against, opposite to, before, for, instead of, in place of someone," and λαμβάνομαι [lambanomai] which means "to take hold of." Romans 8:29 tells us the objective of His help.

> For whom he did foreknow, he also did predestinate to be conformed to the image of his Son, that he might be the firstborn among many brethren.

The Holy Spirit works with us to take us to the destination of having the image of Christ. He has to help us because of our infirmities, which literally means, "the want of strength, weakness, infirmity. Its native weakness and frailty."[6] God knows how weak we are and how impossible that it is for us to arrive at the destination of having the image of Christ in us by ourselves, so His Holy Spirit helps us to do what we need to do to arrive there. One of the ways that He does that is that He intercedes in prayer for us to have the image of Christ because we do not know, in our weakness, how to pray.

Now let us look at another way that the Holy Spirit can be proven to be a Person, not just a force or influence.

The Holy Spirit Is Described in Ways that Could Only Be Used of a Person

There are a number of ways that the Bible describes man's relationship with the Holy Spirit that definitely indicate that He is a Person. These are interactions with the Holy Spirit that could never be described as anything other than a person to Person relationship. These are things that the Bible says that we can do,

---
6 Ibid. #769.

should do, or are doing that indicate that our interaction with the Holy Spirit is with a Person.

A. He can be obeyed

Acts 10:19-21 tells the story of how the Holy Spirit commanded Peter to go with certain Gentile men to the house of Cornelius in Caesarea. Peter obeyed the command of the Holy Spirit, which automatically tells us that the Holy Spirit can be obeyed.

> While Peter thought on the vision, the Spirit said unto him, Behold, three men seek thee. Arise therefore, and get thee down, and go with them, doubting nothing: for I have sent them. Then Peter went down to the men which were sent unto him from Cornelius; and said, Behold, I am he whom ye seek: what is the cause wherefore ye are come?

B. You can lie to Him

It is impossible to lie to an impersonal force or influence. The only one to whom we could lie is another person; thus, when Peter told Ananias that he had lied to the Holy Spirit in Acts 5:3-4, it automatically implies that He is a Person.

> But Peter said, Ananias, why hath Satan filled thine heart to lie to the Holy Ghost, and to keep back part of the price of the land? Whiles it remained, was it not thine own? and after it was sold, was it not in thine own power? why hast thou conceived this thing in thine heart? thou hast not lied unto men, but unto God.

C. He can be resisted

Not only can we lie to the Holy Spirit, but we can also resist Him, as Stephen said in Acts 7:51. It is also interesting to note in this verse that grace is not irresistible since it says that "... ye do always resist the Holy Ghost."

> Ye stiffnecked and uncircumcised in heart and ears, ye do always resist the Holy Ghost: as your fathers did, so do ye.

D. He can be grieved

According to what Paul wrote in Ephesians 4:30, the Holy Spirit can be grieved.

> And grieve not the holy Spirit of God, whereby ye are sealed unto the day of redemption.

The Greek word translated "grieve" is λυπέω [lupeo], which the lexicon[7] defines as:

> λυπέω [lupeo] v. From λύπη [lupe]; 26 occurrences; 1 to make sorrowful. 2 to affect with sadness, cause grief, to throw into sorrow. 3 to grieve, offend. 4 to make one uneasy, cause him a scruple.

The Holy Spirit must be a Person since He can be saddened, made sorrowful and grieved.

E. He can be reverenced

Psalm 51:11 demonstrates the reverence that King David had for the Holy Spirit as he pleaded for forgiveness.

> Cast me not away from thy presence; and take not thy holy spirit from me.

F. He can be blasphemed

It is impossible to blaspheme a force or an influence. For us to speak against someone, that one must be a person. Since Matthew 12:31 says it is possible to blaspheme the Holy Spirit, then the Holy Spirit must be a Person.

---

7 Ibid. #3076.

The Personality of the Holy Spirit

Wherefore I say unto you, All manner of sin and blasphemy shall be forgiven unto men: but the blasphemy against the Holy Ghost shall not be forgiven unto men.

G.   He can be insulted

In Hebrews 10:29, we find the only usage of the Greek word ἐνυβρίζω [*enubrizo*], which was translated "despite." The word literally means[8] "to insult." The Spirit of God can be insulted.

Of how much sorer punishment, suppose ye, shall he be thought worthy, who hath trodden under foot the Son of God, and hath counted the blood of the covenant, wherewith he was sanctified, an unholy thing, and hath done despite unto the Spirit of grace?

There Are Times When the Spirit of God Forced a Grammatical Error in Normal Greek by His Description

There are, what might be considered, "grammatical errors" in the New Testament, which we believe were made on purpose to correctly maintain New Testament doctrine. For example, a grammatical error was created by the usage of the Greek word πνεῦμα [*pneuma*], which is translated "Spirit." The lexicon[9] defines this word in the following way:

The Greek word "Spirit" is πνεῦμα (*pneuma*), ατος (*atos*), τό (*to*): neuter noun, Spirit.

The word πνεῦμα [*pneuma*], which is translated "Spirit," is neuter gender, and therefore has to have neuter adjectives and neuter pronouns. However there are times when the New Testament will use male pronouns and thus create a grammatical error in order to force the reader to conclude that the Holy Spirit is a Person and not a thing. The usage of masculine pronouns clearly shows that

---
8 Ibid. #1796.
9 Swanson, J. (1997). Dictionary of Biblical Languages with Semantic Domains: Greek (New Testament) (electronic ed.). Oak Harbor: Logos Research Systems, Inc., #4460.

He is NOT an impersonal force, but a Person. We can see this in the usage of both personal and relative pronouns in the masculine in two passages that we will examine here.

A. **The usage of a masculine relative pronoun such as ἐκεῖνος [ekeinos][10] (that one, masculine) and of the singular personal pronoun ἑαυτοῦ [heautou][11], ἧς (ēs), οὗ (ou) (which is also reflexive).**

We can see the usage of the masculine relative pronoun ἐκεῖνος [ekeinos] and the reflexive, masculine, personal pronoun ἑαυτοῦ [heautou] in John 16:13-14. The relative pronoun could be translated "he" but could also be translated "that one" in the masculine. This could be considered a grammatical error since Spirit is neuter, but it is doctrinally correct since He is a Person. The same is true for the personal, reflexive pronoun ἑαυτοῦ [heautou] which is translated, "of Himself."

> Howbeit when **he**, the Spirit of truth, is come, he will guide you into all truth: for he shall not speak ***of himself***; but whatsoever he shall hear, that shall he speak: and he will shew you things to come. **He** shall glorify me: for he shall receive of mine, and shall shew it unto you.

In John 16:13-14, Each of the words that are highlighted in the English are likewise bolded in the Greek Textus Receptus.[12]

> ὅταν δὲ ἔλθῃ **ἐκεῖνος**, τὸ πνεῦμα τῆς ἀληθείας, ὁδηγήσει ὑμᾶς εἰς πᾶσαν τὴν ἀλήθειαν· οὐ γὰρ λαλήσει ἀφ' **ἑαυτοῦ**, ἀλλ' ὅσα ἂν ἀκούσῃ λαλήσει, καὶ τὰ ἐρχόμενα ἀναγγελεῖ ὑμῖν. **ἐκεῖνος** ἐμὲ δοξάσει, ὅτι ἐκ τοῦ ἐμοῦ λήψεται, καὶ ἀναγγελεῖ ὑμῖν.

B. **The usage of the masculine relative pronoun in John 15:26**

We can see the same thing in John 15:26 where John used the Greek masculine relative pronoun ἐκεῖνος [ekeinos] ("that

---
10 Strong, J., #1565.
11 Swanson, J., #4460.
12 *Scrivener's 1881 Textus Receptus.*

The Personality of the Holy Spirit

one," masculine) to speak of the Holy Spirit. This again could be considered a grammatical error, but it is doctrinally correct to speak of the Holy Spirit as "He," since He is a person, and not an impersonal force or influence.

> But when the Comforter is come, whom I will send unto you from the Father, even the Spirit of truth, which proceedeth from the Father, he shall testify of me:

Again, in John 15:26, the Textus Receptus[13] uses the masculine, relative pronoun ἐκεῖνος [ekeinos] ("that one," masculine) to describe the Spirit of God.

> ὅταν δὲ ἔλθῃ ὁ παράκλητος, ὃν ἐγὼ πέμψω ὑμῖν παρὰ τοῦ πατρός, τὸ πνεῦμα τῆς ἀληθείας, ὃ παρὰ τοῦ πατρὸς ἐκπορεύεται, ἐκεῖνος μαρτυρήσει περὶ ἐμοῦ·

The Spirit of God Appears in Relation with Other Persons

The Holy Spirit often appears in lists where it is natural to understand that each one, because of his association in the list, is a person. If you have an association of various persons, it does not fit to suddenly insert an impersonal thing in that list. That is the case in each of the verses listed below.

A.   The Spirit and the apostles

First, we will consider Acts 15:28 where the Holy Spirit is included in the grammar with the group of apostles in Jerusalem. Grammatically this verse makes no sense if the Holy Spirit were considered an influence and the apostles considered persons.

> For it seemed good to the Holy Ghost, and to us, to lay upon you no greater burden than these necessary things;

---

13 *Scrivener's 1881 Textus Receptus.*

B. The Spirit and Christ

In John 16:14, the Holy Spirit is spoken of as working together with Christ. Grammatically this verse would make no sense if Christ is a Person, which He clearly is, and the Holy Spirit is just a force.

> He shall glorify me: for he shall receive of mine, and shall shew it unto you.

C. The Spirit and the Father and the Son

II Corinthians 13:14 lists all three Persons of the Godhead. Even the false cults that deny the Personality of the Holy Spirit do not deny the Personality of the Father and the Lord Jesus Christ. Grammatically it makes no sense at all to say that the Father and the Son are Persons (even though you may deny the deity of Christ), but deny that the Holy Spirit, Who is listed in the same sentence, is a Person.

> The grace of the Lord Jesus Christ, and the love of God, and the communion of the Holy Ghost, be with you all. Amen.

D. The Spirit and the power of God

The Unitarians and Jehovah's Witnesses claim that the Holy Spirit is the power of God. This is not possible, however, since the power of God is distinguished from the Spirit of God and the Spirit of God is spoken of as having power also. Luke 4:14, speaks "... of the power of the Spirit," and thus distinguishes between the Spirit and the power of God. If the Spirit of God is the power of God, how does the power of God have its own power?

> And Jesus returned in the power of the Spirit into Galilee: and there went out a fame of him through all the region round about.

In Luke 1:35, the power of the Highest is contrasted with the Holy Ghost Who was to "... come upon" Mary.

> And the angel answered and said unto her, The Holy Ghost shall come upon thee, and the power of the Highest shall overshadow thee: therefore also that holy thing which shall be born of thee shall be called the Son of God.

Again, in Acts 10:38, the Holy Ghost is contrasted with power. This verse says that "... God anointed Jesus of Nazareth with the Holy Ghost and," additionally, "... with power." If Jesus was anointed with two things – the Holy Spirit on the one hand and power on the other hand – then the two things cannot be the same. There is a difference between the power of God and the Spirit of God.

> How God anointed Jesus of Nazareth with the Holy Ghost and with power: who went about doing good, and healing all that were oppressed of the devil; for God was with him.

The Scriptures definitely make a distinction between the Spirit of God, and the power of God. The Spirit is a Person of the Godhead. He is equal with God the Father and the Son of God. He is not an influence or a force. He is the Eternal Spirit.

Chapter Three

THE MINISTRY OF THE HOLY SPIRIT BETWEEN THE OLD AND THE NEW TESTAMENTS

Dispensationalists commonly explain the ministry of the Holy Spirit in the Old Testament versus the New Testament by saying that the Holy Spirit came "over" or "upon" people temporarily in the Old Testament, and when He was done He left, while now, after the day of Pentecost, He comes to live "in" or dwell "within" the believer permanently. This interpretation is based on two different arguments: the existence in the Old Testament of the ministry of the Holy Spirit coming "upon" believers, and Jesus' statement in John 14:17 where it says, "He (the Comforter) dwelleth *with* you, and shall be *in* you." I am a Dispensationalist and was taught this as a student in college and seminary studies, as well as in Bible conferences. This was certainly taught by C. I. Scofield and Lewis Sperry Chafer, and many other Dispensationalists as well.

All Dispensationalists, including Fundamental Baptists make certain distinctions in Biblical interpretation between the Old Testament and the New Testament. Historically we have always agreed on at least that difference. It is why Baptists refused to join the Reformation, which held, and holds, no difference between the Old Testament and the New Testament. In the 1689 London Baptist Confession, Chapter 1 and Section 8 it says:

The Old Testament in Hebrew *(which was the native language of the people of God of old)*, and the New Testament in Greek (which at the time of the writing of it was most generally known to the nations), being immediately inspired by God, and by his singular care and providence kept pure in all ages, are therefore authentic; so as in all controversies of religion, *the church is finally to appeal to them*. But because these original tongues are not known to all the people of God, who have a right unto, and interest in the Scriptures, and are commanded in the fear of God to read and search them, therefore they are to be translated into the vulgar language of every nation unto which they come, that the Word of God dwelling plentifully in all, they may worship him in an acceptable manner, and through patience and comfort of the Scriptures may have hope. (Romans 3:2; Isaiah 8:20; Acts 15:15; John 5:39; 1 Corinthians 14:6, 9, 11, 12, 24, 28; Colossians 3:16)

Independent, Fundamental, Baptists have a history of distinguishing between different dispensations. We have always distinguished between at least two dispensations.

While we have distinguished between the dispensations, we did not differentiate everything between one dispensation and another. We consider that some things have continued the same between dispensations with little or no change. An example of this is found in the fact that man was allowed to eat fruit and vegetables in the Garden of Eden, and man can still eat fruit and vegetables, though he is not limited to this. When Cain killed Abel it was evil, and it is still evil today. God created marriage to be one man and one woman, and that Biblically is still marriage today.

We do not deny that some things did change between dispensations. Animal sacrifices as a means of bringing about atonement came to an end with the sacrifice of Christ on Calvary. There is a difference in the prophetic faith of the Old Testament saint who looked forward to the sacrifice of Christ while he sacrificed an animal, and the historic faith of the New Testament saint who looks back on the sacrifice of Christ. Nonetheless, both are saved by faith in Jesus Christ as "... the Lamb of God, which taketh away the sin of the world" (John 1:29). John, Moses, and Abraham looked to Christ to be the "Lamb of God." With Paul, we look back and say, "Christ our Passover is sacrificed for us" (I Corinthians 5:7).

The doctrine of salvation did not change between dispensations. Only those who trusted in Jesus Christ Alone were saved. Salvation was always a work of God by faith. The security of the Old Testament saint was just as true as that of the New Testament saint. In fact, when Paul defines faith as "... the substance (the security) of things hoped for ..." (Hebrews 11:1), he illustrated it with the elders (verse 2), the creation (verse 3), Abel (verse 4), Enoch (verse 5), Noah (verse 7), Abraham (verses 8-10), Sarah (verse 11), et al. Every illustration of Biblical faith that Paul chose was from the Old Testament. Obviously, the fundamental meaning of faith in salvation had not changed.

Let's consider the work of the Spirit of God in the Old Testament believer and in the New Testament believer. The typical Dispensationalist's explanation is that the Holy Spirit temporarily came upon the Old Testament saint, but He comes to permanently indwell the saint in this dispensation. While this sounds like a good explanation for some Old Testament passages like I Samuel 16:13-14, that seem to indicate that the Holy Spirit "left" someone, there may be a different explanation.

> Then Samuel took the horn of oil, and anointed him in the midst of his brethren: and **the Spirit of the LORD came upon David** from that day forward. So Samuel rose up, and went to Ramah. But **the Spirit of the LORD departed from Saul**, and an evil spirit from the LORD troubled him.

This does not actually say that the Old Testament saint does not have the permanent indwelling of the Holy Spirit. What it does plainly say is that the Holy Spirit came upon David as a recognition that He anointed him to be king of Israel, He had left Saul because he no longer recognized him as king. I will come back to these verses again a little later.

Peter wrote about this question to the Jews of the dispersion in I Peter 1:10–11.

> Of which salvation the prophets have enquired and searched diligently, who prophesied of the grace that should come unto you: Searching what, or what manner of time the Spirit of Christ which was in them did signify, when it testified beforehand the sufferings of Christ, and the glory that should follow.

As Peter wrote to these Jewish believers in Christ, He told them that the Old Testament prophets had "the Spirit of Christ which was in them." But, wait a minute! Weren't we told that the Old Testament saint had the Holy Spirit temporarily "over" him and NOT "in" him? What does the Greek say? It says, τὸ ἐν αὐτοῖς Πνεῦμα Χριστοῦ [to en autois Pneuma Christou][1]. It clearly says, the Spirit of Christ **IN** them. With that in mind, let's reexamine this teaching, and see if there is another way to explain the difference.

A. The Holy Spirit "in" the believer

First, we will consider whether or not there are verses that teach the indwelling of the Holy Spirit in the Old Testament. In Genesis 41:38, the context deals with Joseph who had just been released from prison and interpreted Pharaoh's dream.

> And Pharaoh said unto his servants, Can we find such a one as this is, a man in whom the Spirit of God is?

God told Moses to take Joshua, "… a man in whom is the Spirit." Moses was told by God that Joshua had the Spirit in him. After Moses laid his hands on Joshua, some of Moses' honor would be upon Joshua. That "honor" was the presence of the Holy Spirit "upon" Joshua. The Spirit was already "in" him, and then He was "upon" him according to Numbers 27:18–20.

---

[1] *Scrivener's 1881 Textus Receptus.* (1995). (electronic ed., 1 Pe 1:11). Oak Harbor: Logos Research Systems.

> And the LORD said unto Moses, Take thee Joshua the son of Nun, a man in whom is the spirit, and lay thine hand upon him; And set him before Eleazar the priest, and before all the congregation; and give him a charge in their sight. And thou shalt put some of thine honour upon him, that all the congregation of the children of Israel may be obedient.

In Nehemiah 9:20, it talks about the ministry of the indwelling Holy Spirit in the Children of Israel. "Thy Good Spirit" instructed believers.

> Thou gavest also thy good spirit to instruct them, and withheldest not thy manna from their mouth, and gavest them water for their thirst.

Nehemiah went on in chapter nine to write about the ministry of the inspiration of the Word of God that was performed by the Holy Spirit within the prophets according to verse thirty.

> Yet many years didst thou forbear them, and testifiedst against them by thy spirit in thy prophets: yet would they not give ear: therefore gavest thou them into the hand of the people of the lands.

In Job 27:3, it clearly says that the Spirit of God was "in" Job's nostrils.

> All the while my breath is in me, and the spirit of God is in my nostrils;

Job 32:8 says that there is a Spirit "in" man that is given by the Almighty that gives man "understanding," which is another ministry of the Holy Spirit.

> But there is a spirit in man: and the inspiration of the Almighty giveth them understanding.

Job 32:18 says that the Holy Spirit within him constrained him.

> For I am full of matter, the spirit within me constraineth me.

In Isaiah 63:11, the Bible says that Moses had "... His Holy Spirit within him."

> Then he remembered the days of old, Moses, and his people, saying, Where is he that brought them up out of the sea with the shepherd of his flock? where is he that put his holy Spirit within him?

In Ezekiel 36:26-27, and 29, we find the prophecy of the restoration of Israel from its Babylonian captivity. God promised to put "a new spirit ... within" the Jewish people both in verses 26 and 27. He also promised that they would have "no famine."

> A new heart also will I give you, and a new spirit will I put within you: and I will take away the stony heart out of your flesh, and I will give you an heart of flesh. And I will put my spirit within you, and cause you to walk in my statutes, and ye shall keep my judgments, and do them. ... I will also save you from all your uncleannesses: and I will call for the corn, and will increase it, and lay no famine upon you.

In His explanation of the Valley of Dry Bones, God tells Ezekiel that He shall put His Spirit "in" them. Ezekiel 37:14 makes it clear that the Jewish people understood in the Old Testament that the Spirit of God dwelt in the believer.

> And shall put my spirit in you, and ye shall live, and I shall place you in your own land: then shall ye know that I the LORD have spoken it, and performed it, saith the LORD.

Another reference to the Holy Spirit and His work in the believer is found in John 3:3-10. After explaining to Nicodemus the work of the Holy Spirit in bringing about the new birth, Jesus asked him, "Art thou a master of Israel, and knowest not these things" (verse 10)?

> Jesus answered and said unto him, Verily, verily, I say unto thee, Except a man be born again, he cannot see the kingdom of God. Nicodemus saith unto him, How can a man be born when he is old? can he enter the second time into his mother's womb, and be born? Jesus answered, Verily, verily, I say unto thee, Except a man be born of water and of the Spirit, he cannot enter into the kingdom of God. That which is born of the flesh is flesh; and that which is born of the Spirit is spirit. Marvel not that I said unto thee, Ye must be born again. The wind bloweth where it listeth, and thou hearest the sound thereof, but canst not tell whence it cometh, and whither it goeth: so is every one that is born of the Spirit. Nicodemus answered and said unto him, How can these things be? Jesus answered and said unto him, Art thou a master of Israel, and knowest not these things?

According to Daniel 6:3, Nebuchadnezzar noted that Daniel had "... an excellent Spirit in him."

> Then this Daniel was preferred above the presidents and princes, because an excellent spirit was in him; and the king thought to set him over the whole realm.

The Holy Spirit performed the exact same ministry in the Old Testament that He performs in the New Testament. Salvation did not change from one dispensation to another, and neither did the Holy Spirit's ministry in the life of the believer.

Now let's turn our attention to what the New Testament says about the Holy Spirit indwelling the believer. The New Testament is very specific about the Holy Spirit's ministry in the believer in Romans 8:9, and 11.

> But ye are not in the flesh, but in the Spirit, if so be that the Spirit of God dwell in you. Now if any man have not

the Spirit of Christ, he is none of his. ... But if the Spirit of him that raised up Jesus from the dead dwell in you, he that raised up Christ from the dead shall also quicken your mortal bodies by his Spirit that dwelleth in you.

The church is the corporate dwelling place of the Holy Spirit, and the following verses all speak in the plural, referring to the members of the church. These verses are often quoted in the singular by believers who say, "I am the temple of the Holy Spirit because He lives in me." But in reality, I Corinthians 3:16–17 speaks of the relationship of the Holy Spirit to the church, and all of the references to "you" are in the plural.

Know ye not that ye are the temple of God, and that the Spirit of God dwelleth in you? If any man defile the temple of God, him shall God destroy; for the temple of God is holy, which temple ye are.

The accuracy of the statement that everything is in the plural can be easily seen in the Textus Receptus[2] Greek in I Corinthians 3:16–17 where it uses the second person plural verb ἐστε [*este*] (you (plural) are) and the second person plural personal possessive pronoun ὑμῖν [*humin*] (you (plural)), and the second person plural relative pronoun οἵτινές [*hoitines*] (you (plural)).

Οὐκ οἴδατε ὅτι ναὸς Θεοῦ **ἐστε**, καὶ τὸ Πνεῦμα τοῦ Θεοῦ οἰκεῖ ἐν **ὑμῖν**; εἴ τις τὸν ναὸν τοῦ Θεοῦ φθείρει, φθερεῖ τοῦτον ὁ Θεός· ὁ γὰρ ναὸς τοῦ Θεοῦ ἅγιός ἐστιν, **οἵτινές ἐστε ὑμεῖς**.

Though arguments can be made concerning the indwelling of the Holy Spirit in the individual believer, these particular verses are actually talking about the Holy Spirit dwelling in His temple, which is the church.

Similarly, we find the second person plural, aorist tense, passive voice, indicative conjugation (ἐσφραγίσθητε [*esphragisthete*])

---

2 Ibid. I Corinthians 3:16–17.

of the Greek verb σφραγίζω [sphragizo] which means[3] "you (plural) were sealed," as we find in Ephesians 4:30.

> And grieve not the holy Spirit of God, whereby ye are sealed unto the day of redemption.

Again, the plural pronoun is used in II Timothy 1:14 where the original Greek says, "ἐνοικοῦντος ἐν ἡμῖν" [enoikountos en hemin] which is correctly translated, "dwelleth in us."

> That good thing which was committed unto thee keep by the Holy Ghost which dwelleth in us.

Similarly, in James 4:5, we have the statement that "The Spirit that dwelleth in us. ..." This again identifies the Spirit's dwelling place in the plural and not in the singular.

> Do ye think that the scripture saith in vain, The spirit that dwelleth in us lusteth to envy?

In Ephesians 4:6, God the Father is identified in the same way as the Holy Spirit to be "in you all," which again is "you (plural)," as can be seen in the Greek καὶ ἐν πᾶσιν ὑμῖν.

> One God and Father of all, who is above all, and through all, and in you all.

B. The Holy Spirit came "upon" some believers.

1. In the Old Testament

Now let's look at the places where the Bible speaks of the Holy Spirit coming "upon" or "over" someone. When we analyze the Old Testament usage, we find six different categories where the Holy Spirit is spoken of as coming "upon" someone in the Old Testament. The first category of person over which the Holy Spirit came was the king.

---

[3] Strong, J. (1995). *Enhanced Strong's Lexicon*. Woodside Bible Fellowship, #4972.

a. The king

We find several references to the Spirit of God coming upon Saul as king in the Old Testament. The first place we will look at is I Samuel 10:6, and 10.

> And the Spirit of the LORD will come upon thee, and thou shalt prophesy with them, and shalt be turned into another man. ... And when they came thither to the hill, behold, a company of prophets met him; and the Spirit of God came upon him, and he prophesied among them.

We see it again in I Samuel 11:6.

> And the Spirit of God came upon Saul when he heard those tidings, and his anger was kindled greatly.

In I Samuel 16:13-14, there is an Old Testament reference to the Spirit coming upon David to anoint him as king, while at the same moment leaving Saul, signifying that Saul was no longer chosen by God to be king.

> Then Samuel took the horn of oil, and anointed him in the midst of his brethren: and the Spirit of the LORD came upon David from that day forward. So Samuel rose up, and went to Ramah. But the Spirit of the LORD departed from Saul, and an evil spirit from the LORD troubled him.

The Spirit of God can be seen coming upon King David's allies when in his presence. In I Chronicles 12:17-18 David challenged Amasai to prove his loyalty to King David, and in response, the Holy Spirit came upon him.

> And David went out to meet them, and answered and said unto them, If ye be come peaceably unto me to help me, mine heart shall be knit unto you: but if ye be come to betray me to mine enemies, seeing there is no wrong in mine hands, the God of our fathers look thereon, and rebuke it. Then the spirit came upon Amasai, who was

chief of the captains, and he said, Thine are we, David, and on thy side, thou son of Jesse: peace, peace be unto thee, and peace be to thine helpers; for thy God helpeth thee. Then David received them, and made them captains of the band.

The first category of person upon whom the Holy Spirit came was the king. Let's move on to the second category of person as someone upon whom the Spirit of God came.

b. The priest

II Chronicles 24:20 specifies the second kind of person was the priest. The anointing of the priest with oil, as the king, was merely symbolic of the anointing with the Holy Spirit, which was necessary for both offices.

And the Spirit of God came upon Zechariah the son of Jehoiada the priest, which stood above the people, and said unto them, Thus saith God, Why transgress ye the commandments of the LORD, that ye cannot prosper? because ye have forsaken the LORD, he hath also forsaken you.

This takes us to the third category whose office is equally important with the king and the priest.

c. The judge

The first judge, that we know of, upon whom the Holy Spirit came was Othniel, Caleb's younger brother according to Judges 3:9-10.

And when the children of Israel cried unto the LORD, the LORD raised up a deliverer to the children of Israel, who delivered them, even Othniel the son of Kenaz, Caleb's younger brother. And the Spirit of the LORD came upon him, and he judged Israel, and went out to war: and the LORD delivered Chushanrishathaim king of Mesopotamia into his hand; and his hand prevailed against Chushanrishathaim.

Judges 6:34 tells us that the Holy Spirit also came upon Gideon as a judge.

> But the Spirit of the LORD came upon Gideon, and he blew a trumpet; and Abiezer was gathered after him.

The next judge that we read about upon whom the Spirit of God came was Jephthah. "... The Spirit of the LORD came upon Jephthah," according to Judges 11:29.

> Then the Spirit of the LORD came upon Jephthah, and he passed over Gilead, and Manasseh, and passed over Mizpeh of Gilead, and from Mizpeh of Gilead he passed over unto the children of Ammon.

The next three verses that we will examine all deal with a judge named Samson. In Judges 14:6, and 19 it talks about the Spirit of the LORD coming upon him.

> And the Spirit of the LORD came mightily upon him, and he rent him as he would have rent a kid, and he had nothing in his hand: but he told not his father or his mother what he had done. ... And the Spirit of the LORD came upon him, and he went down to Ashkelon, and slew thirty men of them, and took their spoil, and gave change of garments unto them which expounded the riddle. And his anger was kindled, and he went up to his father's house.

Again, in Judges 15:14, "... the Spirit of the LORD" came upon Samson. Here it specifically mentions that "... the Spirit of the LORD came mightily upon him."

> And when he came unto Lehi, the Philistines shouted against him: and the Spirit of the LORD came mightily upon him, and the cords that were upon his arms became

as flax that was burnt with fire, and his bands loosed from off his hands.

Samson was the twelfth and last judge of the Book of Judges, which takes us to the fourth category.

d. The prophet

The fourth category of people upon whom the Spirit of God came was the prophet. According to Numbers 11:25-26, and 29 God took the Spirit that was upon Moses and put Him over "... the seventy elders" that had been appointed by Moses, and "... they prophesied" also.

> And the LORD came down in a cloud, and spake unto him, and took of the spirit that was upon him, and gave it unto the seventy elders: and it came to pass, that, when the spirit rested upon them, they prophesied, and did not cease. But there remained two of the men in the camp, the name of the one was Eldad, and the name of the other Medad: and the spirit rested upon them; and they were of them that were written, but went not out unto the tabernacle: and they prophesied in the camp. ... And Moses said unto him, Enviest thou for my sake? would God that all the LORD'S people were prophets, and that the LORD would put his spirit upon them!

In Numbers 24:2, the Bible tells us how the Spirit of God came upon a false prophet, Balaam, in order to force him to prophesy the truth.

> And Balaam lifted up his eyes, and he saw Israel abiding in his tents according to their tribes; and the spirit of God came upon him.

Saul sent messengers to take King David, but when they came in contact with the prophets, according to I Samuel 19:20, and 23, they too prophesied.

And Saul sent messengers to take David: and when they saw the company of the prophets prophesying, and Samuel standing as appointed over them, the Spirit of God was upon the messengers of Saul, and they also prophesied. ... And he went thither to Naioth in Ramah: and the Spirit of God was upon him also, and he went on, and prophesied, until he came to Naioth in Ramah.

Before Elijah was taken to heaven, he told Elisha that he could make a request. In II Kings 2:9, the request that Elisha made was for a "... double portion of thy Spirit be upon me."

And it came to pass, when they were gone over, that Elijah said unto Elisha, Ask what I shall do for thee, before I be taken away from thee. And Elisha said, I pray thee, let a double portion of thy spirit be upon me.

In II Kings 2:15, the sons of the prophets stated that, "The Spirit of Elijah doth rest on Elisha." Again, the Spirit of God came upon a prophet.

And when the sons of the prophets which were to view at Jericho saw him, they said, The spirit of Elijah doth rest on Elisha. And they came to meet him, and bowed themselves to the ground before him.

We find another prophet, Azariah, upon whom the Spirit of God came, according to II Chronicles 15:1.

And the Spirit of God came upon Azariah the son of Oded:

We have seen how the Holy Spirit came upon kings, priests, judges, and prophets in the Old Testament. Now let's look at a fifth category.

e. The Messiah

A fifth category of person upon whom the Holy Spirit was prophesied to come was on the Messiah. He was prophesied to come on the Messiah as king in Isaiah 11:1–2.

> And there shall come forth a rod out of the stem of Jesse, and a Branch shall grow out of his roots: And the spirit of the LORD shall rest upon him, the spirit of wisdom and understanding, the spirit of counsel and might, the spirit of knowledge and of the fear of the LORD;

In Isaiah 42:1, the Holy Spirit was prophesied to come upon the Messiah as a priest.

> Behold my servant, whom I uphold; mine elect, in whom my soul delighteth; I have put my spirit upon him: he shall bring forth judgment to the Gentiles.

Isaiah again prophesied the anointing of the Holy Spirit upon the Messiah as a judge in Isaiah 59:20-21.

> And the Redeemer shall come to Zion, and unto them that turn from transgression in Jacob, saith the LORD. As for me, this is my covenant with them, saith the LORD; My spirit that is upon thee, and my words which I have put in thy mouth, shall not depart out of thy mouth, nor out of the mouth of thy seed, nor out of the mouth of thy seed's seed, saith the LORD, from henceforth and for ever.

In Isaiah 61:1, the Spirit was prophesied to come upon the Messiah as the prophet.

> The Spirit of the Lord GOD is upon me; because the LORD hath anointed me to preach good tidings unto the meek; he hath sent me to bind up the brokenhearted, to proclaim liberty to the captives, and the opening of the prison to them that are bound;

f. The Jewish people in the last days

The Old Testament prophesied a time when the Holy Spirit would come upon many Jewish people in the last days, according to Isaiah 44:3.

The Ministry of the Holy Spirit between the Old and the New Testament 103

> For I will pour water upon him that is thirsty, and floods upon the dry ground: I will pour my spirit upon thy seed, and my blessing upon thine offspring:

Joel also prophesied this by firmly stating that the Spirit of God would come upon "... your sons and your daughters ... your old men ..." and "your young men." This was to include also the servants and the handmaids in those days.

> And it shall come to pass afterward, that I will pour out my spirit upon all flesh; and your sons and your daughters shall prophesy, your old men shall dream dreams, your young men shall see visions: And also upon the servants and upon the handmaids in those days will I pour out my spirit (Joel 2:28–29).

Peter said that this prophecy was fulfilled on the day of Pentecost by those present.

> But this is that which was spoken by the prophet Joel; And it shall come to pass in the last days, saith God, I will pour out of my Spirit upon all flesh: and your sons and your daughters shall prophesy, and your young men shall see visions, and your old men shall dream dreams: And on my servants and on my handmaidens I will pour out in those days of my Spirit; and they shall prophesy: And I will shew wonders in heaven above, and signs in the earth beneath; blood, and fire, and vapour of smoke: The sun shall be turned into darkness, and the moon into blood, before that great and notable day of the Lord come: And it shall come to pass, that whosoever shall call on the name of the Lord shall be saved. Ye men of Israel, hear these words; Jesus of Nazareth, a man approved of God among you by miracles and wonders and signs, which God did by him in the midst of you, as ye yourselves also know: Him, being delivered by the determinate counsel and foreknowledge of God, ye have taken, and by wicked

hands have crucified and slain: Whom God hath raised up, having loosed the pains of death: because it was not possible that he should be holden of it (Acts 2:16-24).

Peter stated that the baptism of the Holy Spirit on the day of Pentecost was the fulfillment of Joel's prophecy in which Joel said that the Spirit of God would come "... upon ... your sons and your daughters" in the last days.

2. The Holy Spirit came upon some people during the time of the writing of the New Testament

a. At the birth of Christ

According to Luke 1:35, the virgin conception was made possible by the fact that the Holy Spirit came upon Mary.

> And the angel answered and said unto her, The Holy Ghost shall come upon thee, and the power of the Highest shall overshadow thee: therefore also that holy thing which shall be born of thee shall be called the Son of God.

In Luke 2:25, we see that the Holy Spirit came upon Simeon at the time that Jesus was taken to the temple to offer a sacrifice for Jesus' birth.

> And, behold, there was a man in Jerusalem, whose name was Simeon; and the same man was just and devout, waiting for the consolation of Israel: and the Holy Ghost was upon him.

b. Upon Christ for His ministry

In a very special way, the Lord really began His ministry at His baptism. At the beginning of His ministry as King, Priest, Judge and Prophet, Jesus was anointed by the Holy Spirit Who came upon Him.

> And Jesus, when he was baptized, went up straightway out of the water: and, lo, the heavens were opened unto him, and he saw the Spirit of God descending like a dove,

and lighting upon him (Matthew 3:16) ... And straightway coming up out of the water, he saw the heavens opened, and the Spirit like a dove descending upon him (Mark 1:10) ... And the Holy Ghost descended in a bodily shape like a dove upon him, and a voice came from heaven, which said, Thou art my beloved Son; in thee I am well pleased (Luke 3:22). ... And I knew him not: but he that sent me to baptize with water, the same said unto me, Upon whom thou shalt see the Spirit descending, and remaining on him, the same is he which baptizeth with the Holy Ghost (John 1:33).

At the beginning of His ministry, according to Luke 4:18, Jesus quoted Isaiah 61:1 saying that the Spirit of the LORD was upon Him and the Spirit of God had anointed Him to preach.

> The Spirit of the Lord is upon me, because he hath anointed me to preach the gospel to the poor; he hath sent me to heal the brokenhearted, to preach deliverance to the captives, and recovering of sight to the blind, to set at liberty them that are bruised,

As Peter preached the Gospel to Cornelius and his family, he told them that Jesus had been anointed with the Holy Spirit.

> How God anointed Jesus of Nazareth with the Holy Ghost and with power: who went about doing good, and healing all that were oppressed of the devil; for God was with him (Acts 10:38).

c. Upon the apostles, their helpers, etc.

Jesus referred to the Holy Spirit baptizing the apostles (Acts 1:5) as being synonymous with the Holy Spirit coming "upon" them (Acts 1:8).

> For John truly baptized with water; but ye shall be baptized with the Holy Ghost not many days hence. ... But ye shall receive power, after that the Holy Ghost is

come upon you: and ye shall be witnesses unto me both in Jerusalem, and in all Judaea, and in Samaria, and unto the uttermost part of the earth.

Likewise, in Luke 24:49, where Jesus foretold this event, He said that "I send the promise of my Father **upon** you."

And, behold, I send the promise of my Father upon you: but tarry ye in the city of Jerusalem, until ye be endued with power from on high.

Peter referred to the baptism with the Holy Spirit on the Day of Pentecost as the fulfillment of Joel's prophecy, as we stated above. The baptism with the Holy Spirit, according to Joel's prophecy, was interpreted by Peter to mean that the Holy Spirit came upon the apostles as seen in Acts 2:16-18.

But this is that which was spoken by the prophet Joel; And it shall come to pass in the last days, saith God, I will pour out of my Spirit upon all flesh: and your sons and your daughters shall prophesy, and your young men shall see visions, and your old men shall dream dreams: And on my servants and on my handmaidens I will pour out in those days of my Spirit; and they shall prophesy:

While Peter was preaching the Gospel to Cornelius, the Holy Spirit "... fell on all them which heard the Word."

While Peter yet spake these words, the Holy Ghost fell on all them which heard the word (Acts 10:44). ... Can any man forbid water, that these should not be baptized, which have received the Holy Ghost as well as we (Acts 10:47)?

As Peter explained to the church in Jerusalem what happened at Cornelius's house, he told them in Acts 11:15-16 that the Holy Spirit "... fell on them."

> And as I began to speak, the Holy Ghost fell on them, as on us at the beginning. Then remembered I the word of the Lord, how that he said, John indeed baptized with water; but ye shall be baptized with the Holy Ghost.

Only Jesus Christ could make someone an apostle. Only the apostles could give someone the Holy Spirit upon them. This was only done through the laying on of the hands of an apostle. We can easily see this pattern in Acts 8:14-19 where the apostles had to go personally to Samaria to lay hands on the Samaritan believers so the Holy Spirit would come upon them. But, no amount of money could buy an apostleship; only Jesus Christ could make someone an apostle.

> Now when the apostles which were at Jerusalem heard that Samaria had received the word of God, they sent unto them Peter and John: Who, when they were come down, prayed for them, that they might receive the Holy Ghost: (For as yet he was fallen upon none of them: only they were baptized in the name of the Lord Jesus.) Then laid they their hands on them, and they received the Holy Ghost. And when Simon saw that through laying on of the apostles' hands the Holy Ghost was given, he offered them money, Saying, Give me also this power, that on whomsoever I lay hands, he may receive the Holy Ghost.

As Peter wrote to the Jewish believers of the diaspora, in I Peter 4:14, he told them that the Spirit of God rested upon them.

> If ye be reproached for the name of Christ, happy are ye; for the spirit of glory and of God resteth upon you: on their part he is evil spoken of, but on your part he is glorified.

Modern scholars would say that Peter got it backwards when he said that the Holy Spirit came upon the New Testament believers, and in I Peter 1:10-11, said that the Old Testament prophets had the Spirit of Christ in them. But no, Peter didn't get it backwards.

Of which salvation the prophets have enquired and searched diligently, who prophesied of the grace that should come unto you: Searching what, or what manner of time the Spirit of Christ which was in them did signify, when it testified beforehand the sufferings of Christ, and the glory that should follow.

"In" and "Upon" Explained

A. The Spirit of God was "in" every believer in order to teach, guard, keep, etc.

In Psalm 51:12, David talked about the ministry of the Holy Spirit in him, saying that the Holy Spirit would "uphold" him.

> Restore unto me the joy of thy salvation; and uphold me with thy free spirit.

According to II Corinthians 1:22, the Holy Spirit in the believer "seals" him eternally.

> Who hath also sealed us, and given the earnest of the Spirit in our hearts.

Paul said that the indwelling Holy Spirit is the down-payment that secures our salvation according to II Corinthians 5:5.

> Now he that hath wrought us for the selfsame thing is God, who also hath given unto us the earnest of the Spirit.

Paul summed up both of those things in Ephesians 1:13-14. Here Paul wrote that immediately upon faith in Jesus Christ, God gave us the Holy Spirit as a seal to show ownership since the blood of Jesus Christ purchased us. God declared that His Spirit was our guarantee that, as His purchased possession, we would obtain the inheritance.

> In whom ye also trusted, after that ye heard the word of truth, the gospel of your salvation: in whom also after

that ye believed, ye were sealed with that holy Spirit of promise, Which is the earnest of our inheritance until the redemption of the purchased possession, unto the praise of his glory.

When the Bible speaks about the Holy Spirit indwelling the believer, it is talking about His ministry in the life of the believer. Since He "seals" the believer according to Ephesians 4:30, He cannot leave us. Since He cannot leave us, we should not grieve Him.

And grieve not the holy Spirit of God, whereby ye are sealed unto the day of redemption.

B. The Spirit of God ONLY came "upon" the kings, priests, judges, and prophets

The baptism of the Holy Spirit, or as it was also known, the anointing of the Holy Spirit, or the Spirit coming upon someone, was reserved for kings, priests, judges, prophets, the Messiah or the men who helped these men. We can see this in Acts 2:16-18, and 20, in the prophecy of Joel that was quoted by Peter on the Day of Pentecost.

But this is that which was spoken by the prophet Joel; And it shall come to pass in the last days, saith God, I will pour out of my Spirit upon all flesh: and your sons and your daughters shall prophesy, and your young men shall see visions, and your old men shall dream dreams: And on my servants and on my handmaidens I will pour out in those days of my Spirit; and they shall prophesy ... The sun shall be turned into darkness, and the moon into blood, before that great and notable day of the Lord come:

The Dispensational Difference

There is a dispensational difference, but that difference is not the Holy Spirit's ministry of indwelling or coming upon one of the four designated offices. According to Ephesians 2:12, the real dispensational difference is found in the fact that Gentiles, who at one time had no hope of participation in any future home with the Lord, because they were foreigners to the promises of the new Jerusalem, have now been brought into citizenship rights.

> That at that time ye were without Christ, being aliens from the commonwealth of Israel, and strangers from the covenants of promise, having no hope, and without God in the world:

This new citizenship in the commonwealth of Israel is brought about by the death of Jesus Christ for the sins of all mankind and the creation of a new body.

> And that he might reconcile both unto God in one body by the cross, having slain the enmity thereby (Ephesians 2:16).

The change in dispensations required God to bring the foreigners (Gentiles) near (verse 13), and tear down the wall that separated us (verse 14). It required the destruction of the commandments that divided us and the creation of "one new man" in order to make peace (verse 15). In that new body, the church, we were included in the rights of citizenship, which were denied to us before. Ephesians 2:13–19 lists for us the details of what it cost God to create this new relationship that we can now enjoy. This is the Church Age, or the Dispensation of Grace.

> But now in Christ Jesus ye who sometimes were far off are made nigh by the blood of Christ. For he is our peace, who hath made both one, and hath broken down the middle wall of partition between us; Having abolished in his flesh the enmity, even the law of commandments contained in ordinances; for to make in himself of twain one new man, so making peace; And that he might reconcile both unto God in one body by the cross, having slain the enmity thereby: And came and preached peace

to you which were afar off, and to them that were nigh. For through him we both have access by one Spirit unto the Father. Now therefore ye are no more strangers and foreigners, but fellowcitizens with the saints, and of the household of God;

This new dispensation has a new relationship with the Spirit of God, which according to I Corinthians 12:13, involves all, whether Jew or Gentile, being "... baptized into one body" (εἰς ἓν σῶμα) and drinking "... into one Spirit" (εἰς ἓν Πνεῦμα). We are one through a new work of the Holy Spirit in the Body of Christ.

For by one Spirit are we all baptized into one body, whether we be Jews or Gentiles, whether we be bond or free; and have been all made to drink into one Spirit.

We have briefly considered a few of the differences of the new dispensation. Gentiles are now included through the existence of a new Body, the Body of Christ. But there are still some passages that may be hard to understand in the light of this interpretation. Let's consider them now.

Problematic Texts

A. The Holy Spirit came "upon" someone or something

A very interesting study would be to find the different animals that God used in the Scriptures. Certainly Numbers 22:22-30 tells us of one of those animals that God used, which we should find interesting in several ways. Balaam should have acted surprised that his ass was talking at all, but in his rage, he does not even seem to notice. This always makes me think, if you are arguing with an ass, and the ass is right, that's a good time to quit arguing. Another thing that Numbers 22:22-30 makes me think is, if you have the habit of arguing with an ass and everyone who is watching thinks the animal is right, or can't tell which of you is the prophet and which is the ass, maybe it's time to consider not arguing any more. The one thing that we really need to understand from Numbers 22:22-30 is that God did not call the ass as His prophet. But, God has the right of Creator to use whatever He has created as His instrument. This was *NOT* baptism with the Holy Spirit.

> And God's anger was kindled because he went: and the angel of the LORD stood in the way for an adversary against him. Now he was riding upon his ass, and his two servants were with him. And the ass saw the angel of the LORD standing in the way, and his sword drawn in his hand: and the ass turned aside out of the way, and went into the field: and Balaam smote the ass, to turn her into the way. But the angel of the LORD stood in a path of the vineyards, a wall being on this side, and a wall on that side. And when the ass saw the angel of the LORD, she thrust herself unto the wall, and crushed Balaam's foot against the wall: and he smote her again. And the angel of the LORD went further, and stood in a narrow place, where was no way to turn either to the right hand or to the left. And when the ass saw the angel of the LORD, she fell down under Balaam: and Balaam's anger was kindled, and he smote the ass with a staff. And the LORD opened the mouth of the ass, and she said unto Balaam, What have I done unto thee, that thou hast smitten me these three times? And Balaam said unto the ass, Because thou hast mocked me: I would there were a sword in mine hand, for now would I kill thee. And the ass said unto Balaam, Am not I thine ass, upon which thou hast ridden ever since I was thine unto this day? was I ever wont to do so unto thee? And he said, Nay.

The same thing can be said of the story of Jonah and the great fish that swallowed him up which is found in Jonah 1:17-2:10. People tend to concentrate too much on the great fish that God used rather than the great God Who used a fish. This story is in the Bible to tell us to what great lengths God will go, and has gone, to save man. It is the story of God's love for His prophet Jonah and the city of Nineveh too. It is also the story of how an omnipotent God can even use a

The Ministry of the Holy Spirit between the Old and the New Testament   113

fish. The fish was not baptized with the Spirit of God; the fish was prepared of God.

> Now the LORD had prepared a great fish to swallow up Jonah. And Jonah was in the belly of the fish three days and three nights. Then Jonah prayed unto the LORD his God out of the fish's belly, And said, I cried by reason of mine affliction unto the LORD, and he heard me; out of the belly of hell cried I, and thou heardest my voice. For thou hadst cast me into the deep, in the midst of the seas; and the floods compassed me about: all thy billows and thy waves passed over me. Then I said, I am cast out of thy sight; yet I will look again toward thy holy temple. The waters compassed me about, even to the soul: the depth closed me round about, the weeds were wrapped about my head. I went down to the bottoms of the mountains; the earth with her bars was about me for ever: yet hast thou brought up my life from corruption, O LORD my God. When my soul fainted within me I remembered the LORD: and my prayer came in unto thee, into thine holy temple. They that observe lying vanities forsake their own mercy. But I will sacrifice unto thee with the voice of thanksgiving; I will pay that that I have vowed. Salvation is of the LORD. And the LORD spake unto the fish, and it vomited out Jonah upon the dry land.

Another interesting passage to consider in the light of the Holy Spirit coming upon someone is I Samuel 19:18–24. The passage talks about Saul, who after having sent three different groups of soldiers to kill King David, finally went himself. Just as in the case of each group of soldiers, Saul himself had the Holy Spirit come "upon" him, resulting in him stripping off his armor and prophesying. The Holy Spirit was not anointing Saul again. This act of submission by Saul was due to the power of the anointing of Samuel and King David. The question asked in verse 24 is pertinent: "Is Saul also among the prophets?" The answer is, "no." Saul was an ex-king in rebellion against God and had to be forced to obey God. That is the message of I Samuel 19:18-24.

> So David fled, and escaped, and came to Samuel to Ramah, and told him all that Saul had done to him. And he and Samuel went and dwelt in Naioth. And it was told Saul, saying, Behold, David is at Naioth in Ramah. And Saul sent messengers to take David: and when they saw the company of the prophets prophesying, and Samuel standing as appointed over them, the Spirit of God was upon the messengers of Saul, and they also prophesied. And when it was told Saul, he sent other messengers, and they prophesied likewise. And Saul sent messengers again the third time, and they prophesied also. Then went he also to Ramah, and came to a great well that is in Sechu: and he asked and said, Where are Samuel and David? And one said, Behold, they be at Naioth in Ramah. And he went thither to Naioth in Ramah: and the Spirit of God was upon him also, and he went on, and prophesied, until he came to Naioth in Ramah. And he stripped off his clothes also, and prophesied before Samuel in like manner, and lay down naked all that day and all that night. Wherefore they say, Is Saul also among the prophets?

In Acts chapter ten, the first Gentiles were saved who did not have to be identified with the nation of Israel first by circumcision. Those Gentiles were Cornelius and his family and friends. In Acts chapters eleven and fifteen, Peter, and then all the apostles, had to defend preaching to the Gentiles, and then baptizing these same Gentiles who had not been circumcised. God had to show that He was saving uncircumcised Gentiles through faith alone in Christ alone. How would God show this? Through pouring out the Holy Spirit upon them as proof that He had accepted them already. That is the reason why Acts 10:44-47 was given.

> While Peter yet spake these words, the Holy Ghost fell on all them which heard the word. And they of the circumcision which believed were astonished, as many as came with Peter, because that on the Gentiles also was poured out the gift of the Holy Ghost. For they heard them speak with tongues, and magnify God. Then answered Peter, Can any man forbid water, that these should not be baptized, which have received the Holy Ghost as well as we?

It is also the reason behind Peter's defense of baptizing them which we find in Acts 11:15-16, and the discussion that ensued in the apostolic council in Acts 15. Peter said, in Acts 11:15-16, that what happened at Cornelius's house was identically the same as what happened to the apostles on the Day of Pentecost, thus proving that God approved of them being saved and baptized.

> And as I began to speak, the Holy Ghost fell on them, as on us at the beginning. Then remembered I the word of the Lord, how that he said, John indeed baptized with water; but ye shall be baptized with the Holy Ghost.

There is much more that can be said about this, and I would recommend that you read my book, *Though I Speak, The Biblical Qualifications of a Prophet*, Express Image Publishers, copyright 1984.

B. Remove the Holy Spirit

I Samuel 16:13-16, and 23 has the story of how the Holy Spirit, Who had anointed Saul to be king of Israel, was removed the moment that the Holy Spirit anointed David to be king in his stead. In I Samuel 16:13-16, and 23 we find the tragic results of a life of disobedience and continued lack of confession.

> Then Samuel took the horn of oil, and anointed him in the midst of his brethren: and the Spirit of the LORD came upon David from that day forward. So Samuel rose up, and went to Ramah. But the Spirit of the LORD departed from Saul, and an evil spirit from the LORD troubled him. And

> Saul's servants said unto him, Behold now, an evil spirit from God troubleth thee. Let our lord now command thy servants, which are before thee, to seek out a man, who is a cunning player on an harp: and it shall come to pass, when the evil spirit from God is upon thee, that he shall play with his hand, and thou shalt be well. ... And it came to pass, when the evil spirit from God was upon Saul, that David took an harp, and played with his hand: so Saul was refreshed, and was well, and the evil spirit departed from him.

Saul did not lose his salvation; he lost his throne in God's eyes, and his children would not inherit the kingdom. The very man that Saul needed to comfort him was David, whom he wanted to kill, according to I Samuel 18:10 and I Samuel 19:9.

> And it came to pass on the morrow, that the evil spirit from God came upon Saul, and he prophesied in the midst of the house: and David played with his hand, as at other times: and there was a javelin in Saul's hand. ... And the evil spirit from the LORD was upon Saul, as he sat in his house with his javelin in his hand: and David played with his hand.

Saul and David were both saved men who had the Holy Spirit within, but had very different ways of dealing with sin. After David's sin with Bathsheba, he pleaded with God not to remove the Holy Spirit from over him in Psalm 51:11. In effect, David was asking God to not remove the kingdom from him. His plea had nothing at all to do with removing his salvation. God would not, and could not, remove his salvation and David was secure in that knowledge. However, Psalm 51:11 is a solemn reminder that our ministry may be lost.

> Cast me not away from thy presence; and take not thy holy spirit from me.

C. The usage of the preposition "in" with a future context

There are several passages in the New Testament, especially in the Gospel of John, that speak of the coming of the Holy Spirit as occurring in the future. One such passage is John 7:37-39. Jesus expresses this event of the coming of the Holy Spirit as something that was related to His being "glorified" (John 7:39).

> In the last day, that great day of the feast, Jesus stood and cried, saying, If any man thirst, let him come unto me, and drink. He that believeth on me, as the scripture hath said, out of his belly shall flow rivers of living water. (But this spake he of the Spirit, which they that believe on him should receive: for the Holy Ghost was not yet given; because that Jesus was not yet glorified.)

But John 7:37-39 does not specifically tell us if it is talking about the Holy Spirit coming *upon* or *in* the believer. It also doesn't tell us if this was related to the death of Christ, the resurrection of Christ, or the ascension of Christ. That is also not the case with John 14:16-20. This passage, for the most part, is much more specific. Let's read the passage and then we will examine what it means.

> And I will pray the Father, and he shall give you another Comforter, that he may abide with you for ever; Even the Spirit of truth; whom the world cannot receive, because it seeth him not, neither knoweth him: but ye know him; for he dwelleth with you, and shall be in you. I will not leave you comfortless: I will come to you. Yet a little while, and the world seeth me no more; but ye see me: because I live, ye shall live also. At that day ye shall know that I am in my Father, and ye in me, and I in you.

In this prophecy of the coming Comforter, Jesus informs them of two things right away in verse 16: This Comforter is another Comforter because Jesus is the first Comforter, and secondly, this Comforter would abide (meaning permanently) "forever." In verse 17, Jesus then stated three more things that they needed to understand. The first thing is that the Comforter is the "Spirit of Truth." The second is that "He dwelleth with you." How did He dwell with them? He dwelled with them because Jesus dwelled with them, but that time was going to come to an end at Calvary. So, Jesus went on to tell them the third thing they needed to understand: He "shall be in you."

The Holy Spirit's presence would no longer be with Christ but forever in the believer. This relationship would begin "at that day" (verse 20) that they were to see Him after His resurrection (verse 19). That same resurrection Sunday Jesus appeared and "breathed on them" and said, "Receive ye the Holy Ghost" (John 20:22). Thus Jesus' prophecy of receiving the Holy Spirit to live within them was fulfilled in John 20:19-23.

> Then the same day at evening, being the first day of the week, when the doors were shut where the disciples were assembled for fear of the Jews, came Jesus and stood in the midst, and saith unto them, Peace be unto you. And when he had so said, he shewed unto them his hands and his side. Then were the disciples glad, when they saw the Lord. Then said Jesus to them again, Peace be unto you: as my Father hath sent me, even so send I you. And when he had said this, he breathed on them, and saith unto them, Receive ye the Holy Ghost: Whose soever sins ye remit, they are remitted unto them; and whose soever sins ye retain, they are retained.

Notice that John 14:16-20 **never** says that the Holy Spirit came "over" men in the Old Testament temporarily, and that He will be in the believer of the New Testament permanently and forever. It states that the apostles had the Holy Spirit with them in the Person of Jesus Christ, but they would have Him in them eternally in the Person of the Spirit of God. Jesus let them know that He Personally would be with them when He said, "I will not leave you comfortless: I will come to you" (John 14:18).

In John 16:7-9, the Lord Jesus Christ again talked about the coming of the Holy Spirit to indwell the church. He linked His ministry to the world to the Spirit's presence in the life of the believer. Jesus said that once the Holy Spirit was in the believer, He would "... reprove the world of sin, and of righteousness, and of judgment" (John 16:8).

> Nevertheless I tell you the truth; It is expedient for you that I go away: for if I go not away, the Comforter will not come unto you; but if I depart, I will send him unto you. And when he is come, he will reprove the world of sin, and of righteousness, and of judgment: Of sin, because they believe not on me;

How does the Holy Spirit, in the heart of the believer, perform the conviction of the sin of not believing in Jesus Christ? The Holy Spirit performs His work when the believer gives the Word of God to the unbeliever. That is what we find in Romans 10:17.

> So then faith cometh by hearing, and hearing by the word of God.

In John 14:16-20, the Holy Spirit is referred to as another "Comforter," which is the translation of the Greek word παράκλητος [parakletos][4]. This is the same word that is translated "Advocate" in I John 2:1 where it speaks of Jesus Christ. Christ is our παράκλητος [parakletos] and the Holy Spirit is another, equal παράκλητος [parakletos].

> My little children, these things write I unto you, that ye sin not. And if any man sin, we have an advocate with the Father, Jesus Christ the righteous:

The indwelling ministry of the Holy Spirit was, and is, totally different from the ministry of coming upon the apostles as it was prophesied in Luke 24:49. That event was just for the apostles and their helpers.

---

4 Ibid. #3875.

> And, behold, I send the promise of my Father upon you: but tarry ye in the city of Jerusalem, until ye be endued with power from on high.

Likewise, the prophecy of Acts 1:5-8 has no real relationship with the indwelling of the Holy Spirit. This passage also deals with the Holy Spirit coming upon the apostles to give them the power to do the job that Christ had assigned them to do, namely the writing of the New Testament and the evangelization of the world.

> For John truly baptized with water; but ye shall be baptized with the Holy Ghost not many days hence. When they therefore were come together, they asked of him, saying, Lord, wilt thou at this time restore again the kingdom to Israel? And he said unto them, It is not for you to know the times or the seasons, which the Father hath put in his own power. But ye shall receive power, after that the Holy Ghost is come upon you: and ye shall be witnesses unto me both in Jerusalem, and in all Judaea, and in Samaria, and unto the uttermost part of the earth.

Differentiating the Ministry of the Holy Spirit "In" and "With" the Believer

A. The Son "with."

We need to understand how this actually worked. The Holy Spirit's ministry of indwelling the believers in the Old Testament was performed by the Holy Spirit Himself, but while Christ was on earth Christ performed the ministry of the παράκλητος [*parakletos*]. He was the Comforter during His earthly ministry. What did Christ do that the Holy Spirit did before and does today?

1. Christ taught the believers

Acts 1:1 says that Christ taught truth.

> The former treatise have I made, O Theophilus, of all that Jesus began both to do and teach,

Once again in Matthew 5:2, the Bible specifically tells us that Jesus taught the Word of God which today is a ministry of the Holy Spirit.

> And he opened his mouth, and taught them, saying,

2. Christ illuminated the believers

According to Matthew 15:15-17, Christ performed the ministry of illumination. He constantly gave understanding to His disciples and the apostles.

> Then answered Peter and said unto him, Declare unto us this parable. And Jesus said, Are ye also yet without understanding? Do not ye yet understand, that whatsoever entereth in at the mouth goeth into the belly, and is cast out into the draught?

3. Christ sanctified the believers

In His High Priestly prayer of John 17:14 and 17, Christ twice mentioned the sanctification of the believer as a part of His ministry.

> I have given them thy word; and the world hath hated them, because they are not of the world, even as I am not of the world. ... Sanctify them through thy truth: thy word is truth.

4. Christ kept the believers secure in their salvation

During the earthly ministry of Christ, according to John 17:12, Christ kept the believers secure in their salvation.

> While I was with them in the world, I kept them in thy name: those that thou gavest me I have kept, and none of them is lost, but the son of perdition; that the scripture might be fulfilled.

5. Christ resurrected the believers

In John 11:25, Jesus announced that during His earthly ministry He performed the ministry of resurrection.

> Jesus said unto her, I am the resurrection, and the life: he that believeth in me, though he were dead, yet shall he live:

6. Christ kept the believers from the evil one

Luke 22:31-32 says that during His earthly ministry, the Lord Jesus Christ Himself kept Satan from doing the things that would have destroyed the believers.

> And the Lord said, Simon, Simon, behold, Satan hath desired to have you, that he may sift you as wheat: But I have prayed for thee, that thy faith fail not: and when thou art converted, strengthen thy brethren.

B. While Christ was in the grave, and the Holy Spirit had not yet come, the Father performed these ministries

Who did the necessary ministries that the Holy Spirit did in the Old Testament, and the Son did during His earthly ministry, while Christ was in the grave, and the Holy Spirit had not yet been sent by the Father and the Son? God the Father performed these ministries.

1. God the Father sanctified

During the three days that Jesus spent in the grave, and the Spirit of God was not yet in the world, God the Father sanctified the believers according to Jesus' prayer in John 17:17.

> Sanctify them through thy truth: thy word is truth.

2. God the Father kept the believers secure in their salvation.

In Jesus's High Priestly prayer in John 17:11, Jesus asked God the Father to keep the believers secure in their salvation.

> And now I am no more in the world, but these are in the world, and I come to thee. Holy Father, keep through

thine own name those whom thou hast given me, that
they may be one, as we are.

3. God the Father resurrected the believers

In Romans 6:4, it says that by the glory of God the Father, Christ was raised from the dead.

> Therefore we are buried with him by baptism into death: that like as Christ was raised up from the dead by the glory of the Father, even so we also should walk in newness of life.

4. God the Father kept the believers from the evil one

In Jesus' High Priestly prayer in John 17:15, Jesus prayed that the Father would keep the believers safe from the evil one.

> I pray not that thou shouldest take them out of the world, but that thou shouldest keep them from the evil.

C. The glorified Son of God gave the Holy Spirit to live "in" the believer

Jesus prophesied that, once glorified, He would send the Spirit of God to indwell the believer, according to John 7:39.

> (But this spake he of the Spirit, which they that believe on him should receive: for the Holy Ghost was not yet given; because that Jesus was not yet glorified.)

In John 14:18-20, Jesus clarified the promise to send the Holy Spirit to indwell the believer by saying that He would come to the apostles on "that day," when they would "see" Him alive. "At that day," He would be "in you." The promise of the indwelling Spirit of Christ would be after the resurrection.

> I will not leave you comfortless: I will come to you. Yet a little while, and the world seeth me no more; but ye see

me: because I live, ye shall live also. At that day ye shall know that I am in my Father, and ye in me, and I in you.

In John 17:1, just hours before the death of Christ, Jesus prayed that the Father would glorify Him.

> These words spake Jesus, and lifted up his eyes to heaven, and said, Father, the hour is come; glorify thy Son, that thy Son also may glorify thee:

That glorification of Christ began in the early hours of resurrection Sunday as Christ arose. It was at that time that Christ gave the apostles the indwelling presence of the Holy Spirit, with all of His ministries, according to John 20:19-22.

> Then the same day at evening, being the first day of the week, when the doors were shut where the disciples were assembled for fear of the Jews, came Jesus and stood in the midst, and saith unto them, Peace be unto you. And when he had so said, he shewed unto them his hands and his side. Then were the disciples glad, when they saw the Lord. Then said Jesus to them again, Peace be unto you: as my Father hath sent me, even so send I you. And when he had said this, he breathed on them, and saith unto them, Receive ye the Holy Ghost:

The ministry of the Holy Spirit where He came "upon" the apostles and New Testament prophets was different. That coming of the Holy Spirit, which was prophesied in Acts 1:8, was to empower the apostles to do the work of writing the New Testament, and with the New Testament, evangelize the world.

> But ye shall receive power, after that the Holy Ghost is come upon you: and ye shall be witnesses unto me both in Jerusalem, and in all Judaea, and in Samaria, and unto the uttermost part of the earth.

The Holy Spirit then came upon the apostles (Acts 2:3) on the Day of Pentecost as it is recorded in Acts 2:1-21. Simultaneously, the apostles were also filled with the Holy Spirit (Acts 2:4) and then spoke in twelve different known and spoken languages.

> And when the day of Pentecost was fully come, they were all with one accord in one place. And suddenly there came a sound from heaven as of a rushing mighty wind, and it filled all the house where they were sitting. And there appeared unto them cloven tongues like as of fire, and it sat upon each of them. And they were all filled with the Holy Ghost, and began to speak with other tongues, as the Spirit gave them utterance. And there were dwelling at Jerusalem Jews, devout men, out of every nation under heaven. Now when this was noised abroad, the multitude came together, and were confounded, because that every man heard them speak in his own language. And they were all amazed and marvelled, saying one to another, Behold, are not all these which speak Galilaeans? And how hear we every man in our own tongue, wherein we were born? Parthians, and Medes, and Elamites, and the dwellers in Mesopotamia, and in Judaea, and Cappadocia, in Pontus, and Asia, Phrygia, and Pamphylia, in Egypt, and in the parts of Libya about Cyrene, and strangers of Rome, Jews and proselytes, Cretes and Arabians, we do hear them speak in our tongues the wonderful works of God. And they were all amazed, and were in doubt, saying one to another, What meaneth this? Others mocking said, These men are full of new wine. But Peter, standing up with the eleven, lifted up his voice, and said unto them, Ye men of Judaea, and all ye that dwell at Jerusalem, be this known unto you, and hearken to my words: For these are not drunken, as ye suppose, seeing it is but the third hour of the day. But this is that which was spoken by the prophet Joel; And it shall come to pass in the last days, saith God, I will pour out of my Spirit upon all flesh: and your sons and your daughters shall prophesy, and your young men shall see visions, and your old men shall dream dreams:

> And on my servants and on my handmaidens I will pour out in those days of my Spirit; and they shall prophesy: And I will shew wonders in heaven above, and signs in the earth beneath; blood, and fire, and vapour of smoke: The sun shall be turned into darkness, and the moon into blood, before that great and notable day of the Lord come: And it shall come to pass, that whosoever shall call on the name of the Lord shall be saved.

Jesus gave the apostles the indwelling Holy Spirit on resurrection Sunday. Upon His resurrection, He had to ascend to Heaven and offer His blood in the heavenly sanctuary. For that reason, when Mary saw Him immediately after His resurrection, she was not permitted to touch Him until He had finished His work as the High Priest according to John 20:17.

> Jesus saith unto her, Touch me not; for I am not yet ascended to my Father: but go to my brethren, and say unto them, I ascend unto my Father, and your Father; and to my God, and your God.

Fifty days later on that Sunday in Jerusalem, Jesus, now glorified at the right hand of God the Father, sent the Holy Spirit upon the apostles to write the New Testament and to begin a new dispensation: the church age.

Chapter Four

THE BAPTISM AND FILLING OF THE HOLY SPIRIT

With the growth of the experience-centered Charismatic movement and Pentecostalism, there is a corresponding growth in the number of errors that are propagated about the Person, the ministry, the baptisms, and the filling of the Holy Spirit. Since the end of World War II there has been a definite shift in Christianity away from, "Thus saith the Lord," to "I feel." This philosophy has invaded our educational system to where the greatest perceived need of the student is that no one challenge his thinking and make him feel insecure. Politicians prey on this insecurity, promising everything to make a man feel better with no human effort.

I'm not sure which came first: the offer of a religion of human "feelings" that is nowhere based on the Word of God and requires no study of the Bible to construct a Biblical doctrine, or a lazy, emotional people who would be attracted to such a system. This is an important distinction, and one, which should be studied, but it is neither the purpose of this chapter, nor of this book, except to say that this study will not follow this type of an approach.

Two Baptisms of the Holy Spirit

The Scriptures speak of two baptisms of the Holy Spirit. We need to distinguish between these baptisms before we can consider the subject of the filling of the Holy Spirit.

A. Baptism with (in) the Holy Spirit

The first kind of baptism that involved the Holy Spirit was baptism with (or in) the Holy Spirit. This baptism was prophesied by John the Baptist in Matthew 3:11.

> I indeed baptize you with water unto repentance: but he that cometh after me is mightier than I, whose shoes I am not worthy to bear: he shall baptize you with the Holy Ghost, and with fire:

Let's take a look at Matthew 3:11 in the Greek Textus Receptus.

> ἐγὼ μὲν βαπτίζω ὑμᾶς ἐν ὕδατι εἰς μετάνοιαν· ὁ δὲ ὀπίσω μου ἐρχόμενος ἰσχυρότερός μού ἐστιν, οὗ οὐκ εἰμὶ ἱκανὸς τὰ ὑποδήματα βαστάσαι· αὐτὸς ὑμᾶς βαπτίσει ἐν Πνεύματι Ἁγίῳ καὶ πυρί·

John the Baptist said, "βαπτίζω ὑμᾶς ἐν ὕδατι," "I baptize you (plural) in water," but Christ, "βαστάσαι· αὐτὸς ὑμᾶς βαπτίσει ἐν Πνεύματι Ἁγίῳ," "shall baptize you (plural) in the Holy Spirit." Just as John had baptized in water, Jesus was going to baptize in the Holy Spirit. We see this same truth in Mark 1:8, which is a parallel passage.

> I indeed have baptized you with water: but he shall baptize you with the Holy Ghost.

Luke 3:16 is another parallel passage which, like Matthew 3:11, not only speaks of baptism in the Holy Spirit, but also in fire.

> John answered, saying unto them all, I indeed baptize you with water; but one mightier than I cometh, the latchet of whose shoes I am not worthy to unloose: he shall baptize you with the Holy Ghost and with fire:

The statements that are found in Matthew, Mark, and Luke all seem to have been made in connection with a conversation between John the Baptist and the Pharisees, before the baptism of

Christ. In John 1:32-33, we find another similar account that talks about baptism in the Holy Spirit, which seems to have taken place after the Lord's baptism.

> And John bare record, saying, I saw the Spirit descending from heaven like a dove, and it abode upon him. And I knew him not: but he that sent me to baptize with water, the same said unto me, Upon whom thou shalt see the Spirit descending, and remaining on him, the same is he which baptizeth with the Holy Ghost.

In Acts 1:2-5, and 8, the Lord Jesus Christ was quoted by Luke who again referred to John's prophecy about a coming baptism in the Holy Spirit.

> Until the day in which he was taken up, after that he through the Holy Ghost had given commandments unto the apostles whom he had chosen: To whom also he shewed himself alive after his passion by many infallible proofs, being seen of them forty days, and speaking of the things pertaining to the kingdom of God: And, being assembled together with them, commanded them that they should not depart from Jerusalem, but wait for the promise of the Father, which, saith he, ye have heard of me. For John truly baptized with water; but ye shall be baptized with the Holy Ghost not many days hence. ... But ye shall receive power, after that the Holy Ghost is come upon you: and ye shall be witnesses unto me both in Jerusalem, and in all Judaea, and in Samaria, and unto the uttermost part of the earth.

In Acts 1:5, Jesus told the apostles that they would "... be baptized with the Holy Ghost not many days hence." In verse 8, however, Jesus described this baptism as "... the Holy Ghost is come upon you." The apostles were baptized in the Holy Spirit on the Day of Pentecost. This was synonymous with having the Holy Spirit come upon them.

Luke 24:33 says that the eleven living apostles were all gathered together in Jerusalem where Christ later would find them.

> And they rose up the same hour, and returned to Jerusalem, and found the eleven gathered together, and them that were with them,

Then in Luke 24:49, Christ again promised the Apostles that the Holy Spirit, the promise of God the Father, would come "upon you."

> And, behold, I send the promise of my Father upon you: but tarry ye in the city of Jerusalem, until ye be endued with power from on high.

Peter further mentioned the baptism in the Holy Spirit in reference to what occurred in Cornelius' house in Acts 11:15–16. Peter referred to this event as having been baptized in the Holy Ghost.

> And as I began to speak, the Holy Ghost fell on them, as on us at the beginning. Then remembered I the word of the Lord, how that he said, John indeed baptized with water; but ye shall be baptized with the Holy Ghost.

There are three distinguishing characteristics to the baptism "in" the Holy Spirit. Let's look at them and see how this is distinguished from the next baptism.

1. **Jesus Christ did the baptizing**
2. **Only the apostles were baptized**
3. **The Holy Spirit was the "fluid" into which the apostles were baptized**

B. Baptism by the Holy Spirit or in Jesus Christ

The second type of Spirit baptism is Baptism by the Holy Spirit, or baptism into Jesus Christ. This is the baptism that is physically demonstrated by water baptism. As the believer goes into the water, he is identified with the death of Christ. When he is immersed, he is identified with the burial of Christ. As the believer comes out of the water he symbolically announces his identification with the resurrection of Christ. Water baptism demonstrates a relationship to Christ that took place spiritually when the Holy Spirit baptized the believer into the body of Christ, that is, into His death, His burial, and His resurrection. This is the baptism spoken of in Romans 6:3-5.

> Know ye not, that so many of us as were baptized into Jesus Christ were baptized into his death? Therefore we are buried with him by baptism into death: that like as Christ was raised up from the dead by the glory of the Father, even so we also should walk in newness of life. For if we have been planted together in the likeness of his death, we shall be also in the likeness of his resurrection:

In I Corinthians 12:12-13, Paul again referred to the baptism by the Spirit of God into the Body of Christ.

> For as the body is one, and hath many members, and all the members of that one body, being many, are one body: so also is Christ. For by one Spirit are we all baptized into one body, whether we be Jews or Gentiles, whether we be bond or free; and have been all made to drink into one Spirit.

In I Corinthians 12:12-13, Paul mentions the unity that exists in the Body of Christ where "Jews or Gentiles" and "bond or free" are "all made to drink into one Spirit" through the baptism into the Body of Christ by the Holy Spirit. The Apostle Paul again emphasized that unity of the Body of Christ in Ephesians 4:5 saying,

> One Lord, one faith, one baptism,

It is necessary, therefore, to point out the differences that exist between the baptisms in (or with) the Holy Spirit, and into the Body of Christ. In the baptism with the Holy Spirit: 1. Jesus Christ did the baptizing. 2. Only the apostles were baptized. 3. The Holy Spirit was the "fluid" into which they were baptized. But the baptism into the Body of Christ would be expressed in these three ways:

1. **The Holy Spirit does the baptizing**
2. **Every believer receives this baptism**
3. **The Body of Christ (His death, burial, and resurrection) is the "fluid" into which all were baptized**

The Prophecies that Were Fulfilled by the Baptism WITH the Holy Spirit

There were three major prophecies that were given about the baptism with the Holy Spirit. Baptism with the Holy Spirit was also called baptism in the Holy Spirit or having the Holy Spirit come upon a person. The first of the three prophecies that we will examine is that of John the Baptist. This prophecy was stated in all four Gospel accounts. In Matthew 3:11 it says:

> I indeed baptize you with water unto repentance: but he that cometh after me is mightier than I, whose shoes I am not worthy to bear: he shall baptize you with the Holy Ghost, and with fire:

It is found again in Mark 1:8 where Mark wrote:

> I indeed have baptized you with water: but he shall baptize you with the Holy Ghost.

In Luke 3:16, we see a similar statement as that of Matthew.

> John answered, saying unto them all, I indeed baptize you with water; but one mightier than I cometh, the

latchet of whose shoes I am not worthy to unloose: he shall baptize you with the Holy Ghost and with fire:

The Apostle John also listed John the Baptist's prophecy in John 1:32-33.

And John bare record, saying, I saw the Spirit descending from heaven like a dove, and it abode upon him. And I knew him not: but he that sent me to baptize with water, the same said unto me, Upon whom thou shalt see the Spirit descending, and remaining on him, the same is he which baptizeth with the Holy Ghost.

The second major prophecy about the baptism with the Holy Spirit on the day of Pentecost was the prophecy of Joel 2:28-32.

And it shall come to pass afterward, that I will pour out my spirit upon all flesh; and your sons and your daughters shall prophesy, your old men shall dream dreams, your young men shall see visions: And also upon the servants and upon the handmaids in those days will I pour out my spirit. And I will shew wonders in the heavens and in the earth, blood, and fire, and pillars of smoke. The sun shall be turned into darkness, and the moon into blood, before the great and the terrible day of the LORD come. And it shall come to pass, that whosoever shall call on the name of the LORD shall be delivered: for in mount Zion and in Jerusalem shall be deliverance, as the LORD hath said, and in the remnant whom the LORD shall call.

The third major prophecy of the baptism of the Holy Spirit was given by the Lord Jesus Christ Himself. We find that prophecy in Luke 24:49.

And, behold, I send the promise of my Father upon you: but tarry ye in the city of Jerusalem, until ye be endued with power from on high.

In John's Gospel, Jesus specifically prophesied about the baptism of the Holy Spirit at least three times where it was directly tied to the writing of the Word of God by the apostles. The first passage that we will look at is John 14:16-27.

> And I will pray the Father, and he shall give you another Comforter, that he may abide with you for ever; Even the Spirit of truth; whom the world cannot receive, because it seeth him not, neither knoweth him: but ye know him; for he dwelleth with you, and shall be in you. I will not leave you comfortless: I will come to you. Yet a little while, and the world seeth me no more; but ye see me: because I live, ye shall live also. At that day ye shall know that I am in my Father, and ye in me, and I in you. He that hath my commandments, and keepeth them, he it is that loveth me: and he that loveth me shall be loved of my Father, and I will love him, and will manifest myself to him. Judas saith unto him, not Iscariot, Lord, how is it that thou wilt manifest thyself unto us, and not unto the world? Jesus answered and said unto him, If a man love me, he will keep my words: and my Father will love him, and we will come unto him, and make our abode with him. He that loveth me not keepeth not my sayings: and the word which ye hear is not mine, but the Father's which sent me. These things have I spoken unto you, being yet present with you. But the Comforter, which is the Holy Ghost, whom the Father will send in my name, he shall teach you all things, and bring all things to your remembrance, whatsoever I have said unto you. Peace I leave with you, my peace I give unto you: not as the world giveth, give I unto you. Let not your heart be troubled, neither let it be afraid.

Again, the coming of the Holy Spirit on the day of Pentecost was prophesied in John 15:26-27 where it was again tied to His ministry in the writing of the New Testament by the apostles.

The Baptism and the Filling of the Holy Spirit

> But when the Comforter is come, whom I will send unto you from the Father, even the Spirit of truth, which proceedeth from the Father, he shall testify of me: And ye also shall bear witness, because ye have been with me from the beginning.

The third place in the Gospel of John where Jesus prophesied of the baptism with the Holy Spirit in the day of Pentecost is found in John 16:7-16. Because of the baptism with the Holy Spirit, Jesus prophesied that the Holy Spirit would lead the apostles "into all truth" (John 16:13) guaranteeing not only the historical accuracy of what the apostles wrote ("… and bring all things to your remembrance, whatsoever I have said unto you" [John 14:26].), but even guaranteeing those things that they could not "bear" (John 16:12) at that moment. So the things that the apostles wrote about the past (John 14:26), the things that they wrote about truth that the Holy Spirit revealed to them (John 16:13), and the "things to come" (John 16:13), which are the future things, were all inspired as a result of the baptism with the Holy Spirit. That is all found in Christ's prophecy concerning the baptism with the Holy Spirit on the day of Pentecost as seen in John 16:7-16.

> Nevertheless I tell you the truth; It is expedient for you that I go away: for if I go not away, the Comforter will not come unto you; but if I depart, I will send him unto you. And when he is come, he will reprove the world of sin, and of righteousness, and of judgment: Of sin, because they believe not on me; Of righteousness, because I go to my Father, and ye see me no more; Of judgment, because the prince of this world is judged. I have yet many things to say unto you, but ye cannot bear them now. Howbeit when he, the Spirit of truth, is come, he will guide you into all truth: for he shall not speak of himself; but whatsoever he shall hear, that shall he speak: and he will shew you things to come. He shall glorify me: for he shall receive of mine, and shall shew it unto you. All things that the Father hath are mine: therefore said I, that he

shall take of mine, and shall shew it unto you. A little while, and ye shall not see me: and again, a little while, and ye shall see me, because I go to the Father.

All three of the prophecies, that is, the prophecy of Joel, the prophecy of John the Baptist, and the prophecy of Jesus Christ were fulfilled by the baptism with the Holy Spirit on the day of Pentecost. The Apostle Peter specifically stated that Joel's prophecy was fulfilled on the day of Pentecost in Acts 2:16–21, where he said:

> But ***this is that which was spoken by the prophet Joel***; And it shall come to pass in the last days, saith God, I will pour out of my Spirit upon all flesh: and your sons and your daughters shall prophesy, and your young men shall see visions, and your old men shall dream dreams: And on my servants and on my handmaidens I will pour out in those days of my Spirit; and they shall prophesy: And I will shew wonders in heaven above, and signs in the earth beneath; blood, and fire, and vapour of smoke: The sun shall be turned into darkness, and the moon into blood, before that great and notable day of the Lord come: And it shall come to pass, that whosoever shall call on the name of the Lord shall be saved.

The prophecy of John the Baptist was likewise fulfilled on the day of Pentecost. Jesus had personally tied the prophecy of John the Baptist to the coming of the Holy Spirit upon the apostles on the day of Pentecost in saying:

> And, being assembled together with them, commanded them that they should not depart from Jerusalem, but wait for the promise of the Father, which, saith he, ye have heard of me. ***For John truly baptized with water; but ye shall be baptized with the Holy Ghost not many days hence*** (Acts 1:4–5).

The Baptism and the Filling of the Holy Spirit

In this same passage (Acts 1:4–5), Jesus said that His Own prophecy of the baptism with the Holy Spirit was fulfilled. Once this prophecy was fulfilled, it will not be fulfilled again.

> And, being assembled together with them, commanded them that they should not depart from Jerusalem, but **wait for the promise of the Father, which, saith he, ye have heard of me.** For John truly baptized with water; but ye shall be baptized with the Holy Ghost not many days hence (Acts 1:4–5).

Baptism in Fire

Baptism in fire is often confused with baptism in the Holy Spirit and baptism by the Holy Spirit. There is so much confusion about this baptism that even the lost will refer to some difficult event as being a "baptism in fire." Pentecostals will often refer to a baptism in fire as being synonymous with baptism with the Holy Spirit. To defend this interpretation, they will quote Acts 2:3 where the manifestation of the baptism with the Holy Spirit was spoken of as "cloven tongues like as of fire." But the very terminology of being "baptized," that is, immersed in fire sounds like Hell and is therefore something that should be avoided rather than sought.

In order to understand correctly what the Bible means by baptism in fire, we need to carefully study the passages where baptism in fire is mentioned. One such passage is Matthew 3:7–12, where John the Baptist prophesied of the coming "baptism with the Holy Ghost, and with fire."

> But when he saw many of the Pharisees and Sadducees come to his baptism, he said unto them, O generation of vipers, who hath warned you to flee from the wrath to come? Bring forth therefore fruits meet for repentance: And think not to say within yourselves, We have Abraham to our father: for I say unto you, that God is able of these stones to raise up children unto Abraham. And now also the axe is laid unto the root of the trees: therefore

every tree which bringeth not forth good fruit is hewn down, and cast into the fire. I indeed baptize you with water unto repentance: but he that cometh after me is mightier than I, whose shoes I am not worthy to bear: he shall baptize you with the Holy Ghost, and with fire: Whose fan is in his hand, and he will throughly purge his floor, and gather his wheat into the garner; but he will burn up the chaff with unquenchable fire.

There are several things in this passage that need to be understood in order to be able to interpret it properly. First of all, as John spoke about baptism with the Holy Ghost and with fire, he had a mixed audience as is stated in Matthew 3:7. There were the disciples of John, there were Pharisees, and there were Sadducees all present. He addressed the Pharisees and Sadducees as a "generation of vipers." John told them to "... bring forth therefore fruits meet for repentance" (Matthew 3:8). He said that judgment was coming, and as such that "... the axe is laid unto the root of the trees." This is not just a pruning, but a total judgment.

This then leads us to the second question: what is "the root of the trees?" The root is singular even though the trees are spoken of as being plural. The root of the trees suffered the judgment. The Apostle Paul declared that the root was Jesus Christ in Romans 11:16-18. He also stated that the Jews were the natural olive tree, while the Gentiles were the "wild olive tree:" two trees with just one root.

> For if the firstfruit be holy, the lump is also holy: and if the root be holy, so are the branches. And if some of the branches be broken off, and thou, being a wild olive tree, wert graffed in among them, and with them partakest of the root and fatness of the olive tree; Boast not against the branches. But if thou boast, thou bearest not the root, but the root thee.

The end result is that the tree "which bringeth not forth good fruit is hewn down, and cast into the fire" (Matthew 3:10), whether it be a natural olive or a wild olive tree. Baptism with fire was for the Pharisees and Sadducees. The axe fell on Jesus Christ, the Holy Root, but for those who do not trust Him, there is coming a baptism with fire. John made that very clear in Matthew 3:12 when he said that Christ "... will throughly purge his floor, and gather his wheat into the garner; but he will burn up the chaff with unquenchable fire." There is a baptism for the wheat "into the garner." There is a baptism in fire for "the chaff with unquenchable fire." This is a baptism that we must avoid. It is the baptism the Apostle John wrote about in Revelation 20:11–15.

> And I saw a great white throne, and him that sat on it, from whose face the earth and the heaven fled away; and there was found no place for them. And I saw the dead, small and great, stand before God; and the books were opened: and another book was opened, which is the book of life: and the dead were judged out of those things which were written in the books, according to their works. And the sea gave up the dead which were in it; and death and hell delivered up the dead which were in them: and they were judged every man according to their works. And death and hell were cast into the lake of fire. This is the second death. And whosoever was not found written in the book of life was cast into the lake of fire.

How to Receive the Holy Spirit

Many people say they want to receive the Holy Spirit but have no idea how to receive Him. The indwelling of the Holy Spirit should not be a mystery. According to John 20:22, on that very Sunday in which Christ arose, He gave the Holy Spirit to believers.

> And when he had said this, he breathed on them, and saith unto them, Receive ye the Holy Ghost:

The Bible makes it clear in Ephesians 1:12-14 that the receiving of the Holy Spirit, and His sealing of us as children of God, was permanently given to us the moment that we believed in Christ.

> That we should be to the praise of his glory, who first trusted in Christ. In whom ye also trusted, after that ye heard the word of truth, the gospel of your salvation: in whom also after that ye believed, ye were sealed with that holy Spirit of promise, Which is the earnest of our inheritance until the redemption of the purchased possession, unto the praise of his glory.

Paul is emphatic that the Holy Spirit's indwelling is at the moment that we have believed "... the word of truth, the gospel of your salvation." The indwelling of the Holy Spirit comes "... after that ye believed" as a result of faith in the Gospel, and not as the result of any prayer, pleading, or other type of works. Paul made that abundantly clear in Galatians 3:2-3 as he defended the Gospel against the heresy of the Judaizers who wanted to add works as a requirement for receiving the Holy Spirit.

> This only would I learn of you, Received ye the Spirit by the works of the law, or by the hearing of faith? Are ye so foolish? having begun in the Spirit, are ye now made perfect by the flesh?

Some people think that they can receive more of the Holy Spirit than others can. Instead of seeking to surrender more of their lives to the Holy Spirit, they seek to have more of the Holy Spirit in their lives. But Jesus denied this possibility in John 3:34 when He said that "God giveth not the Spirit by measure."

> For he whom God hath sent speaketh the words of God: for God giveth not the Spirit by measure (*unto him*).

Notice that "unto him" is italicized, meaning it was added by the translators of the King James and is not found in the original text, as can be seen in John 3:34 in the Greek Textus Receptus.

The Baptism and the Filling of the Holy Spirit 141

> ὃν γὰρ ἀπέστειλεν ὁ Θεός, τὰ ῥήματα τοῦ Θεοῦ λαλεῖ· οὐ γὰρ ἐκ μέτρου δίδωσιν ὁ Θεὸς τὸ Πνεῦμα.

God does not measure the Holy Spirit. This was not only true for the Lord Jesus Christ, but for everyone who receives the Holy Spirit. The fact that God does not give the Holy Spirit by measure leads us to three distinct conclusions. First, the Holy Spirit cannot be divided up, or measured, since He is a Person. Second, He is present or absent in someone. There is no beginning, intermediate, or advanced level of having the Holy Spirit. Third, you cannot have more or less of the Spirit of God. Since God does not give the Spirit by measure, it is impossible to obtain more of the Spirit than you have right now.

One passage that seemingly contradicts these conclusions is II Kings 2:8–15 where Elisha requested a double portion of the Holy Spirit that was upon Elijah.

> And Elijah took his mantle, and wrapped it together, and smote the waters, and they were divided hither and thither, so that they two went over on dry ground. And it came to pass, when they were gone over, that Elijah said unto Elisha, Ask what I shall do for thee, before I be taken away from thee. And Elisha said, I pray thee, let a double portion of thy spirit be upon me. And he said, Thou hast asked a hard thing: nevertheless, if thou see me when I am taken from thee, it shall be so unto thee; but if not, it shall not be so. And it came to pass, as they still went on, and talked, that, behold, there appeared a chariot of fire, and horses of fire, and parted them both asunder; and Elijah went up by a whirlwind into heaven. And Elisha saw it, and he cried, My father, my father, the chariot of Israel, and the horsemen thereof. And he saw him no more: and he took hold of his own clothes, and rent them in two pieces. He took up also the mantle of Elijah that fell from him, and went back, and stood by the bank of Jordan; And he took the mantle of Elijah that fell

from him, and smote the waters, and said, Where is the LORD God of Elijah? and when he also had smitten the waters, they parted hither and thither: and Elisha went over. And when the sons of the prophets which were to view at Jericho saw him, they said, The spirit of Elijah doth rest on Elisha. And they came to meet him, and bowed themselves to the ground before him.

This passage does not deal with receiving the Holy Spirit to indwell a believer, but rather with the baptism with the Holy Spirit. That is clearly stated in II Kings 2:9 where it says, "... let a double portion of thy spirit be **upon** me." Elisha had received a ministry as Elijah's helper, that is, he was the "son of the prophet." Now he wanted another ministry – he wanted to be a prophet in the place of Elijah. "When the sons of the prophets which were to view at Jericho" referred to Elisha, they did not say that a double portion of the Spirit of Elijah was upon Elisha, but rather "The spirit of Elijah doth rest on Elisha" (II Kings 2:15). The Bible says that the Spirit was "upon" Elisha. He was recognized as being now a prophet just as Elijah had been. This had to do with a double ministry, not receiving more of the Holy Spirit to indwell him. Elisha had been the "son of the prophet" and he was now a prophet.

We said that we do not receive the Spirit of God by prayer, but Luke 11:13 seems to contradict that. In this verse the Lord Jesus Christ told the apostles,

If ye then, being evil, know how to give good gifts unto your children: how much more shall your heavenly Father give the Holy Spirit to them that ask him?

During the earthly ministry of Christ, the Holy Spirit was with the believers in the Person of Christ. He would come to indwell them on resurrection Sunday when "He breathed on them, and saith unto them, Receive ye the Holy Ghost" (John 20:22). But a special promise was given just for that period of time, that is, during the earthly ministry of Christ, and just for the apostles. They could ask the Father for the Holy Spirit and He would give the Holy Spirit to them. There are two things that we can conclude from this promise: first, nowhere does the Bible say that any of the apostles actually asked for the Holy Spirit, and secondly, in the end, Christ Himself prayed for them to receive the Holy Spirit, according to John 14:16.

> And I will pray the Father, and he shall give you another Comforter, that he may abide with you for ever;

How to Be Filled with the Holy Spirit

If God the Father does not give the Spirit by measure, then how can a person be filled with the Holy Spirit? The filling of the Holy Spirit must be understood so as not to be contradictory to the other teachings of the Scriptures about the Person, works, attributes, and ministries of the Holy Spirit according to the Word of God.

I have heard many people compare the filling of the Holy Spirit to the filling of a glass with water. Some have said that the glass is not full if it is only half full. Others have said that if the glass is already half full of dirt, you cannot fill it with water. But we already know that God does not give the Holy Spirit by measure, so these illustrations that deal with a glass and water are clearly erroneous and must be rejected. Our problem is one of understanding the word "filling," especially as it relates to something non-material, such as the Holy Spirit. The dictionary is not our authority, but a dictionary definition of the word "filling" just might help. The MacMillan Dictionary[1], in its sixth definition of "fill," says:

> [transitive] if something fills you with a particular emotion, you feel that emotion very strongly. fill someone with something: (e.g.) The sound of his voice filled me with dread. (or) His heart was filled with joy. Collocates: fill: Nouns frequently used with fill – apprehension, dread, fear, foreboding, horror, remorse, terror, trepidation

---

1 https://www.macmillandictionary.com/us/dictionary/american/fill_1

The American Heritage Dictionary[2] gives many definitions for the word filled. Its ninth definition says:

9. To occupy the whole of (the mind or thoughts, for example); consume: ...

The above definitions have more to do with the Biblical usage of the word "filling" than the illustrations we read about filling a glass with water. So, let's take a look at the Biblical usage of the word "filling." The word "fill" is used negatively to talk about "something [that] fills you with a particular emotion," such as wrath.

And all they in the synagogue, when they heard these things, were filled with wrath (Luke 4:28). ... And when they heard these sayings, they were full of wrath, and cried out, saying, Great is Diana of the Ephesians (Acts 19:28).

Certainly, madness is a negative emotion that Luke 6:11 tells us "filled" certain men.

And they were filled with madness; and communed one with another what they might do to Jesus.

Sorrow was a negative emotion that Jesus reproved in the apostles according to John 16:6.

But because I have said these things unto you, sorrow hath filled your heart.

In the case of Ananias, Peter said that Satan had filled his heart and caused him to lie to the Holy Spirit in Acts 5:3.

But Peter said, Ananias, why hath Satan filled thine heart to lie to the Holy Ghost, and to keep back part of the price of the land?

---

[2] *The American Heritage Dictionary of the English Language* Houghton Mifflin Company/ Boston William Morris, editor. 1976 edition.

It is interesting to note that the Bible never talks of someone being half filled with wrath, madness, sorrow or with Satan. Either Satan controlled a person, or he didn't. The same thing is true of "indignation" or "envy" which are different translations of the same Greek root word.

> Then the high priest rose up, and all they that were with him, (which is the sect of the Sadducees,) and were filled with indignation (Acts 5:17). ... But when the Jews saw the multitudes, they were filled with envy, and spake against those things which were spoken by Paul, contradicting and blaspheming (Acts 13:45).

In Acts 13:10, Paul accused Elymas the sorcerer of being full of "subtilty," which means "deceit," and "mischief" which is the translation of ῥᾳδιουργία [rhadiourgia] and is defined by the lexicon[3] as:

> 1 ease in doing, faculty. 2 levity or easiness in thinking or acting. 2A love of a lazy effeminate life. 3 unscrupulous, cunning, mischief.

Paul accused Elymas of being full of all deceit and a lazy, effeminate life in Acts 13:10. Neither of these things were tolerable to the Apostle Paul.

> And said, O full of all subtilty and all mischief, thou child of the devil, thou enemy of all righteousness, wilt thou not cease to pervert the right ways of the Lord?

Luke wrote that the city of Ephesus "... was filled with confusion" in Acts 19:29.

> And the whole city was filled with confusion: and having caught Gaius and Aristarchus, men of Macedonia, Paul's companions in travel, they rushed with one accord into the theatre.

---

3   Strong, J. (1995). *Enhanced Strong's Lexicon*. Woodside Bible Fellowship, #4468.

The word confusion has to do with tumult, outbreak or riot. None of these items would make sense to speak of them as being "half filled," and neither would any of the sins listed in Romans 1:29-31.

> Being filled with all unrighteousness, fornication, wickedness, covetousness, maliciousness; full of envy, murder, debate, deceit, malignity; whisperers, Backbiters, haters of God, despiteful, proud, boasters, inventors of evil things, disobedient to parents, Without understanding, covenantbreakers, without natural affection, implacable, unmerciful:

There are positive usages in the Scriptures of the word "filling" as well. Paul prayed for the Colossian believers to "... be filled with the knowledge of" God's will "in all wisdom."

> For this cause we also, since the day we heard it, do not cease to pray for you, and to desire that ye might be filled with the knowledge of his will in all wisdom and spiritual understanding (Colossians 1:9).

In Luke 2:40, the Bible also describes Jesus Christ as being "... filled with wisdom" even at an early age.

> And the child grew, and waxed strong in spirit, filled with wisdom: and the grace of God was upon him.

The Apostle Paul spoke of himself as being filled with παράκλησις [paraklesis], which is translated "comfort" in II Corinthians 7:4. The Greek word παράκλησις [paraklesis] is from the same root word that was translated "Comforter" in John 14:16 and 26. Paul chose that Greek word to tell the Corinthians, in II Corinthians 7:4, that he too would come alongside them to comfort them.

> Great is my boldness of speech toward you, great is my glorying of you: I am filled with comfort, I am exceeding joyful in all our tribulation.

Philippians 1:11 talks about "... being filled with the fruits of righteousness."

> Being filled with the fruits of righteousness, which are by Jesus Christ, unto the glory and praise of God.

Paul wanted to see Timothy in order to "... be filled with joy" according to II Timothy 1:4.

> Greatly desiring to see thee, being mindful of thy tears, that I may be filled with joy;

None of these quotes can be interpreted in such a way as to mean quantity, such as "completely full," "half full" or "half empty." Instead, the word "filled" in the Bible means to be controlled by something or some emotion.

The Bible also uses the word "filled" in a neutral sense. What I mean by a neutral sense is that I cannot determine whether it was used in a positive way, such as being filled with comfort, or a negative way, such as being filled with wrath. One way that the Bible speaks of being filled is found in Luke 5:26 where it says that they were filled with fear. Fear of God can be a good thing, but these men were filled with fear after seeing Christ heal a lame man. While it may have been a fear of God, the passage doesn't actually specify that. They concluded "... saying, We have seen strange things to day."

> And they were all amazed, and they glorified God, and were filled with fear, saying, We have seen strange things to day (Luke 5:26).

Another one that I have not been able to determine, is found in Acts 3:10 where it says that the people were filled with amazement.

> And they knew that it was he which sat for alms at the Beautiful gate of the temple: and they were filled with wonder and amazement at that which had happened unto him.

We cannot be half filled with amazement. Obviously being filled with the Holy Spirit is not the quantity of the Holy Spirit that we may have, but whether or not the Holy Spirit controls our lives.

So, let's consider how to be filled with the Holy Spirit. This filling is not an option since God definitely commands us to be filled with the Holy Spirit in Ephesians 5:18.

> And be not drunk with wine, wherein is excess; but be filled with the Spirit;

To not be filled with the Spirit of God is disobedience. God commands us to be filled. If we compare the command to be filled in Ephesians 5:18 with the command in Colossians 3:16 to "Let the word of Christ dwell in you richly in all wisdom. ..." and then compare the results, it might give us a hint as to how to be filled with the Holy Spirit.

1. The command

Ephesians 5:18	Colossians 3:16a
And be not drunk with wine, wherein is excess; but be filled with the Spirit;	Let the word of Christ dwell in you richly in all wisdom ...

2. How filling affects our worship of God

Ephesians 5:19-21	Colossians 3:16b-17
19 Speaking to yourselves in psalms and hymns and spiritual songs, singing and making melody in your heart to the Lord; 20 Giving thanks always for all things unto God and the Father in the name of our Lord Jesus Christ; 21 Submitting yourselves one to another in the fear of God.	... teaching and admonishing one another in psalms and hymns and spiritual songs, singing with grace in your hearts to the Lord. 17 And whatsoever ye do in word or deed, do all in the name of the Lord Jesus, giving thanks to God and the Father by him.

3. How filling affects our marriages

Ephesians 5:22–33	Colossians 3:18–19
22 Wives, submit yourselves unto your own husbands, as unto the Lord.	18 Wives, submit yourselves unto your own husbands, as it is fit in the Lord.
23 For the husband is the head of the wife, even as Christ is the head of the church: and he is the saviour of the body.	
24 Therefore as the church is subject unto Christ, so let the wives be to their own husbands in every thing.	
25 Husbands, love your wives, even as Christ also loved the church, and gave himself for it;	19 Husbands, love your wives, and be not bitter against them.
26 That he might sanctify and cleanse it with the washing of water by the word,	
27 That he might present it to himself a glorious church, not having spot, or wrinkle, or any such thing; but that it should be holy and without blemish.	
28 So ought men to love their wives as their own bodies. He that loveth his wife loveth himself.	
29 For no man ever yet hated his own flesh; but nourisheth and cherisheth it, even as the Lord the church:	
30 For we are members of his body, of his flesh, and of his bones.	
31 For this cause shall a man leave his father and mother, and shall be joined unto his wife, and they two shall be one flesh.	
32 This is a great mystery: but I speak concerning Christ and the church.	
33 Nevertheless let every one of you in particular so love his wife even as himself; and the wife see that she reverence her husband.	

a. How filling affects the wife

Ephesians 5:22–24, 33b	Colossians 3:18
22 Wives, submit yourselves unto your own husbands, as unto the Lord.	Wives, submit yourselves unto your own husbands, as it is fit in the Lord.
23 For the husband is the head of the wife, even as Christ is the head of the church: and he is the saviour of the body.	
24 Therefore as the church is subject unto Christ, so let the wives be to their own husbands in every thing.	
33b ... and the wife see that she reverence her husband.	

b. How filling affects the husband

Ephesians 5:25-33a	Colossians 3: 19
25 Husbands, love your wives, even as Christ also loved the church, and gave himself for it;	Husbands, love your wives, and be not bitter against them.
26 That he might sanctify and cleanse it with the washing of water by the word,	
27 That he might present it to himself a glorious church, not having spot, or wrinkle, or any such thing; but that it should be holy and without blemish.	
28 So ought men to love their wives as their own bodies. He that loveth his wife loveth himself.	
29 For no man ever yet hated his own flesh; but nourisheth and cherisheth it, even as the Lord the church:	
30 For we are members of his body, of his flesh, and of his bones.	
31 For this cause shall a man leave his father and mother, and shall be joined unto his wife, and they two shall be one flesh.	
32 This is a great mystery: but I speak concerning Christ and the church.	
33 Nevertheless let every one of you in particular so love his wife even as himself; ...	

4. How filling affects the family

Ephesians 6:1–4	Colossians 3:20–21
1 Children, obey your parents in the Lord: for this is right. 2 Honour thy father and mother; (which is the first commandment with promise;) 3 That it may be well with thee, and thou mayest live long on the earth. 4 And, ye fathers, provoke not your children to wrath: but bring them up in the nurture and admonition of the Lord.	20 Children, obey your parents in all things: for this is well pleasing unto the Lord. 21 Fathers, provoke not your children to anger, lest they be discouraged.

5. How filling affects our work

Ephesians 6:5–9	Colossians 3:22–4:1
5 Servants, be obedient to them that are your masters according to the flesh, with fear and trembling, in singleness of your heart, as unto Christ;	22 Servants, obey in all things your masters according to the flesh; not with eyeservice, as menpleasers; but in singleness of heart, fearing God:
6 Not with eyeservice, as menpleasers; but as the servants of Christ, doing the will of God from the heart;	23 And whatsoever ye do, do it heartily, as to the Lord, and not unto men;
7 With good will doing service, as to the Lord, and not to men:	24 Knowing that of the Lord ye shall receive the reward of the inheritance: for ye serve the Lord Christ.
8 Knowing that whatsoever good thing any man doeth, the same shall he receive of the Lord, whether he be bond or free.	25 But he that doeth wrong shall receive for the wrong which he hath done: and there is no respect of persons.
9 And, ye masters, do the same things unto them, forbearing threatening: knowing that your Master also is in heaven; neither is there respect of persons with him.	1 Masters, give unto your servants that which is just and equal; knowing that ye also have a Master in heaven.

a. How filling affects the employee

Ephesians 6:5-8	Colossians 3:22-25
5 Servants, be obedient to them that are your masters according to the flesh, with fear and trembling, in singleness of your heart, as unto Christ; 6 Not with eyeservice, as menpleasers; but as the servants of Christ, doing the will of God from the heart; 7 With good will doing service, as to the Lord, and not to men: 8 Knowing that whatsoever good thing any man doeth, the same shall he receive of the Lord, whether he be bond or free.	22 Servants, obey in all things your masters according to the flesh; not with eyeservice, as menpleasers; but in singleness of heart, fearing God: 23 And whatsoever ye do, do it heartily, as to the Lord, and not unto men; 24 Knowing that of the Lord ye shall receive the reward of the inheritance: for ye serve the Lord Christ. 25 But he that doeth wrong shall receive for the wrong which he hath done: and there is no respect of persons.

b. How filling affects the employer

Ephesians 6:9	Colossians 4:1
And, ye masters, do the same things unto them, forbearing threatening: knowing that your Master also is in heaven; neither is there respect of persons with him.	Masters, give unto your servants that which is just and equal; knowing that ye also have a Master in heaven.

6. How filling affects our prayers

Ephesians 6:18–19	Colossians 4:2–4
18 Praying always with all prayer and supplication in the Spirit, and watching thereunto with all perseverance and supplication for all saints; 19 And for me, that utterance may be given unto me, that I may open my mouth boldly, to make known the mystery of the gospel,	2 Continue in prayer, and watch in the same with thanksgiving; 3 Withal praying also for us, that God would open unto us a door of utterance, to speak the mystery of Christ, for which I am also in bonds: 4 That I may make it manifest, as I ought to speak.

Since the effects of being filled with the Holy Spirit are identical with the effects of letting the Word of Christ dwell in us richly, we can conclude that being filled with the Word of Christ is the same thing as being filled with the Holy Spirit. Both are commands, and both produce the exact same results in the life of the believer. Being filled with the Holy Spirit is not an experience, it is obedience to the Word of God. There is no way to be filled with the Holy Spirit and disobey the Word of Christ. The filling of the Spirit requires a disciplined life of filling our hearts and minds with the Word of the Spirit.

According to Colossians 1:9-14, being filled with the Spirit is also synonymous with being filled with the knowledge of His will and obeying His will.

> For this cause we also, since the day we heard it, do not cease to pray for you, and to desire that ye might be filled with the knowledge of his will in all wisdom and spiritual understanding; That ye might walk worthy of the Lord unto all pleasing, being fruitful in every good work, and increasing in the knowledge of God; Strengthened

with all might, according to his glorious power, unto all patience and longsuffering with joyfulness; Giving thanks unto the Father, which hath made us meet to be partakers of the inheritance of the saints in light: Who hath delivered us from the power of darkness, and hath translated us into the kingdom of his dear Son: In whom we have redemption through his blood, even the forgiveness of sins:

Romans 15:14 sums up the filling of the Spirit of God saying that we must be filled with all knowledge.

> And I myself also am persuaded of you, my brethren, that ye also are full of goodness, filled with all knowledge, able also to admonish one another.

Being filled with the Holy Spirit is also equivalent to being filled with God the Father according to Ephesians 3:14-21.

> For this cause I bow my knees unto the Father of our Lord Jesus Christ, Of whom the whole family in heaven and earth is named, That he would grant you, according to the riches of his glory, to be strengthened with might by his Spirit in the inner man; That Christ may dwell in your hearts by faith; that ye, being rooted and grounded in love, May be able to comprehend with all saints what is the breadth, and length, and depth, and height; And to know the love of Christ, which passeth knowledge, that ye might be filled with all the fulness of God. Now unto him that is able to do exceeding abundantly above all that we ask or think, according to the power that worketh in us, Unto him be glory in the church by Christ Jesus throughout all ages, world without end. Amen.

Of course, the Bible also tells us that being filled with the Holy Spirit is synonymous with being filled with Christ according to Ephesians 1:22-23.

> And hath put all things under his feet, and gave him to be the head over all things to the church, Which is his body, the fulness of him that filleth all in all.

How do we explain this close association of the Holy Spirit to the Word of Christ? It's actually not hard to understand. Allowing the Holy Spirit to control our lives is only possible as we obey the Word that He has inspired. Too many people want a cheap filling that requires no effort on their part, while being filled with the Word of Christ takes effort and years of study and obedience to the Word of God. In Ephesians 6:17, Paul closely identified the Spirit of God and the Word of God, saying:

> And take the helmet of salvation, and the sword of the Spirit, which is the word of God:

Jesus Christ Himself made that kind of comparison in John 6:63.

> It is the spirit that quickeneth; the flesh profiteth nothing: the words that I speak unto you, they are spirit, and they are life.

Chapter Five

THE GIFTS OF THE HOLY SPIRIT

With the rise of Pentecostalism and the Charismatic movement there has been a tremendous increase in the number of books that have been written about "spiritual gifts," especially about the gift of tongues, interpretation of tongues, healing and prophecy. As a part of my research on this chapter alone, I read more than one hundred books, most of them written by Pentecostals or Charismatics. Some of the Charismatics with whom I have spoken go so far as to say that a person is not saved unless he has demonstrated his salvation by the use of some spiritual gift. But this adds another requirement on top of faith alone, in Christ alone, for salvation. In his declaration of the Gospel, in I Corinthians 15:1-4, Paul never included anything about a demonstration of any spiritual gift as a proof of salvation.

> Moreover, brethren, I declare unto you the gospel which I preached unto you, which also ye have received, and wherein ye stand; By which also ye are saved, if ye keep in memory what I preached unto you, unless ye have believed in vain. For I delivered unto you first of all that which I also received, how that Christ died for our sins according to the scriptures; And that he was buried, and that he rose again the third day according to the scriptures:

The Bible clearly declares that salvation is appropriated by faith, not by speaking in tongues, healing, etc. This can be easily seen in Acts 16:30-31 where the Philippian jailor asked, "What must I do to be saved?" The answer was unambiguous: "Believe on the Lord Jesus Christ."

> And brought them out, and said, Sirs, what must I do to be saved? And they said, Believe on the Lord Jesus Christ, and thou shalt be saved, and thy house.

When Nicodemus asked how to be born again, Jesus did not tell him that he needed to speak in tongues, but instead that he needed to believe in the only begotten Son of God, according to John 3:15-18.

> That whosoever believeth in him should not perish, but have eternal life. For God so loved the world, that he gave his only begotten Son, that whosoever believeth in him should not perish, but have everlasting life. For God sent not his Son into the world to condemn the world; but that the world through him might be saved. He that believeth on him is not condemned: but he that believeth not is condemned already, because he hath not believed in the name of the only begotten Son of God.

Nowhere does the Bible give some spiritual gift as evidence that a person is saved. The thing that we see in the Bible as evidence of salvation is baptism, according to Acts 2:41.

> Then they that gladly received his word were baptized: and the same day there were added unto them about three thousand souls.

We could argue from Romans 10:8-17 that confession is possibly an evidence of salvation, but nowhere are spiritual gifts listed as an evidence of salvation.

> But what saith it? The word is nigh thee, even in thy mouth, and in thy heart: that is, the word of faith, which we preach; That if thou shalt confess with thy mouth the Lord Jesus, and shalt believe in thine heart that God

hath raised him from the dead, thou shalt be saved. For with the heart man believeth unto righteousness; and with the mouth confession is made unto salvation. For the scripture saith, Whosoever believeth on him shall not be ashamed. For there is no difference between the Jew and the Greek: for the same Lord over all is rich unto all that call upon him. For whosoever shall call upon the name of the Lord shall be saved. How then shall they call on him in whom they have not believed? and how shall they believe in him of whom they have not heard? and how shall they hear without a preacher? And how shall they preach, except they be sent? as it is written, How beautiful are the feet of them that preach the gospel of peace, and bring glad tidings of good things! But they have not all obeyed the gospel. For Esaias saith, Lord, who hath believed our report? So then faith cometh by hearing, and hearing by the word of God.

The New-Testament Spiritual Gifts

In this chapter, we will be discussing the purpose of spiritual gifts, but before we get to that, we should at least develop a list of the things that are called spiritual gifts in the Bible. First, we will consider the list that the Apostle Paul gave us in I Corinthians 12:8-10. We will examine this passage in both English and in the Greek Textus Receptus.

> For to one is given by the Spirit the word of wisdom; to another the word of knowledge by the same Spirit; To **another** faith by the same Spirit; to another the gifts of healing by the same Spirit; To another the working of miracles; to another prophecy; to another discerning of spirits; to **another** divers kinds of tongues; to another the interpretation of tongues:

Now let's look at I Corinthians 12:8-10 in the Greek Textus Receptus.

The Gifts of the Holy Spirit

> ᾧ μὲν γὰρ διὰ τοῦ Πνεύματος δίδοται λόγος σοφίας, ἄλλῳ δὲ λόγος γνώσεως, κατὰ τὸ αὐτὸ Πνεῦμα· **ἑτέρῳ** δὲ πίστις, ἐν τῷ αὐτῷ Πνεύματι· ἄλλῳ δὲ χαρίσματα ἰαμάτων ἐν τῷ αὐτῷ πνεύματι· ἄλλῳ δὲ ἐνεργήματα δυνάμεων, ἄλλῳ δὲ προφητεία, ἄλλῳ δὲ διακρίσεις πνευμάτων, **ἑτέρῳ** δὲ γένη γλωσσῶν, ἄλλῳ δὲ ἑρμηνεία γλωσσῶν·

I have put the word ἑτέρῳ [*heteroi*] in bold type above. This word was translated "**another**" in the Authorized Version. Paul used the word ἑτέρῳ [*heteroi*] to divide the list of spiritual gifts into three major groups. The Greek word ἑτέρῳ [*heteroi*] comes from the word ἕτερος [*heteros*], which means "another, one of two things, different, or foreign," or as it says in El Diccionario de Idiomas Bíblicos (The Dictionary of Biblical Languages),

> 2283 ἕτερος [*heteros*]: adjective; different, from another type or class.

In I Corinthians 12:8-10, three different groups are given which are all separated from one another by the Greek word ἑτέρῳ [*heteroi*].

There is another Greek word in this passage, which is also translated as "another." That particular Greek word is ἄλλῳ. The word ἄλλῳ comes from the word ἄλλος, and is likewise translated as "another" in English. What is the difference between the two words? The Greek word ἄλλος means "another equal, or another which is the same," while the word ἕτερος means "another which is different." The difference in the meanings of these two words can be easily seen in a couple of passages. First, look at Galatians 1:6-9 where the Apostle Paul used these same two words to contrast the truth of the uniqueness of the Gospel with any other gospel.

> I marvel that ye are so soon removed from him that called you into the grace of Christ unto another gospel (ἕτερον εὐαγγέλιον "another different gospel"): Which is not another (ὃ οὐκ ἔστιν ἄλλο "which is not another that is equal or the same"); but there be some that trouble

you, and would pervert the gospel of Christ. But though we, or an angel from heaven, preach any other gospel unto you than that which we have preached unto you, let him be accursed. As we said before, so say I now again, If any man preach any other gospel unto you than that ye have received, let him be accursed.

Galatians 1:6-9 in the Greek Textus Receptus, bears out what we have said above, saying:

> Θαυμάζω ὅτι οὕτω ταχέως μετατίθεσθε ἀπὸ τοῦ καλέσαντος ὑμᾶς ἐν χάριτι Χριστοῦ εἰς ἕτερον εὐαγγέλιον· ὃ οὐκ ἔστιν ἄλλο, εἰ μή τινές εἰσιν οἱ ταράσσοντες ὑμᾶς καὶ θέλοντες μεταστρέψαι τὸ εὐαγγέλιον τοῦ Χριστοῦ. ἀλλὰ καὶ ἐὰν ἡμεῖς ἢ ἄγγελος ἐξ οὐρανοῦ εὐαγγελίζηται ὑμῖν παρ᾽ ὃ εὐηγγελισάμεθα ὑμῖν, ἀνάθεμα ἔστω. ὡς προειρήκαμεν, καὶ ἄρτι πάλιν λέγω, εἴ τις ὑμᾶς εὐαγγελίζεται παρ᾽ ὃ παρελάβετε, ἀνάθεμα ἔστω.

Another passage where the meaning of the Greek word ἄλλος is very clear is John 14:16 where Jesus prophesied that He would send ἄλλον παράκλητον, another (equal or the same) Comforter.

> And I will pray the Father, and he shall give you another Comforter, that he may abide with you for ever;

As we read John 14:16 in the Greek, it should be obvious to us that the παράκλητον had to be the same as Christ. Christ was God, and the Comforter is God, equal to the Father and to the Son. He is ἄλλον παράκλητον.

> καὶ ἐγὼ ἐρωτήσω τὸν πατέρα, καὶ ἄλλον παράκλητον δώσει ὑμῖν, ἵνα μένῃ μεθ᾽ ὑμῶν εἰς τὸν αἰῶνα,

Let's review what we have learned about the words that are translated "another" in the Bible. Paul wrote that there is only one Gospel, and that another, different (ἕτερος) Gospel is not the same (ἄλλος), since there is no other which is the same (ἄλλος), even though it seems to be parallel. On the other hand, the Spirit is Another Comforter (ἄλλον παράκλητον), which is equal to Christ.

Now if we look back on how Paul divided up spiritual gifts in I Corinthians 12:8-10, we see the following lists develop from this passage.

A. The first group is formed before the first usage of ἑτέρῳ
   1. Word of wisdom
   2. Word of knowledge
B. The second group is formed before the second usage of ἑτέρῳ
   1. Faith
   2. Healing
   3. Miracles
   4. Prophecy
   5. Discerning of Spirits
C. The third group is formed after the second usage of ἑτέρῳ
   1. Tongues
   2. The interpretation of tongues

More spiritual gifts could be added to the lists that we developed from I Corinthians 12:8-10 by including the spiritual gifts listed in Mark 16:17-20.

> And these signs shall follow them that believe; In my name shall they cast out devils; they shall speak with new tongues; They shall take up serpents; and if they drink any deadly thing, it shall not hurt them; they shall lay hands on the sick, and they shall recover. So then after the Lord had spoken unto them, he was received up into heaven, and sat on the right hand of God. And they went forth, and preached every where, the Lord

working with them, and confirming the word with signs following. Amen.

Let's examine Mark 16:17-20 in the Greek Textus Receptus.

σημεῖα δὲ τοῖς πιστεύσασι ταῦτα παρακολουθήσει· ἐν τῷ ὀνόματί μου δαιμόνια ἐκβαλοῦσι· γλώσσαις λαλήσουσι καιναῖς, ὄφεις ἀροῦσι· κἂν θανάσιμόν τι πίωσιν, οὐ μὴ αὐτοὺς βλάψει, ἐπὶ ἀρρώστους χεῖρας ἐπιθήσουσι, καὶ καλῶς ἕξουσιν. Ὁ μὲν οὖν Κύριος, μετὰ τὸ λαλῆσαι αὐτοῖς, ἀνελήφθη εἰς τὸν οὐρανὸν, καὶ ἐκάθισεν ἐκ δεξιῶν τοῦ Θεοῦ. ἐκεῖνοι δὲ ἐξελθόντες ἐκήρυξαν πανταχοῦ, τοῦ Κυρίου συνεργοῦντος, καὶ τὸν λόγον βεβαιοῦντος διὰ τῶν ἐπακολουθούντων σημείων. Ἀμήν.

Now let's compare the lists that we have seen of spiritual gifts from I Corinthians 12:8-10 with those spiritual gifts that we find in Mark 16:17-20. In comparing the two lists we find two spiritual gifts, or signs, that overlap. Both of these lists include the gift of tongues and the gift of healing.

Furthermore, we need to examine what gifts are found in Mark 16:17-20 that are not found in I Corinthians 12:8-10. There are three signs or spiritual gifts that are found in Mark 16:17-20 that are not found in I Corinthians 12:8-10. Those three spiritual gifts are: the casting out of demons, the taking up of serpents in the hands, and the attempts to kill the apostles by getting them to drink poison would have no harmful effect.

At this point we can combine the three lists that comprise spiritual gifts from I Corinthians 12:8-10 and Mark 16:17-20 and outline them in the following manner.

A. The first group is called "Wonders"
    1. Word of wisdom
    2. Word of knowledge

The Gifts of the Holy Spirit

B. **The second group is called "Miracles"**
   1. **Faith**
   2. **Healing**
   3. **Miracles**
   4. **Prophecy**
   5. **Discerning of Spirits**
   6. **Casting out of demons**

C. **The third group is called "Signs"**
   1. **Tongues**
   2. **The interpretation of tongues**
   3. **Taking up serpents in the hands**
   4. **Being unharmed by someone trying to poison them**

The twelve spiritual gifts that we have listed, along with the three categories of "signs," "wonders," and "miracles" are together called the "signs of an apostle." Paul had performed these signs in Corinth and when he wrote to the church in I Corinthians 9:2, he mentioned that they were "… the seal of mine apostleship."

> If I be not an apostle unto others, yet doubtless I am to you: for the seal of mine apostleship are ye in the Lord.

More specifically Paul wrote in II Corinthians 12:11-12 that he had "… the signs of an apostle." He then divided the signs of an apostle into three categories: "signs, and wonders, and mighty deeds."

> I am become a fool in glorying; ye have compelled me: for I ought to have been commended of you: for in nothing am I behind the very chiefest apostles, though I be nothing. Truly the signs of an apostle were wrought among you in all patience, in signs, and wonders, and mighty deeds.

In Hebrews 2:1-4, Paul again stated that the Gospel was confirmed to us "... by them (the apostles) that heard him (Christ)" (Hebrews 2:3). Paul went on to say that God bore witness to the apostles, "... with signs and wonders, and with divers miracles" (Hebrews 2:4) which were also called "... gifts of the Holy Ghost."

> Therefore we ought to give the more earnest heed to the things which we have heard, lest at any time we should let them slip. For if the word spoken by angels was stedfast, and every transgression and disobedience received a just recompence of reward; How shall we escape, if we neglect so great salvation; which at the first began to be spoken by the Lord, and was confirmed unto us by them that heard him; God also bearing them witness, both with signs and wonders, and with divers miracles, and gifts of the Holy Ghost, according to his own will?

Mark chapter 16 ends by letting us know that only the apostles had the signs of an apostle. Verse 20 clearly states that the apostles "... went forth" and God confirmed His Word "... with signs following." The signs followed the apostolic Word, not the church.

> And they went forth, and preached every where, the Lord working with them, and confirming the word with signs following. Amen.

In Romans 15:14-20, Paul again enumerated the three categories of spiritual gifts or the signs of an apostle. He said that his job was "... to make the Gentiles obedient, by word and deed" (Romans 15:18). He did that "... through mighty signs and wonders, by the power (miracles) of the Spirit of God" (Romans 15:19).

> And I myself also am persuaded of you, my brethren, that ye also are full of goodness, filled with all knowledge, able also to admonish one another. Nevertheless, brethren, I have written the more boldly unto you in some sort, as putting you in mind, because of the grace that is given to me of God, That I should be the minister of Jesus Christ

> to the Gentiles, ministering the gospel of God, that the offering up of the Gentiles might be acceptable, being sanctified by the Holy Ghost. I have therefore whereof I may glory through Jesus Christ in those things which pertain to God. For I will not dare to speak of any of those things which Christ hath not wrought by me, to make the Gentiles obedient, by word and deed, Through mighty signs and wonders, by the power of the Spirit of God; so that from Jerusalem, and round about unto Illyricum, I have fully preached the gospel of Christ. Yea, so have I strived to preach the gospel, not where Christ was named, lest I should build upon another man's foundation:

Jesus promised to send the apostles and their assistants, which are called the New Testament prophets, to write the New Testament. Jesus clearly stated that in Luke 11:49.

> Therefore also said the wisdom of God, I will send them prophets and apostles, and some of them they shall slay and persecute:

That doesn't really explain, though, why the apostles and prophets had the signs of an apostle. What was the purpose in having these signs?

The Purpose of Spiritual Gifts

These spiritual gifts were called the signs of an apostle because they demonstrated who was an apostle or a New Testament prophet. They were rightly called signs, because a sign points to something. In that sense they were like a military uniform where the insignias on the uniform not only inform the soldier's rank, but also whose side he is on.

Since the signs could be conferred through a letter of commendation from an apostle, or by the laying on of his hands, these signs also demonstrated who was authorized by the apostle, and who was not.

We should also mention that the signs were given only to the Jewish people. These were signs to the Jewish people who were charged with the writing, the copying, and the preserving of the Word of God. In Romans 3:1-4, Paul wrote:

> What advantage then hath the Jew? or what profit is there of circumcision? Much every way: chiefly, because that unto them were committed the oracles of God. For what if some did not believe? shall their unbelief make the faith of God without effect? God forbid: yea, let God be true, but every man a liar; as it is written, That thou mightest be justified in thy sayings, and mightest overcome when thou art judged.

For that reason, "... the Jews require a sign" (I Corinthians 1:22) which is something Moses required of them in order to determine what was legitimately the Word of God.

How and When Did the Signs of an Apostle End?

Only the apostles were given the ability to confer a spiritual gift, either through personally laying on their hands, or by a letter of commendation. The men who received this spiritual gift from the apostles could not confer this gift to another. For that reason, when the last apostle died, spiritual gifts, or the signs of an apostle, came to an end. The Lord Himself prophesied of an end of the apostolic age. The date that He gave for that was the destruction of the temple in A.D. 70. We find this prophecy in Matthew 23:29-38.

> Woe unto you, scribes and Pharisees, hypocrites! because ye build the tombs of the prophets, and garnish the sepulchres of the righteous, And say, If we had been in the days of our fathers, we would not have been partakers with them in the blood of the prophets. Wherefore ye be witnesses unto yourselves, that ye are the children of them which killed the prophets. Fill ye up then the measure of your fathers. Ye serpents, ye generation of vipers, how can ye escape the damnation

of hell? Wherefore, behold, I send unto you prophets, and wise men, and scribes: and some of them ye shall kill and crucify; and some of them shall ye scourge in your synagogues, and persecute them from city to city: That upon you may come all the righteous blood shed upon the earth, from the blood of righteous Abel unto the blood of Zacharias son of Barachias, whom ye slew between the temple and the altar. Verily I say unto you, All these things shall come upon this generation. O Jerusalem, Jerusalem, thou that killest the prophets, and stonest them which are sent unto thee, how often would I have gathered thy children together, even as a hen gathereth her chickens under her wings, and ye would not! **Behold, your house is left unto you desolate.**

Jesus said that He was going to "... send unto you prophets, and wise men, and scribes" (Matthew 23:34). The blood of all the prophets would come "... upon this generation" (Matthew 23:36), and that time period would be marked by "Behold, your house is left unto you desolate," which was the destruction of the temple by the Roman emperor, Titus. In Luke 11:49–51, we find a parallel passage to Matthew 23.

Therefore also said the wisdom of God, I will send them prophets and apostles, and some of them they shall slay and persecute: That the blood of all the prophets, which was shed from the foundation of the world, may be required of this generation; From the blood of Abel unto the blood of Zacharias, which perished between the altar and the temple: verily I say unto you, It shall be required of this generation.

In Luke 11:49, Jesus called the men that He was sending, "prophets and apostles." There were only twelve apostles and there were never going to be more than twelve. At the very end of time, in eternity, there will still only be twelve apostles as we see in Revelation 21:14.

And the wall of the city had twelve foundations, and in them the names of the twelve apostles of the Lamb.

This means that all of the apostles were dead and the New Testament was finished by A.D. 70. I know that some are already saying, "Wait a minute! The Gospel according to John was not written until A.D. 95." Who says so? Many modern scholars say so. But the Bible does not say so. It is easy enough to see in John 5:1-2 that these verses were written before the destruction of the temple.

After this there was a feast of the Jews; and Jesus went up to Jerusalem. Now there is at Jerusalem by the sheep market a pool, which is called in the Hebrew tongue Bethesda, having five porches.

John used the past tense in verse 1 where he wrote that "... there was a feast" and "... Jesus went up to Jerusalem," but suddenly when he wrote about the existence of Jerusalem, the sheep gate, the pool of Bethesda, and its five porches, he changed to present tense. He said, "Now there IS at Jerusalem." Jerusalem and all the other things that he mentioned in present tense still existed, and that would not have been the case in A.D. 95. There is not even a mention of the siege of Jerusalem by Titus. John had finished his part of the writing of the New Testament by the fall of Jerusalem.

The Lord clearly stated in the passages we just read that there were never going to be more than twelve apostles. Spiritual gifts would cease to exist at the death of the last apostle, which took place before the destruction of the temple in A.D. 70.

The Apostle Paul also stated that spiritual gifts had to end, by presenting a logical argument to show that they would end. He chose the three most important gifts, one sign, one wonder, and one miracle. He reasoned that the most important sign gift was tongues, since the interpretation of tongues cannot exist if there are no tongues to interpret. The indispensable sign, therefore, is tongues. If no one can speak a language, then interpretation likewise cannot exist. The same was true for the wonder gifts of knowledge and

The Gifts of the Holy Spirit

wisdom. Wisdom is the interpretation of knowledge. If there is no knowledge, there is no need for the gift of "word of wisdom." The same can be stated for the miracles. The reason for all of the miracles was to confirm the word of prophecy. Prophecy is the indispensable miracle, for without prophecy there is no need to prove who is a prophet. For that reason, if you were to do away with the word of knowledge and prophecy, all of the gifts would cease. That is Paul's argument in I Corinthians 13:8b.

> ... but whether there be prophecies, they shall fail ; whether there be tongues, they shall cease ; whether there be knowledge, it shall vanish away.

Notice carefully the Greek of I Corinthians 13:8b, particularly the verbs that are translated "they shall fail," "they shall cease," and, "it shall vanish away."

> ... εἴτε δὲ προφητεῖαι, καταργηθήσονται· εἴτε γλῶσσαι, παύσονται· εἴτε γνῶσις, καταργηθήσεται.

The Greek verb which is translated "they shall fail" is καταργηθήσονται [katargethesontai], which is future tense, passive voice, indicative mood, third person plural conjugation of the verb καταργέω [katargeo] which the lexicon[1] defines as:

> 1 to render idle, unemployed, inactivate, inoperative. 1A to cause a person or thing to have no further efficiency. 1B to deprive of force, influence, power. 2 to cause to cease, put an end to, do away with, annul, abolish. 2A to cease, to pass away, be done away. 2B to be severed from, separated from, discharged from, loosed from any one. 2C to terminate all intercourse with one.

Something was going to cause prophecies to be "idle, unemployed, inactivate, inoperative." Prophecies would come to an end by an outside force. At the same time, the verb, which is translated "it shall vanish away," is καταργηθήσεται [katargethesetai]

---

1 Strong, J. (1995). *Enhanced Strong's Lexicon*. Woodside Bible Fellowship, #2673.

which is the future tense, passive voice, indicative mood, third person singular conjugation of the same exact verb καταργέω [katargeo]. The gift of "word of wisdom" shall also be brought to an end by an outside force and will be rendered "idle, unemployed, inactivate, inoperative." Before we discuss what force would have done this, let's first find out what happens to tongues. I Corinthians 13:8b says of tongues, "... they shall cease." The Greek verb that is translated "they shall cease" is παύσονται [pausontai], which is the future tense, middle voice, indicative mood, third person plural conjugation of the verb παύω [pauo], which means[2]:

> 1 to make to cease or desist. 2 to restrain a thing or person from something. 3 to cease, to leave off.

Tongues shall cease all by themselves. There is no need for an outside influence. They would have to cease or "desist" since there was no longer a need for them.

Paul then wrote in verse 9 that the gifts of prophecy and knowledge were "in part," that is, "incomplete."

For we know *in part*, and we prophesy *in part*.

The word "part" is the translation of the Greek word, μέρος [meros], which the lexicon[3] defines as:

> 1 a part. 1A a part due or assigned to one. 1B lot, destiny. 2 one of the constituent parts of a whole. 2A in part, partly, in a measure, to some degree, as respects a part, severally, individually. 2B any particular, in regard to this, in this respect.

By revelation, Paul knew some truth that Peter or John did not know. Each had some things revealed to them, and they each prophesied their part. Each of them was incomplete by themselves. But the day would come when their revelation and prophecy would be joined together in one place. There would finally be the complete

---

2 Ibid. #3973.
3 Ibid. #3313.

The Gifts of the Holy Spirit

revelation and prophecy that was incomplete until that moment. So Paul wrote in I Corinthians 13:10:

> But when that which is perfect is come, then that which is in part shall be done away.

That which "... shall be done away" (again Paul used the Greek verb καταργέω [katargeo][4]) to again state that something was going to cause prophecies and knowledge to be "idle, unemployed, inactivate, inoperative." That thing that would bring the gifts of knowledge and prophecy to an end was when all the prophecy and knowledge were combined in "that which is perfect." That which is perfect is the complete knowledge and prophecy. It is not an allusion to the second coming of Christ. It is a direct comparison to that which is in part. Furthermore "that" is neuter, not masculine. If it were to refer to Christ it would have to be masculine and say, "When He which is perfect shall come." This is a reference to the completion of the New Testament. Spiritual gifts would end with the finishing of the New Testament.

The word that is translated "perfect" is the Greek word τέλειος [teleios], which the lexicon[5] defines as:

> 1 brought to its end, finished. 2 wanting nothing necessary to completeness. 3 perfect. 4 that which is perfect. 4A consummate human integrity and virtue. 4B of men. 4B1 full grown, adult, of full age, mature.

Paul wrote that when the New Testament was "finished," then the incomplete gifts of knowledge and prophecy would end. Since the word translated "perfect" also means to be "full grown, adult, of full age, mature," Paul continued with an illustration about becoming an adult in I Corinthians 13:11:

> When I was a child, I spake as a child (tongues), I understood as a child (knowledge), I thought as a child

---

4 Ibid. #2673.
5 Ibid. #5046

(prophecy): but when I became a man, I put away (καταργέω [katargeo]) childish things.

Paul compared spiritual gifts to "childish things." These were the things that he "put away" when he "became a man." He used the exact same verb (καταργέω [katargeo]) that he had used in I Corinthians 13:8 where he had said that prophecies "shall fail" and knowledge "shall vanish away." In verse 11, it was translated "I put away." Just like the childish things of his youth that Paul had "put away," when the New Testament was complete, the incomplete gifts of the Spirit were "put away." The Holy Spirit no longer needed the sign gifts once the New Testament was complete. These spiritual gifts were then rendered idle, unemployed, inactive and inoperative by the existence of the superior, complete Word of God. With that in mind, the Apostle Paul wrote about the superiority of the written Word of God in I Corinthians 14:37 saying:

> If any man think himself to be a prophet, or spiritual, let him acknowledge that the things that I write unto you are the commandments of the Lord.

Another illustration of the superiority of the completed Scriptures in comparison to the spiritual gifts is found in I Corinthians 13:12. Here Paul compared the partial revelation and prophecy to the completed New Testament using terminology that was similar to what he used to speak of the giving of the Law to Moses.

> For now we see through a glass, darkly; but then face to face: now I know in part; but then shall I know even as also I am known.

Paul stated that, at that moment ("now"), he, and the other writers of the New Testament, could know in part. The Greek says, ἄρτι γινώσκω ἐκ μέρους [arti ginosko ek merous]. Paul then said, in comparison that he would know τότε δὲ ἐπιγνώσομαι καθὼς καὶ ἐπεγνώσθην [*tote de epignosomai kathos kai epegnosthen*][6]. Notice the change in the verb translated "I know." First Paul said that he knew "γινώσκω" only his part, but once the New Testament was completed, "I shall know" (ἐπιγνώσομαι) which is the future tense, middle voice, indicative mood, first person singular conjugation of the Greek verb ἐπιγινώσκω [*epiginosko*], which according to the lexicon[7] means:

> 1 to become thoroughly acquainted with, to know thoroughly. 1A to know accurately, know well. 2 to know. 2A to recognise. 2A1 by sight, hearing, of certain signs, to perceive who a person is. 2B to know i.e. to perceive. 2C to know i.e. to find out, ascertain. 2D to know i.e. to understand.

Paul's knowledge was like looking through a dark glass at that moment. He could not see the entire picture. He only knew his part of the prophecy. But once all the parts were put together, he would know, ἐπιγινώσκω [*epiginosko*], thoroughly, accurately, and well everything that had been revealed and prophesied.

In a similar way, Paul compared the New Testament to the giving of the Law to Moses in II Corinthians 3:14–15, and 18.

> But their minds were blinded: for until this day remaineth the same vail untaken away in the reading of the old testament; which vail is done away in Christ. But even unto this day, when Moses is read, the vail is upon their heart. ... But we all, with open face beholding as in a glass the glory of the Lord, are changed into the same image from glory to glory, even as by the Spirit of the Lord.

James used the same kind of an illustration about the value of the written Word of God in James 1:22–25.

---

6 *Scrivener's 1881 Textus Receptus*. (1995). (electronic ed., I Co 13:12). Oak Harbor: Logos Research Systems.
7 Strong, J. (1995). *Enhanced Strong's Lexicon*. Woodside Bible Fellowship, #1921.

> But be ye doers of the word, and not hearers only, deceiving your own selves. For if any be a hearer of the word, and not a doer, he is like unto a man beholding his natural face in a glass: For he beholdeth himself, and goeth his way, and straightway forgetteth what manner of man he was. But whoso looketh into the perfect law of liberty, and continueth therein, he being not a forgetful hearer, but a doer of the work, this man shall be blessed in his deed.

Having the completed Word of God is far better than spiritual gifts, as long as we read it, study it, and obey it today. As James said, "This man shall be blessed in his deed."

The Purpose of Tongues in Particular

Paul wrote I Corinthians chapters thirteen and fourteen so that we could understand the purpose of tongues during the apostolic age. As we have seen in I Corinthians thirteen, the sign of tongues was temporary in nature along with the gifts of word of knowledge and prophecy. In chapter fourteen Paul wrote specifically of the purpose of tongues while this gift temporarily existed. Paul makes these instructions clear by stating many times to whom he was writing. We could sum up his reasoning by combining I Corinthians 14:23 and 40 where he said that the corporate meeting of the church must be done decently and in order in the use of spiritual gifts.

> If therefore the whole church be come together into one place, and all speak with tongues, and there come in those that are unlearned, or unbelievers, will they not say that ye are mad? ... Let all things be done decently and in order.

A correct interpretation of chapter fourteen should answer the question, "To whom was this chapter written?" The chapter was written to a local church congregation in Corinth. Paul used several things to indicate that it is not written to an individual. One strong indication is the constant usage of the second person

The Gifts of the Holy Spirit

plural pronoun "ye" or "you (plural)." Another word that Paul used frequently in this passage to show that it was written to the entire church as a body is the word "brethren." It can also be seen in the conjugation of the verbs, which are in the second person plural imperative, such as *"Follow* after charity" in verse 1.

> *Follow* after charity, and *desire* spiritual gifts, but rather that ye may prophesy (I Corinthians 14:1) ... I would that ye all spake with tongues, but rather that ye prophesied: for greater is he that prophesieth than he that speaketh with tongues, except he interpret, that the church may receive edifying. Now, brethren, if I come unto you speaking with tongues, what shall I profit you, except I shall speak to you either by revelation, or by knowledge, or by prophesying, or by doctrine (I Corinthians 14:5-6)? ... So likewise ye, except ye utter by the tongue words easy to be understood, how shall it be known what is spoken? for ye shall speak into the air (I Corinthians 14:9). ... Even so ye, forasmuch as ye are zealous of spiritual gifts, seek that ye may excel to the edifying of the church (I Corinthians 14:12). ... Brethren, *be* not children in understanding: howbeit in malice be ye children, but in understanding *be* men (I Corinthians 14:20). ... How is it then, brethren? when ye come together, every one of you hath a psalm, hath a doctrine, hath a tongue, hath a revelation, hath an interpretation. *Let* all things be done unto edifying (I Corinthians 14:26). ... Let the prophets speak two or three, and let the other judge (I Corinthians 14:29). ... For ye may all prophesy one by one, that all may learn, and all may be comforted (I Corinthians 14:31). ... Let your women keep silence in the churches: for it is not permitted unto them to speak; but they are commanded to be under obedience, as also saith the law (I Corinthians 14:34). ... What? came the word of God out from you? or came it unto you only (I Corinthians 14:36)?

> ... Wherefore, brethren, covet to prophesy, and forbid not to speak with tongues (I Corinthians 14:39).

Another strong indication that I Corinthians chapter fourteen, was written to the church as a body and not to an individual is found in the many verses where Paul used the word "church" in such a way as to identify to whom he was writing. This can be found in the following verses of I Corinthians chapter fourteen.

> He that speaketh in an unknown tongue edifieth himself; but he that prophesieth edifieth the church. I would that ye all spake with tongues, but rather that ye prophesied: for greater is he that prophesieth than he that speaketh with tongues, except he interpret, that the church may receive edifying (I Corinthians 14:4-5). ... Even so ye, forasmuch as ye are zealous of spiritual gifts, seek that ye may excel to the edifying of the church (I Corinthians 14:12). ... Yet in the church I had rather speak five words with my understanding, that by my voice I might teach others also, than ten thousand words in an unknown tongue (I Corinthians 14:19). ... If therefore the whole church be come together into one place, and all speak with tongues, and there come in those that are unlearned, or unbelievers, will they not say that ye are mad (I Corinthians 14:23)? ... But if there be no interpreter, let him keep silence in the church; and let him speak to himself, and to God (I Corinthians 14:28). ... For God is not the author of confusion, but of peace, as in all churches of the saints. Let your women keep silence in the churches: for it is not permitted unto them to speak; but they are commanded to be under obedience, as also saith the law. And if they will learn any thing, let them ask their husbands at home: for it is a shame for women to speak in the church (I Corinthians 14:33-35).

In I Corinthians 14:20, Paul stated that the way to understand the purpose of tongues was to quit trying to understand it as a child (παιδίον [*paidion*]) but rather as men (τέλειος [*teleios*]). This was the same word that was used in I Corinthians 13:10 and was translated there as "perfect" where Paul said, "But when that which is perfect is come ..." In order to understand the purpose of tongues, you must study it as a mature, complete, and perfect man and not as a child. Paul wrote I Corinthians 14:20–25 so that we could have that perfect understanding of the purpose of tongues.

> Brethren, be not children in understanding: howbeit in malice be ye children, but in understanding be men. In the law it is written, With men of other tongues and other lips will I speak unto this people; and yet for all that will they not hear me, saith the Lord. Wherefore tongues are for a sign, not to them that believe, but to them that believe not: but prophesying serveth not for them that believe not, but for them which believe. If therefore the whole church be come together into one place, and all speak with tongues, and there come in those that are unlearned, or unbelievers, will they not say that ye are mad? But if all prophesy, and there come in one that believeth not, or one unlearned, he is convinced of all, he is judged of all: And thus are the secrets of his heart made manifest; and so falling down on his face he will worship God, and report that God is in you of a truth.

Paul stated definitively that "... tongues are for a sign, not to them that believe, but to them that believe not" in verse 22. Tongues were prophesied all the way back in the Law. They were prophesied to be for "this people," that is, the Jewish people as a sign of impending judgement (verse 21). If they were used in the church, people would say that the Christians were "mad." The Greek word that Paul used that was translated "mad" in verse 23 is the word μαίνομαι [*mainomai*] which the *Enhanced Strong's Lexicon*[8] defines as:

> 1 to be mad, to rave. 1A of one who so speaks that he seems not to be in his right mind.

---
8 Ibid. #3105.

If tongues were used in the church, the conclusion that people would make is that someone was crazy or speaking as if he were not "in his right mind." Why was that the case? Tongues were not to be used in the church, because tongues were a sign of impending judgment on **Israel** for not listening to the Word of God in Hebrew. It was never intended as a mark of spirituality or having the Spirit of God. Paul commanded the Corinthians to quit thinking as children. Instead, he commanded them to understand as men. It's even in the Law. First, it was given by Moses in Deuteronomy 28:45-51.

> Moreover all these curses shall come upon thee, and shall pursue thee, and overtake thee, till thou be destroyed; **because thou hearkenedst not unto the voice of the LORD thy God,** to keep his commandments and his statutes which he commanded thee: And they shall be upon thee for a sign and for a wonder, and upon thy seed for ever. Because thou servedst not the LORD thy God with joyfulness, and with gladness of heart, for the abundance of all things; Therefore shalt thou serve thine enemies which the LORD shall send against thee, in hunger, and in thirst, and in nakedness, and in want of all things: and he shall put a yoke of iron upon thy neck, until he have destroyed thee. The LORD shall bring a nation against thee from far, from the end of the earth, as swift as the eagle flieth; a nation **whose tongue thou shalt not understand**; A nation of fierce countenance, which shall not regard the person of the old, nor shew favour to the young: And he shall eat the fruit of thy cattle, and the fruit of thy land, until thou be destroyed: which also shall not leave thee either corn, wine, or oil, or the increase of thy kine, or flocks of thy sheep, until he have destroyed thee.

God had warned the Jewish people that He would use the tongues of foreigners to speak to them harshly if they would not listen to Hebrew. When that judgment was near arrival Isaiah again warned the nation of Judah. Judgment was coming from Babylon and they would hear "stammering lips and another tongue" (Isaiah

28:11). The purpose of tongues was not their salvation, but their punishment. Isaiah said that the result was that "they might go, and fall backward, and be broken, and snared, and taken" (Isaiah 28:13). I Corinthians 14:20–21 seems to be taken from Isaiah 28:7–13, which is a warning about the coming Babylonian captivity, followed by the Medo-Persian Empire, the Greco-Macedonian Empire, the empires of Ptolemy and that of the Seleucids, and finally of the Romans. Each of them came speaking a different language.

> But they also have erred through wine, and through strong drink are out of the way; the priest and the prophet have erred through strong drink, they are swallowed up of wine, they are out of the way through strong drink; they err in vision, they stumble in judgment. For all tables are full of vomit and filthiness, so that there is no place clean. Whom shall he teach knowledge? and whom shall he make to understand doctrine? them that are weaned from the milk, and drawn from the breasts. For precept must be upon precept, precept upon precept; line upon line, line upon line; here a little, and there a little: For with stammering lips and another tongue will he speak to this people. To whom he said, This is the rest wherewith ye may cause the weary to rest; and this is the refreshing: yet they would not hear. But the word of the LORD was unto them precept upon precept, precept upon precept; line upon line, line upon line; here a little, and there a little; that they might go, and fall backward, and be broken, and snared, and taken.

Tongues were always a sign of coming judgment. The very first usage of the sign of tongues is found in Genesis 11:1–8. Here we find the Biblical account of the creation of languages. When speaking just one language, mankind created a unified religion against God. A single idolatrous religion and a single government for all mankind then united man, who was already united by a common language. At that point God judged man, creating many languages and making a worldwide religion and government much more difficult. God's judgment came in the form of languages.

> And the whole earth was of one language, and of one speech. And it came to pass, as they journeyed from the east, that they found a plain in the land of Shinar; and they dwelt there. And they said one to another, Go to, let us make brick, and burn them throughly. And they had brick for stone, and slime had they for morter. And they said, Go to, let us build us a city and a tower, whose top may reach unto heaven; and let us make us a name, lest we be scattered abroad upon the face of the whole earth. And the LORD came down to see the city and the tower, which the children of men builded. And the LORD said, Behold, the people is one, and they have all one language; and this they begin to do: and now nothing will be restrained from them, which they have imagined to do. Go to, let us go down, and there confound their language, that they may not understand one another's speech. So the LORD scattered them abroad from thence upon the face of all the earth: and they left off to build the city.

In Acts chapter two, the usage of tongues again announced coming judgment. That judgment finally came when the Romans, under Titus, destroyed the temple and carried off all the precious things of the temple to Rome, along with the Jewish people who were taken as slaves and sold. The announcement of this coming judgment is found in the tongues that were used on the day of Pentecost in Acts 2:1–42.

> And when the day of Pentecost was fully come, they were all with one accord in one place. And suddenly there came a sound from heaven as of a rushing mighty wind, and it filled all the house where they were sitting. And there appeared unto them cloven tongues like as of fire, and it sat upon each of them. And they were all filled with the Holy Ghost, and began to speak with other tongues, as

The Gifts of the Holy Spirit

the Spirit gave them utterance. And there were dwelling at Jerusalem Jews, devout men, out of every nation under heaven. Now when this was noised abroad, the multitude came together, and were confounded, because that every man heard them speak in his own language. And they were all amazed and marvelled, saying one to another, Behold, are not all these which speak Galilaeans? And how hear we every man in our own tongue, wherein we were born? Parthians, and Medes, and Elamites, and the dwellers in Mesopotamia, and in Judaea, and Cappadocia, in Pontus, and Asia, Phrygia, and Pamphylia, in Egypt, and in the parts of Libya about Cyrene, and strangers of Rome, Jews and proselytes, Cretes and Arabians, we do hear them speak in our tongues the wonderful works of God. And they were all amazed, and were in doubt, saying one to another, What meaneth this? Others mocking said, These men are full of new wine. But Peter, standing up with the eleven, lifted up his voice, and said unto them, Ye men of Judaea, and all ye that dwell at Jerusalem, be this known unto you, and hearken to my words: For these are not drunken, as ye suppose, seeing it is but the third hour of the day. But this is that which was spoken by the prophet Joel; And it shall come to pass in the last days, saith God, I will pour out of my Spirit upon all flesh: and your sons and your daughters shall prophesy, and your young men shall see visions, and your old men shall dream dreams: And on my servants and on my handmaidens I will pour out in those days of my Spirit; and they shall prophesy: And I will shew wonders in heaven above, and signs in the earth beneath; blood, and fire, and vapour of smoke: The sun shall be turned into darkness, and the moon into blood, before that great and notable day of the Lord come: And it shall come to pass, that whosoever shall call on the name of the Lord shall be saved. Ye men of Israel, hear these words; Jesus of Nazareth, a man approved of God among you by miracles and wonders and signs, which God did by him in the midst of you, as ye yourselves also know: Him, being delivered by the determinate counsel and foreknowledge of God, ye have taken, and by wicked hands have crucified and slain: Whom God hath raised up, having loosed the pains of death: because it was not possible that he should be holden of it. For David speaketh concerning him, I foresaw the Lord always before my face, for he is on my right hand, that I should not be moved: Therefore did my heart rejoice, and my tongue was glad; moreover also my flesh shall rest in hope: Because thou wilt not leave my soul in hell, neither wilt thou suffer thine Holy One to see corruption. Thou hast made known to me the ways of life; thou shalt make me full of joy with thy countenance. Men and brethren, let me freely speak unto you of the patriarch David, that he is both dead and buried, and his sepulchre is with us unto this day. Therefore being a prophet, and knowing that God had sworn with an oath to him, that of the fruit of his loins, according to the flesh, he would raise up Christ to sit on his throne; He seeing this before spake of the resurrection of Christ, that his soul was not left in hell, neither his flesh did see corruption. This Jesus hath God raised up, whereof we all are witnesses. Therefore being by the right hand of God exalted, and having received of the Father the promise of the Holy Ghost, he hath shed forth this, which ye now see and hear. For David is not ascended into the heavens: but he saith himself, The LORD said unto my Lord, Sit thou on my right hand, Until I make thy foes thy footstool. Therefore let all the house of Israel know assuredly, that God hath made that same Jesus, whom ye have crucified, both Lord and Christ. Now when they heard this, they were pricked in their heart, and said unto Peter and to the rest of the apostles, Men and brethren, what shall we do? Then Peter said unto them, Repent, and be baptized every one of you in the name of Jesus Christ for the

The Gifts of the Holy Spirit

remission of sins, and ye shall receive the gift of the Holy Ghost. For the promise is unto you, and to your children, and to all that are afar off, even as many as the Lord our God shall call. And with many other words did he testify and exhort, saying, Save yourselves from this untoward generation. Then they that gladly received his word were baptized: and the same day there were added unto them about three thousand souls. And they continued stedfastly in the apostles' doctrine and fellowship, and in breaking of bread, and in prayers.

Luke wrote in Acts 1:26, that there were twelve different languages that were spoken by the eleven apostles plus Matthias.

And they gave forth their lots; and the lot fell upon Matthias; and he was numbered with the eleven apostles.

These twelve men were gathered together "in one place" and "all with one accord" (Acts 2:1). Luke lists twelve languages that were spoken on that day (Acts 2:9-11). Peter preached a message of coming judgment. He said, "The sun shall be turned into darkness, and the moon into blood, before that great and notable day of the Lord come" (verse 20). He laid the blame squarely on them for Israel's rejection of their Messiah, saying in verses 22-23:

Ye men of Israel, hear these words; Jesus of Nazareth, a man approved of God among you by miracles and wonders and signs, which God did by him in the midst of you, as ye yourselves also know: Him, being delivered by the determinate counsel and foreknowledge of God, ye have taken, and by wicked hands have crucified and slain:

He again laid the guilt of the death of the Son of God on the "house of Israel" and warned them to be saved "from this untoward generation" in Acts 2:36-40.

Therefore let all the house of Israel know assuredly, that God hath made that same Jesus, whom ye have crucified, both Lord and Christ. Now when they heard this, they were pricked in their heart, and said unto Peter and to the rest of the apostles, Men and brethren, what shall we do? Then Peter said unto them, Repent, and be baptized every one of you in the name of Jesus Christ for the remission of sins, and ye shall receive the gift of the Holy Ghost. For the promise is unto you, and to your children, and to all that are afar off, even as many as the Lord our God shall call. And with many other words did he testify and exhort, saying, Save yourselves from this untoward generation.

Judgment was coming within a few years because of Israel's rejection of the Messiah. John 1:11 says, "He came unto his own, and his own received him not." Their rejection had brought about the sign of tongues in Acts chapter two.

Paul told the believers in Corinth that they needed to understand the usage of tongues as something that was given to the unbelieving Jewish people. It was not given to the church, and it was not given to Gentiles. It was a sign to the Jewish people that comes from the Law of Moses.

One of the rules of Biblical interpretation is that a correct hermeneutic must be directional. To whom is a verse or passage directed? That is an important question to answer. Paul answered that when he said that tongues are a sign to the unbelievers of the Jewish people – "… this people" (I Corinthians 14:21). As the Sabbath day was clearly stated to be a sign for the Jewish people and not for the church or Gentiles, according to Exodus 31:16-17, so was the sign of tongues.

> Wherefore the children of Israel shall keep the sabbath, to observe the sabbath throughout their generations, for a perpetual covenant. It is a sign between me and the children of Israel for ever: for in six days the LORD made heaven and earth, and on the seventh day he rested, and was refreshed.

Chapter Six

THE RELATIONSHIP OF THE HOLY SPIRIT TO THE TRINITY AND THE WORKS OF GOD

In Chapter 1, we studied the deity of the Holy Spirit and proved that He is a coequal member of the Trinity. We further stated that the Spirit of God participates in the works of God. In this chapter we are not just trying to show that He participates, but also defining what His role has been in the different things in which He has participated. While a complete list could easily fill a book all by itself, we will define the role of the Holy Spirit in just seven areas.

The seven areas that we will discuss

We can easily demonstrate the roles that the Holy Spirit played or is playing in these seven areas. What is or was His relationship to the creation? The same question could be asked about the Spirit's relationship to the Word of God. What does the Spirit do, or what did He do in relation to the Word of God? We will also study the relationship of the Spirit of God to the Old Testament saints. In the fourth place we want to know what His relationship was and is to the Son of God. We will also study the relationship that the Holy Spirit has to the world. What does the Spirit do in relation to unbelievers? In the sixth place we will look at the relationship of the Holy Spirit to the believer. What does the Holy Spirit do in the life of the believer today? The last thing that we will seek to understand is His relationship to spiritual gifts. In relationship to spiritual gifts, what does the Spirit do, or what did He do?

The relationship of the Spirit of God to the creation

A. The Spirit participated in the creation of all things

We can easily see that the Spirit of God participated in the creation of everything that exists. From the very beginning of creation, He was active, and His work as seen in Genesis 1:2-3.

> And the earth was without form, and void; and darkness was upon the face of the deep. And the Spirit of God moved upon the face of the waters. And God said, Let there be light: and there was light.

The Holy Spirit was active in the creation of man as well. In Genesis 2:7, the Bible mentions the way that God gave man life. The Father designed his body, the Son molded his body from the dust of the earth, and the Spirit of life made that dust into a living soul.

> And the LORD God formed man of the dust of the ground, and breathed into his nostrils the breath of life; and man became a living soul.

There are three things that can be seen in the way that the Holy Spirit participated in the creation of all things. First, the Spirit brought order out of disorder. The world was "... without form, and void" (Genesis 1:2) and the Spirit brought order. Second, He brought light out of darkness. The Bible describes this work of the Holy Spirit when it describes the condition of the creation at the time as "... darkness was upon the face of the deep" (Genesis 1:2). The Spirit of God then said, "Let there be light: and there was light" (Genesis 1:3). Third, He is the One who brought life out of matter. God the Father designed the creation, the Son of God gave form to the creation, and then the Spirit of God gave life to that creation. Paul affirms this in Acts 17:28.

> For in him we live, and move, and have our being; as certain also of your own poets have said, For we are also his offspring.

B. The Spirit of God participates in upholding the creation

The second way in which the Spirit of God participates in the work of creation is that He upholds the creation. Psalm 104:29-30 states that He renews "the face of the earth."

> Thou hidest thy face, they are troubled: thou takest away their breath, they die, and return to their dust. Thou sendest forth thy spirit, they are created: and thou renewest the face of the earth.

The relationship of the Spirit of God to the Word of God

A second way in which we see the relationship of the Spirit to the Father and to the Son is His work in relationship to the Word of God. This is a multifaceted work, which is related to the giving of the Word of God. In the first place, the Spirit of God gave the prophet, or the apostle, revelation.

A. He gave revelation to the prophets and apostles

What do we mean by revelation? We are talking about how the prophet could know truth which was previously unknown. II Samuel 23:2-3 says:

> The Spirit of the LORD spake by me, and his word was in my tongue. The God of Israel said, the Rock of Israel spake to me, He that ruleth over men must be just, ruling in the fear of God.

1. The Holy Spirit took the Word of Christ, and placed it in the prophet

God the Father gave the Word, and the Son of God spoke the Word. At that point the Holy Spirit took the Word of Christ and placed it in the mouth of the prophet, even as Christ prophesied that He would in John 16:13-15.

> Howbeit when he, the Spirit of truth, is come, he will guide you into all truth: for he shall not speak of himself; but whatsoever he shall hear, that shall he speak: and he will shew you things to come. He shall glorify me: for he shall receive of mine, and shall shew it unto you. All things that the Father hath are mine: therefore said I, that he shall take of mine, and shall shew it unto you.

In that way, the Word of God is the Word of the Father, the Word of the Son of God, and the Word of the Spirit as well.

2. He carried the prophet to fulfill the purposes of God

Prophecy was always given through a prophet or an apostle. This was not because of any desire on the part of the man who was chosen by God to be a prophet, but rather the will of God who "carried" him by the Holy Spirit as it says in II Peter 1:21.

> For the prophecy came not in old time by the will of man: but holy men of God spake as they were moved (φερόμενοι) by the Holy Ghost.

The word, "moved" is the translation of the Greek word, φερόμενοι [*pheromenoi*], which is the present tense, passive voice, plural, nominative case, masculine gender participle of the verb φέρω [*phero*] which means[1],

> 1 to carry. 1A to carry some burden. 1A1 to bear with one's self. 1B to move by bearing; move or, to be conveyed or borne, with the suggestion of force or speed. 1B1 of persons borne in a ship over the sea. 1B2 of a gust of wind, to rush. 1B3 of the mind, to be moved inwardly, prompted. 1C to bear up i.e. uphold (keep from falling). 1C1 of Christ, the preserver of the universe. 2 to bear, i.e.

---
1 Strong, J. (1995). *Enhanced Strong's Lexicon*. Woodside Bible Fellowship, #5342.

endure, to endure the rigour of a thing, to bear patiently one's conduct, or spare one (abstain from punishing or destroying). 3 to bring, bring to, bring forward. 3A to move to, apply. 3B to bring in by announcing, to announce. 3C to bear i.e. bring forth, produce; to bring forward in a speech. 3D to lead, conduct.

This same verb was used in Luke 23:26, where it was translated "bear."

> And as they led him away, they laid hold upon one Simon, a Cyrenian, coming out of the country, and on him they laid the cross, that he might *bear* it after Jesus.

The same verb was again used in Hebrews 1:3 where it was translated "upholding" to speak of Christ as carrying the weight of the entire creation, as it were, on His shoulder.

> Who being the brightness of his glory, and the express image of his person, and upholding all things by the word of his power, when he had by himself purged our sins, sat down on the right hand of the Majesty on high;

The Holy Spirit's work was to "bear" the prophet as Simon of Cyrene had to "bear" on his shoulder the cross of Christ. His work in relationship to the giving of the Word of God was to carry, as it were on His shoulder, the prophet in the same way that Christ carries the entire creation on His shoulder. This may explain Ezekiel 8:1-3 where Ezekiel says that "… the Spirit lifted me up between the earth and the heaven, and brought me in the visions of God to Jerusalem" (Ezekiel 8:3).

> And it came to pass in the sixth year, in the sixth month, in the fifth day of the month, as I sat in mine house, and the elders of Judah sat before me, that the hand of the Lord GOD fell there upon me. Then I beheld, and lo a likeness as the appearance of fire: from the appearance of his loins even downward, fire; and from his loins even

upward, as the appearance of brightness, as the colour of amber. And he put forth the form of an hand, and took me by a lock of mine head; and the spirit lifted me up between the earth and the heaven, and brought me in the visions of God to Jerusalem, to the door of the inner gate that looketh toward the north; where was the seat of the image of jealousy, which provoketh to jealousy.

B. The Holy Spirit gave the very Words of God to the prophet and guaranteed them in the prophecy and in the written Word

I Corinthians 2:4-16 is a very important passage in the Word of God because of its description of the process and method that the Holy Spirit used in giving the Word of God through the prophet and apostle. First Paul stated in verse 4 that the Holy Spirit did not use either great oratory or human wisdom in giving us the Word. The Spirit used "... the wisdom of God in a mystery (I Corinthians 2:7), that is, He gave the prophets and apostles previously unknown wisdom that they would write. The wisdom that the Holy Spirit revealed (I Corinthians 2:10) was unknown (I Corinthians 2:8), unseen, unheard, and unimagined (I Corinthians 2:9). That part was revelation and it was only given to the prophets and apostles. Then the Holy Spirit guaranteed the Word as they spoke it, choosing the words "... which the Holy Ghost teacheth" (I Corinthians 2:13). The Holy Spirit then illumines "... he that is spiritual" (I Corinthians 2:15) and gives him "... the mind of Christ" (I Corinthians 2:16).

> And my speech and my preaching was not with enticing words of man's wisdom, but in demonstration of the Spirit and of power: That your faith should not stand in the wisdom of men, but in the power of God. Howbeit we speak wisdom among them that are perfect: yet not the wisdom of this world, nor of the princes of this world, that come to nought: But we speak the wisdom of God in a mystery, even the hidden wisdom, which God ordained before the world unto our glory: Which none

of the princes of this world knew: for had they known it, they would not have crucified the Lord of glory. But as it is written, Eye hath not seen, nor ear heard, neither have entered into the heart of man, the things which God hath prepared for them that love him. But God hath revealed them unto us by his Spirit: for the Spirit searcheth all things, yea, the deep things of God. For what man knoweth the things of a man, save the spirit of man which is in him? even so the things of God knoweth no man, but the Spirit of God. Now we have received, not the spirit of the world, but the spirit which is of God; that we might know the things that are freely given to us of God. Which things also we speak, not in the words which man's wisdom teacheth, but which the Holy Ghost teacheth; comparing spiritual things with spiritual. But the natural man receiveth not the things of the Spirit of God: for they are foolishness unto him: neither can he know them, because they are spiritually discerned. But he that is spiritual judgeth all things, yet he himself is judged of no man. For who hath known the mind of the Lord, that he may instruct him? But we have the mind of Christ (I Corinthians 2:4-16).

An error that people frequently make is to call someone the author of a book of the Bible. You will read, for example, in commentaries on the Gospel according to Saint Luke that Luke was the author. What we just read in I Corinthians 2:4-16, as well as the other passages that we studied, is that the Spirit of God was the Author, and Luke was the writer. That leads us to the next point about the relationship of the Holy Spirit to the Word of God.

C. The New Testament affirms that the Spirit is the Author of everything written in the Old Testament

In Mark 12:36, He is seen as the Author of the writing of Psalm 110.

For David himself said by the Holy Ghost, The LORD said to my Lord, Sit thou on my right hand, till I make thine enemies thy footstool (Mark 12:36).

In Mark 12:36, Jesus Himself confirms two different things when He quoted Psalm 110:1. First, he confirmed that David wrote this Psalm, and second, that the Holy Spirit was the Author. Let's take a look at this entire Psalm that the Holy Spirit authored.

The LORD said unto my Lord, Sit thou at my right hand, until I make thine enemies thy footstool. The LORD shall send the rod of thy strength out of Zion: rule thou in the midst of thine enemies. Thy people shall be willing in the day of thy power, in the beauties of holiness from the womb of the morning: thou hast the dew of thy youth. The LORD hath sworn, and will not repent, Thou art a priest for ever after the order of Melchizedek. The Lord at thy right hand shall strike through kings in the day of his wrath. He shall judge among the heathen, he shall fill the places with the dead bodies; he shall wound the heads over many countries. He shall drink of the brook in the way: therefore shall he lift up the head (Psalm 110:1-7).

In Acts 1:16-20, Peter stated that the Holy Spirit was the Author of Psalms 41, 69, and 109.

Men and brethren, this scripture must needs have been fulfilled, which the Holy Ghost by the mouth of David spake before concerning Judas, which was guide to them that took Jesus. For he was numbered with us, and had obtained part of this ministry. Now this man purchased a field with the reward of iniquity; and falling headlong, he burst asunder in the midst, and all his bowels gushed out. And it was known unto all the dwellers at Jerusalem; insomuch as that field is called in their proper tongue, Aceldama, that is to say, The field of blood. For it is written in the book of Psalms, Let his habitation be desolate, and let no man dwell therein: and his bishoprick let another take.

Peter refers to these three passages that follow, saying "... this scripture must needs have been fulfilled, which the Holy Ghost by the mouth of David spake before" (Acts 1:16). He calls these verses "Scripture," and says that the Holy Spirit was the Author and that David was the writer. He further stated that the Old Testament Scriptures, written "before," had to be "fulfilled."

> Yea, mine own familiar friend, in whom I trusted, which did eat of my bread, hath lifted up his heel against me (Psalm 41:9). ... Let their habitation be desolate; and let none dwell in their tents (Psalm 69:25). ... Let his days be few; and let another take his office (Psalm 109:8).

The apostles confirmed that the Holy Spirit was the Author of the books of the Old Testament. Peter stated that the Holy Spirit was the Author of the Psalms that David wrote, and Paul stated, in Acts 28:25-27, that the Holy Spirit spoke Isaiah 6:9-10 "... by Esaias the prophet."

> And when they agreed not among themselves, they departed, after that Paul had spoken one word, Well spake the Holy Ghost by Esaias the prophet unto our fathers, Saying, Go unto this people, and say, Hearing ye shall hear, and shall not understand; and seeing ye shall see, and not perceive: For the heart of this people is waxed gross, and their ears are dull of hearing, and their eyes have they closed; lest they should see with their eyes, and hear with their ears, and understand with their heart, and should be converted, and I should heal them (Acts 28:25-27).

When Paul quoted Isaiah 6:9-10, he said that the Holy Spirit spoke these words. They are not the words of the man Isaiah, even though Isaiah wrote them. The Holy Spirit is the Author of the

Word of God. He took the words and placed them in the mouth of the prophet.

> And he said, Go, and tell this people, Hear ye indeed, but understand not; and see ye indeed, but perceive not. Make the heart of this people fat, and make their ears heavy, and shut their eyes; lest they see with their eyes, and hear with their ears, and understand with their heart, and convert, and be healed (Isaiah 6:9-10).

The relationship of the Holy Spirit to people during Old Testament times

We studied this relationship in greater detail in Chapter 3. Here we will look at other details about the relationship of the Holy Spirit to the saints of the Old Testament. Before we study His relationship with the saved, let's consider what relationship the Holy Spirit had with the lost in the Old Testament.

A. His relationship to the unsaved was to convict of sin, and restrain it

According to Genesis 6:3, the Holy Spirit's ministry with the lost in the Old Testament was practically identical to His ministry in the New Testament. God stated that the Spirit's ministry, up to the time of the flood, was to "strive with man."

> And the LORD said, My spirit shall not always strive with man, for that he also is flesh: yet his days shall be an hundred and twenty years.

The word "strive" is the translation of the Hebrew word יָדוֹן [yadown] which means to judge, contend, plead, strive, or to plead a cause. This particular word is very similar to the Greek word ἐλέγχω [elegcho] which is translated "reprove" in John 16:8. ἐλέγχω [elegcho] means[2]:

---

2 Strong, J. (1995). *Enhanced Strong's Lexicon*. Woodside Bible Fellowship, #1651.

1 to convict, refute, confute. 1A generally with a suggestion of shame of the person convicted. 1B by conviction to bring to the light, to expose. 2 to find fault with, correct. 2A by word. 2A1 to reprehend severely, chide, admonish, reprove. 2A2 to call to account, show one his fault, demand an explanation. 2B by deed. 2B1 to chasten, to punish.

The Holy Spirit's ministry toward the lost in the Old Testament was nearly identical to His ministry in the New Testament.

B. His relationship to believers in the Old Testament, for the most part, if not totally and exclusively, was limited to Israel

Israel was God's chosen instrument to write and preserve the Word of God[3]. Israel was also to be a nation of priests to the Gentile world[4], giving God's Word to all nations. In the Old Testament,

---

3 Romans 3:1-4 says that God "committed" this to the Jewish people: "What advantage then hath the Jew? or what profit is there of circumcision? Much every way: chiefly, because that unto them were committed the oracles of God. For what if some did not believe? shall their unbelief make the faith of God without effect? God forbid: yea, let God be true, but every man a liar; as it is written, That thou mightest be justified in thy sayings, and mightest overcome when thou art judged."

4 There are two passages that speak of Israel's job of giving Gentile nations God's Word. First is Exodus 19:5-6 which says: "Now therefore, if ye will obey my voice indeed, and keep my covenant, then ye shall be a peculiar treasure unto me above all people: for all the earth is mine: And ye shall be unto me a kingdom of priests, and an holy nation. These are the words which thou shalt speak unto the children of Israel." The second passage is found in I Peter 2:5-9 where Peter wrote to the believing Jews of the dispersion, saying:

"Ye also, as lively stones, are built up a spiritual house, an holy priesthood, to offer up spiritual sacrifices, acceptable to God by Jesus Christ. Wherefore also it is contained in the scripture, Behold, I lay in Sion a chief corner stone, elect, precious: and he that believeth on him shall not be confounded. Unto you therefore which believe he is precious: but unto them which be disobedient, the stone which the builders disallowed, the same is made the head of the corner, And a stone of stumbling, and a rock of offence, even to them which stumble at the word, being disobedient: whereunto also they were appointed. But ye are a chosen generation, a royal priesthood, an holy nation, a peculiar people; that ye should shew forth the praises of him who hath called you out of darkness into his marvellous light:"

after the call of Abraham, the Holy Spirit's ministry was limited to working through the Jewish people.

According to Deuteronomy 7:6-8, God did not call Israel to this task because of any special ability Israel possessed or because of its mighty army. In fact, the opposite was true.

> For thou art an holy people unto the LORD thy God: the LORD thy God hath chosen thee to be a special people unto himself, above all people that are upon the face of the earth. The LORD did not set his love upon you, nor choose you, because ye were more in number than any people; for ye were the fewest of all people: But because the LORD loved you, and because he would keep the oath which he had sworn unto your fathers, hath the LORD brought you out with a mighty hand, and redeemed you out of the house of bondmen, from the hand of Pharaoh king of Egypt.

In Nehemiah 9:20, Nehemiah wrote that even at the time that Israel was taken out of Egypt, God gave the Holy Spirit to Israel to instruct them, which is one of the ministries of the Holy Spirit in the church today.

> Thou gavest also thy good spirit to instruct them, and withheldest not thy manna from their mouth, and gavest them water for their thirst.

God's Holy Spirit limited His ministry to the nation of Israel after the call of Abraham. This is evidenced clearly in Isaiah 63:10-11, and 14 where Isaiah explains that the captivity was the result of having "... vexed His Holy Spirit." Isaiah longed for the days when God "... brought them up out of the sea" and "... put His Holy Spirit within" Moses.

> But they rebelled, and vexed his holy Spirit: therefore he was turned to be their enemy, and he fought against them. Then he remembered the days of old, Moses, and his people, saying, Where is he that brought them up out

of the sea with the shepherd of his flock? where is he that put his holy Spirit within him? ... As a beast goeth down into the valley, the Spirit of the LORD caused him to rest: so didst thou lead thy people, to make thyself a glorious name.

The relationship of the Spirit to the Son of God

This is the fourth relationship that we will consider. What we specifically want to examine is the relationship of the Spirit of God to the Son of God during the earthly ministry of Jesus Christ. The only exception to that will be our first point.

A. In eternity, the Holy Spirit is the Third Person of the Trinity; He proceeds from the Father and the Son

Eternally, there is a relationship that exists between the Father, the Son, and the Holy Spirit. In relation to the other members of the Trinity, the position of the Holy Spirit is called the procession of the Holy Spirit. This relationship is thoroughly discussed in Chapter 1, but at least a brief explanation here would be profitable.

Catholics, Protestants, and Baptists alike generally consider John 15:26 as a key verse that deals with the procession of the Holy Spirit.

> But when the Comforter is come, whom I will send unto you from the Father, even the Spirit of truth, which proceedeth from the Father, he shall testify of me:

This verse states clearly that the Holy Spirit proceeds (ἐκπορεύεται [ekporeuetai]) from the Father, while also stating that the Lord Jesus "will send" (πέμψω [pempso]) Him. This indicates automatically a voluntary submission by the Holy Spirit both to the Father and to the Son as well. In addition, John 15:26 says that Christ will send the Holy Spirit from the Father, while John 14:26 states that the Father will send the Holy Spirit in the name of Christ.

> But the Comforter, which is the Holy Ghost, whom the Father will send in my name, he shall teach you all things, and bring all things to your remembrance, whatsoever I have said unto you (John 14:26).

John 14:26 clearly affirms that "... the Father will send" (πέμψει [*pempsei*]) the Holy Spirit while John 15:26 says that the Son of God will send Him. The Holy Spirit is thus seen to be voluntarily submissive to the Father and the Son.

In no way does the Spirit's submission to the Father and the Son represent the idea of inferiority or make Him less than God or a lesser god. Voluntary submission is observed in human relationships where one person is submissive to the will of another and yet still equal. In Chapter 1, I used the illustration of a husband and wife. We could also use the illustration of a person who voluntarily submits to an order by a policeman to move from a particular place. When a man voluntarily submits to governmental authority, he does it with no sense of inequality.

B. We can see the relationship of the Holy Spirit to the Son of God in the conception of Christ

1. The Holy Spirit was the Agent of the virgin birth

When we talk about the miracle of the virgin birth, for the most part, we are talking about the virgin conception. Yes, Christ was born of a virgin, but He was conceived in a virgin whose name was Mary. In Luke 1:35, the angel Gabriel told Mary that this conception would be the work of the Holy Spirit.

> And the angel answered and said unto her, The Holy Ghost shall come upon thee, and the power of the Highest shall overshadow thee: therefore also that holy thing which shall be born of thee shall be called the Son of God.

The Holy Spirit alone conceived the body of the Lord Jesus Christ in Mary's womb according to Luke 1:26-38.

Matthew agrees with Luke in Matthew 1:16, saying that Joseph was "… the husband of Mary, of whom was born Jesus, who is called Christ." The phrase "of whom" in Greek is in the feminine gender meaning that Mary alone conceived Christ with no help from Joseph. This was repeated by the angel to Joseph in verse 20, where the angel spoke with Joseph saying, "… that which is conceived in her is of the Holy Ghost." Joseph's account of the virgin conception is recorded for us in Matthew 1:16-23.

> And Jacob begat Joseph the husband of Mary, of whom was born Jesus, who is called Christ. So all the generations from Abraham to David are fourteen generations; and from David until the carrying away into Babylon are fourteen generations; and from the carrying away into Babylon unto Christ are fourteen generations. Now the birth of Jesus Christ was on this wise: When as his mother Mary was espoused to Joseph, before they came together, she was found with child of the Holy Ghost. Then Joseph her husband, being a just man, and not willing to make her a publick example, was minded to put her away privily. But while he thought on these things, behold, the angel of the Lord appeared unto him in a dream, saying, Joseph, thou son of David, fear not to take unto thee Mary thy wife: for that which is conceived in her is of the Holy Ghost. And she shall bring forth a son, and thou shalt call his name JESUS: for he shall save his people from their sins. Now all this was done, that it might be fulfilled which was spoken of the Lord by the prophet, saying, Behold, a virgin shall be with child, and shall bring forth a son, and they shall call his name Emmanuel, which being interpreted is, God with us.

2. The result of His work in the virgin birth was the hypostatic union

The Holy Spirit's conception of Jesus Christ directly made the hypostatic union possible. The hypostatic union is the doctrine which treats the uniting into One Person, the deity of Christ with the humanity of Christ. The Holy Spirit was the Agent that made this possible by creating a perfect body for Christ, within the womb of Mary. There could have been no union of the humanity of Christ and the deity of Christ except that a very special body was prepared by the Holy Spirit for the Son of God. This is stated in Hebrews 10:5 saying,

> Wherefore when he cometh into the world, he saith, Sacrifice and offering thou wouldest not, but a body hast thou prepared me:

A more thorough study of the doctrine of the Hypostatic Union can be found in my book, *The Son of the Father*, Chapter 4.

C. The relationship of the Holy Spirit to the life of Christ. The anointing of the Spirit identified Him as the Lamb of God

The visible presence of the Holy Spirit made it possible for people to identify Jesus as the Messiah. Jesus Christ demonstrated through His power a divine presence in His life, and that was because of the anointing of the Holy Spirit. Peter referred to the anointing of the Holy Spirit as he preached the Gospel to Cornelius in Acts 10:38.

> How God anointed Jesus of Nazareth with the Holy Ghost and with power: who went about doing good, and healing all that were oppressed of the devil; for God was with him.

The prayer of the church in Jerusalem included a reference to Christ being anointed by God the Father with the Holy Spirit (Acts 4:27). This was stated to be His source of power.

> And when they heard that, they lifted up their voice to God with one accord, and said, Lord, thou art God, which hast made heaven, and earth, and the sea, and all that in them is: Who by the mouth of thy servant David hast said,

> Why did the heathen rage, and the people imagine vain things? The kings of the earth stood up, and the rulers were gathered together against the Lord, and against his Christ. For of a truth against thy holy child Jesus, whom thou hast anointed, both Herod, and Pontius Pilate, with the Gentiles, and the people of Israel, were gathered together, For to do whatsoever thy hand and thy counsel determined before to be done (Acts 4:24–28).

Oil was a frequently used symbol for the Holy Spirit in the Bible. Paul used that symbolic reference to the Holy Spirit in Hebrews 1:9 where he stated that Christ was "anointed" by God with "... the oil of gladness above thy fellows."

> Thou hast loved righteousness, and hated iniquity; therefore God, even thy God, hath anointed thee with the oil of gladness above thy fellows.

John the Baptist was the forerunner of the Lord Jesus Christ. His job was to prepare the nation of Israel for the coming of Messiah. God had already informed John of how he would know Who the Messiah was. He would know Him by the anointing of the Holy Spirit. The Spirit would not only anoint Him, but be a permanent anointing that would abide with Him (John 1:32). In that way, John the Baptist could twice identify Christ according to John 1:29–36.

> The next day John seeth Jesus coming unto him, and saith, Behold the Lamb of God, which taketh away the sin of the world. This is he of whom I said, After me cometh a man which is preferred before me: for he was before me. And I knew him not: but that he should be made manifest to Israel, therefore am I come baptizing with water. And John bare record, saying, I saw the Spirit descending from heaven like a dove, and it abode upon him. And I knew him not: but he that sent me to baptize with water, the same said unto me, Upon whom thou shalt see the Spirit descending, and remaining on him, the same is he

which baptizeth with the Holy Ghost. And I saw, and bare record that this is the Son of God. Again the next day after John stood, and two of his disciples; And looking upon Jesus as he walked, he saith, Behold the Lamb of God!

D. The filling of the Holy Spirit empowered Him to serve

Not only was Christ anointed with the Holy Spirit, but He was filled with the Holy Spirit, which was another relationship that the Holy Spirit had with Him. During the earthly ministry of Christ, the filling of the Holy Spirit was first mentioned immediately after His baptism, and immediately preceding His temptation by the devil. The importance of the Holy Spirit's relationship with Christ is demonstrated from the very beginning of His ministry in both His baptism as well as His temptation.

> And Jesus being full of the Holy Ghost returned from Jordan, and was led by the Spirit into the wilderness (Luke 4:1).

In John 3:34, the filling of the Holy Spirit is again referenced with the ministry of the Lord Jesus Christ, saying:

> For he whom God hath sent speaketh the words of God: for God giveth not the Spirit by measure unto him.

Even the Old Testament prophecies that dealt with the coming of Jesus Christ reveal the importance of the relationship of the Holy Spirit with the Son of God. That can certainly be seen in Isaiah 11:1–3.

> And there shall come forth a rod out of the stem of Jesse, and a Branch shall grow out of his roots: And the spirit of the LORD shall rest upon him, the spirit of wisdom and understanding, the spirit of counsel and might, the spirit of knowledge and of the fear of the LORD; And shall make him of quick understanding in the fear of the LORD: and he shall not judge after the sight of his eyes, neither reprove after the hearing of his ears:

In Isaiah 42:1-8, we again notice the importance of the filling of the Holy Spirit being mentioned in the life of Christ. In this passage, Isaiah spoke about the relationship between all the members of the Triune God. The Father calls the Son of God, "My Servant," and "Mine Elect" in verse 1. Then the Father says that He has "... put My Spirit upon Him" and gives the direct results in Jesus' earthly ministry. The Father is thus seen as sending the Holy Spirit to fill the Lord Jesus Christ, and again showing both the voluntary submission of the Son of God to God the Father, but also of the Holy Spirit to the Father. Isaiah 42:1-8 specifically links the different ministries of the Son of God to the presence of the Holy Spirit.

> Behold my servant, whom I uphold; mine elect, in whom my soul delighteth; I have put my spirit upon him: he shall bring forth judgment to the Gentiles. He shall not cry, nor lift up, nor cause his voice to be heard in the street. A bruised reed shall he not break, and the smoking flax shall he not quench: he shall bring forth judgment unto truth. He shall not fail nor be discouraged, till he have set judgment in the earth: and the isles shall wait for his law. Thus saith God the LORD, he that created the heavens, and stretched them out; he that spread forth the earth, and that which cometh out of it; he that giveth breath unto the people upon it, and spirit to them that walk therein: I the LORD have called thee in righteousness, and will hold thine hand, and will keep thee, and give thee for a covenant of the people, for a light of the Gentiles; To open the blind eyes, to bring out the prisoners from the prison, and them that sit in darkness out of the prison house. I am the LORD: that is my name: and my glory will I not give to another, neither my praise to graven images.

E. The guidance of the Holy Spirit in the life of Christ

There is a definite relationship established in the Scriptures between the guidance of the Holy Spirit and the ministry of the

Lord Jesus Christ. Luke 4:1 states that Christ "... was led by the Spirit into the wilderness."

> And Jesus being full of the Holy Ghost returned from Jordan, and was led by the Spirit into the wilderness,

The purpose of that leading was detailed by the Apostle Matthew in Matthew 4:1 where it says:

> Then was Jesus led up of the Spirit into the wilderness to be tempted of the devil.

Let's discuss something that we covered in *The Son of the Father*, which is a study on the doctrine of Christology. How could the Holy Spirit lead the Lord Jesus Christ into temptation if God cannot be tempted and tempts no one, according to James 1:13?

> Let no man say when he is tempted, I am tempted of God: for God cannot be tempted with evil, neither tempteth he any man:

The fact that God "... cannot be tempted with evil" was the purpose of the temptation "... of the devil" (Matthew 4:1). Our Savior had to be tempted just as Adam and Eve, perfect sinless humans, were tempted by the devil.

> Forasmuch then as the children are partakers of flesh and blood, he also himself likewise took part of the same; that through death he might destroy him that had the power of death, that is, the devil; And deliver them who through fear of death were all their lifetime subject to bondage. For verily he took not on him the nature of angels; but he took on him the seed of Abraham. Wherefore in all things it behoved him to be made like unto his brethren, that he might be a merciful and faithful high priest in things pertaining to God, to make reconciliation for the sins of the people. For in that he himself hath suffered being tempted, he is able to succour them that are tempted (Hebrews 2:14–18).

The temptation of Christ happened to show us that a perfect man, with the guidance of the Holy Spirit, is able to resist temptation. The temptation of Christ was accomplished to prove his impeccability, not His ability to be tempted.

F. The rejoicing of the Spirit of God

Another relationship that the Holy Spirit had with the Son of God can be seen in Luke 10:21. The presence of the Holy Spirit in the life of our Lord gave Him the ability to rejoice.

> In that hour Jesus rejoiced in spirit, and said, I thank thee, O Father, Lord of heaven and earth, that thou hast hid these things from the wise and prudent, and hast revealed them unto babes: even so, Father; for so it seemed good in thy sight.

G. The power of the Spirit of God

The relationship between the Spirit of God and the Lord Jesus Christ is evident in the miracles that Christ performed. One area of miracles that was definitely linked to the Holy Spirit's presence in the Lord Jesus Christ was the casting out of demons. When the Pharisees heard that Jesus was casting out demons by the power of the Holy Spirit, they tried to pass it off as though this were by the power of the devil (Matthew 12:24). Jesus reasoned that a nation divided against itself could not stand (Matthew 12:25), and that Satan could not be "... divided against himself" (Matthew 12:26).

He further questioned that if He were casting out demons by the power of the devil, then by whose power were the Pharisees doing it? Then He reasoned with them that if He were casting out demons by the power of the Spirit of God, "... then the kingdom of God is come unto you" (Matthew 12:28). Christ made it a crucial matter to believe that He performed miracles by the power of the Holy Spirit. To attribute the miracles of Christ to the devil during the His earthly ministry was blasphemy of the Holy Spirit. If Satan is a corrupt tree, a corrupt tree can never bring forth good fruit (Matthew 12:33).

> But when the Pharisees heard it, they said, This fellow doth not cast out devils, but by Beelzebub the prince of the devils. And Jesus knew their thoughts, and said unto them, Every kingdom divided against itself is brought to desolation; and every city or house divided against itself shall not stand: And if Satan cast out Satan, he is divided against himself; how shall then his kingdom stand? And if I by Beelzebub cast out devils, by whom do your children cast them out? therefore they shall be your judges. But if I cast out devils by the Spirit of God, then the kingdom of God is come unto you. Or else how can one enter into a strong man's house, and spoil his goods, except he first bind the strong man? and then he will spoil his house. He that is not with me is against me; and he that gathereth not with me scattereth abroad. Wherefore I say unto you, All manner of sin and blasphemy shall be forgiven unto men: but the blasphemy against the Holy Ghost shall not be forgiven unto men. And whosoever speaketh a word against the Son of man, it shall be forgiven him: but whosoever speaketh against the Holy Ghost, it shall not be forgiven him, neither in this world, neither in the world to come. Either make the tree good, and his fruit good; or else make the tree corrupt, and his fruit corrupt: for the tree is known by his fruit (Matthew 12:24-33).

The ministry of Christ throughout Galilee was directly linked to the presence of the Holy Spirit Who empowered Him. Luke 4:14-15, and 18 teaches that the source of power that the Lord had, during His earthly ministry, was the Holy Spirit.

> And Jesus returned in the power of the Spirit into Galilee: and there went out a fame of him through all the region round about. And he taught in their synagogues, being glorified of all. ... The Spirit of the Lord is upon me, because he hath anointed me to preach the gospel to the poor; he hath sent me to heal the brokenhearted,

to preach deliverance to the captives, and recovering of sight to the blind, to set at liberty them that are bruised,

The ministry of the Holy Spirit in salvation

There are many aspects to the ministry of the Holy Spirit in salvation. Let's begin with what the Holy Spirit does for the lost which is intended to bring them to salvation.

A. The Holy Spirit's ministry toward the unbelieving world

The Spirit of God is good to all people, both the saved and the lost. God displays His goodness by giving good gifts to men. In everything, we would have to say that this is generally called the goodness of God. In Psalm 145:9 we read of His goodness to all men.

> The LORD is good to all: and his tender mercies are over all his works.

Another area of the general goodness of God can be seen in the fact that God provides sunshine and rain equally to the saved as well as the lost.

> That ye may be the children of your Father which is in heaven: for he maketh his sun to rise on the evil and on the good, and sendeth rain on the just and on the unjust (Matthew 5:45).

God's Holy Spirit expects the believer to be kind, even to his enemies, because the Holy Spirit is kind, even to the enemies of God.

> But love ye your enemies, and do good, and lend, hoping for nothing again; and your reward shall be great, and ye shall be the children of the Highest: for he is kind unto the unthankful and to the evil (Luke 6:35).

The Holy Spirit provides mankind with the fruit of the earth. In Acts 14:17, we are told that the Holy Spirit has left a witness of His goodness, giving us rain and fruitful seasons.

> Nevertheless he left not himself without witness, in that he did good, and gave us rain from heaven, and fruitful seasons, filling our hearts with food and gladness.

The greatest witness to the goodness of God is His provision of a Savior. While Christ is the Savior of all men, He is especially the Savior, in the most specific way, of those that believe according to I Timothy 4:10.

> For therefore we both labour and suffer reproach, because we trust in the living God, who is the Saviour of all men, specially of those that believe.

In Romans 2:4, Paul sums up all the truth about the "... goodness and forbearance and longsuffering" of God, reminding us "... that the goodness of God" was intended by God, to lead us to repentance.

> Or despisest thou the riches of his goodness and forbearance and longsuffering; not knowing that the goodness of God leadeth thee to repentance?

In the first place, we have seen how the Holy Spirit is good to all men by giving us good things such as sunshine, rain, food, etc. The second way that the Holy Spirit is good to all men is that He restrains sin. He does that immediately, which means He Personally interferes with the development and progress of sin. He also does it intermediately, that is, He uses others and other things to restrain sin. Let's consider His immediate means first. We read how the Holy Spirit restrained sin in the Old Testament, even striving with man according to Genesis 6:3.

> And the LORD said, My spirit shall not always strive with man, for that he also is flesh: yet his days shall be an hundred and twenty years.

The New Testament demonstrates clearly in II Thessalonians 2:6-7, that the Holy Spirit even retards the manifestation of the man of sin so that in our day he has not yet been revealed.

> And now ye know what withholdeth that he might be revealed in his time. For the mystery of iniquity doth already work: only he who now letteth will let, until he be taken out of the way.

There are many intermediate means by which the Holy Spirit interferes with the development of sinful practices and the spread of sin. The first way is the Holy Spirit's use of prophets. In Isaiah 63:10–11, God's Word discusses the use of prophets as intermediaries to try to turn Israel away from sin. This is a part of the goodness of God, since allowing sin to continue its downward spiral is what led to the flood, the destruction of Sodom and Gomorrah, and the Babylonian captivity.

> But they rebelled, and vexed his holy Spirit: therefore he was turned to be their enemy, and he fought against them. Then he remembered the days of old, Moses, and his people, saying, Where is he that brought them up out of the sea with the shepherd of his flock? where is he that put his holy Spirit within him?

In Romans 13:1–4, Paul laid out a defense of the Holy Spirit's use of governments as a means of His goodness toward man in restraining sin. Paul wrote that governments were established by God as an "ordinance of God" (verse 2) to punish evil (verse 3). This was God's goodness.

> Let every soul be subject unto the higher powers. For there is no power but of God: the powers that be are ordained of God. Whosoever therefore resisteth the power, resisteth the ordinance of God: and they that resist shall receive to themselves damnation. For rulers are not a terror to good works, but to the evil. Wilt thou then not be afraid of the power? do that which is good, and thou shalt have praise of the same: For he is the minister of God to thee for good. But if thou do that which is evil, be afraid; for he beareth not the sword in vain: for he is the minister

of God, a revenger to execute wrath upon him that doeth evil.

God is good in restraining sin. When sin was left practically unrestrained, humanity had to be destroyed in the days of Noah. Another way that the Holy Spirit restrains sin in the world is that He uses believers as the salt of the earth, according to Matthew 5:13.

> Ye are the salt of the earth: but if the salt have lost his savour, wherewith shall it be salted? it is thenceforth good for nothing, but to be cast out, and to be trodden under foot of men.

Another intermediate way that the Holy Spirit restrains sin is by using man's conscience. Everyone, saved and unsaved alike, was given a conscience. The Holy Spirit uses the conscience of men as an indirect way of convicting of sin, and by that, restraining sin. Paul wrote in Romans 2:15 that conscience has the law written into the hearts of men, thus forcing them to be accused or excused for everything they do.

> Which shew the work of the law written in their hearts, their conscience also bearing witness, and their thoughts the mean while accusing or else excusing one another;)

Conscience, however, is a very imperfect way of judging what is right and wrong, since one man's conscience can differ greatly from another man's conscience. What one man may consider to be justifiable homicide, someone else may consider murder. What one man excuses, according to Romans 2:15, another man condemns. Regardless, the Holy Spirit, in His goodness, uses man's conscience.

All of the different types of psychology have placed the existence of the conscience as one of their primary objectives for destruction. They reason that if man no longer had a conscience, then he would no longer suffer the psychological effects of the conscience, thus limiting the Holy Spirit's restraint of sin.

While conscience is an imperfect intermediate means that is used by the Holy Spirit, the Scriptures are a perfect intermediate means. While men may fight over what the Scriptures mean, they detail exactly what God considers to be sin, and thus restrain sin. Because God's will is so explicitly stated in the Bible, all of the devil's forces have been aimed against man knowing what is in the Bible. In II Timothy 2:15, Paul stated that a study of the Word of God would make Timothy, or anyone else, an approved workman.

> Study to shew thyself approved unto God, a workman that needeth not to be ashamed, rightly dividing the word of truth.

The Holy Spirit convicts man of sin in all the ways that we have discussed, but the way that is most effective is when that conviction is tied to the declaration of the truth. In John 16:8-11, the Lord Jesus Christ defined the convicting work of the Holy Spirit in three areas: reproving the world of sin, of righteousness, and of judgment. But all three of these areas were tied to the declaration of truth. "... Of sin, because they believe not on me" assumes that man has heard the truth, since it is not possible to "... believe in him of whom they have not heard" (Romans 10:14).

> And when he is come, he will reprove the world of sin, and of righteousness, and of judgment: Of sin, because they believe not on me; Of righteousness, because I go to my Father, and ye see me no more; Of judgment, because the prince of this world is judged.

In II Thessalonians 2:13-14, the Apostle Paul detailed the convicting work of the Holy Spirit by stating that the Spirit of God separated us to conviction when we were called by the proclamation of the Gospel.

> But we are bound to give thanks alway to God for you, brethren beloved of the Lord, because God hath from the beginning chosen you to salvation through sanctification of the Spirit and belief of the truth: Whereunto he called

you by our gospel, to the obtaining of the glory of our Lord Jesus Christ.

Some people object to the idea that the Holy Spirit "sanctifies" an unbeliever, saying that the work of sanctification is what He does for the believer alone. But there is a sense in which the unbeliever is "sanctified," that is, "set apart" by the Holy Spirit for conviction. We see the word used in that way in I Corinthians 7:13-16 when Paul speaks of the "unbelieving husband" or the "unbelieving wife."

> And the woman which hath an husband that believeth not, and if he be pleased to dwell with her, let her not leave him. For the unbelieving husband is sanctified by the wife, and the unbelieving wife is sanctified by the husband: else were your children unclean; but now are they holy. But if the unbelieving depart, let him depart. A brother or a sister is not under bondage in such cases: but God hath called us to peace. For what knowest thou, O wife, whether thou shalt save thy husband? or how knowest thou, O man, whether thou shalt save thy wife?

The Holy Spirit restrains sin and convicts the unbeliever of sin through the preaching of the Word of God by the saved. This is the most effective way for the Holy Spirit to accomplish conviction.

B. The Holy Spirit's ministry of regeneration

After convicting man of sin, of righteousness, and of judgment, another aspect of the Holy Spirit's work in relation to the salvation of man is regeneration. The Greek word that is translated "regeneration" is the word παλιγγενεσίας [palingenesias] which means "a new Genesis" or "a new beginning." In order to save the believer, the Spirit of Christ had to begin a new "creation," of which Christ is its Head, like Adam was the head of the first creation. The provision of the new creation was for all men, but only believers benefit fully from the new creation.

The Bible uses the word "regeneration" in two different ways. The first way that we will look at is where the "new Genesis" speaks of the coming millennial reign of Christ. That is the usage of the word "regeneration" that we find in Matthew 19:28.

> And Jesus said unto them, Verily I say unto you, That ye which have followed me, in the *regeneration* when the Son of man shall sit in the throne of his glory, ye also shall sit upon twelve thrones, judging the twelve tribes of Israel.

According to Matthew 19:28, the παλιγγενεσίας [*palingenesias*], that is, the "... new beginning is Christ's kingdom. This has nothing to do with the usage of παλιγγενεσίας [*palingenesias*] in Titus 3:5. In this verse it deals with the work of the Holy Spirit in the salvation of the believer where he is washed, given a new "Genesis," and renewed by the Spirit.

> Not by works of righteousness which we have done, but according to his mercy he saved us, by the washing of *regeneration*, and renewing of the Holy Ghost;

C. The Holy Spirit's ministry in the salvation of man

The Spirit of God operates in the salvation of man. We have seen first of all, how the Holy Spirit operated in the provision of a Savior. He was the Agent of the virgin birth of Christ.

In the second place, the Holy Spirit is also the One who baptizes every believer into the Body of Christ as can be seen in I Corinthians 12:13.

> For by one Spirit are we all baptized into one body, whether we be Jews or Gentiles, whether we be bond or free; and have been all made to drink into one Spirit.

In Ephesians 1:12-14, we see the third and the fourth ways in which the Holy Spirit operates in His ministry in the salvation of mankind. He seals every believer to preserve his salvation, and He gives the believer the "earnest" of his inheritance. "... The earnest of our inheritance" (Ephesians 1:14) is His presence in us as a down payment of our future inheritance.

> That we should be to the praise of his glory, who first trusted in Christ. In whom ye also trusted, after that ye heard the word of truth, the gospel of your salvation: in whom also after that ye believed, ye were sealed with that holy Spirit of promise, Which is the earnest of our inheritance until the redemption of the purchased possession, unto the praise of his glory (Ephesians 1:12-14).

A fifth thing that the Holy Spirit does in His work of saving man is that He gives the believer security of his salvation. The very presence of the Holy Spirit in the life of the believer is proof enough of his salvation according to Romans 8:9.

> But ye are not in the flesh, but in the Spirit, if so be that the Spirit of God dwell in you. Now if any man have not the Spirit of Christ, he is none of his.

Jesus spoke of that security in the parable of the Good Shepherd, which is found in John chapter 10. First of all, He gave the parable in verses 1-5. When those present did not understand the parable (verse 6), Jesus explained the parable (verses 7-18). Here we will highlight several things that were stated in the explanation.

The salvation of the believer is only accomplished by Jesus Christ, who stated: "by me if any man enter in, he shall be saved" (verse 9). He also said, "I am the good shepherd, and know my sheep" (verse 14). Our security is that Christ *knows* His sheep. Jesus then said what the Holy Spirit does to make salvation possible: man must "hear" the Word of Christ. The Holy Spirit must open the eyes of his understanding so that he can be saved. Jesus said, "My sheep hear my voice, and I know them, and they follow me: And I give unto them eternal life; and they shall never perish, neither shall any man pluck them out of my hand. My Father, which gave them me, is greater than all; and no man is able to pluck them out of my Father's hand" (verses 27-29).

> Verily, verily, I say unto you, He that entereth not by the door into the sheepfold, but climbeth up some other way,

the same is a thief and a robber. But he that entereth in by the door is the shepherd of the sheep. To him the porter openeth; and the sheep hear his voice: and he calleth his own sheep by name, and leadeth them out. And when he putteth forth his own sheep, he goeth before them, and the sheep follow him: for they know his voice. And a stranger will they not follow, but will flee from him: for they know not the voice of strangers. This parable spake Jesus unto them: but they understood not what things they were which he spake unto them. Then said Jesus unto them again, Verily, verily, I say unto you, I am the door of the sheep. All that ever came before me are thieves and robbers: but the sheep did not hear them. I am the door: by me if any man enter in, he shall be saved, and shall go in and out, and find pasture. The thief cometh not, but for to steal, and to kill, and to destroy: I am come that they might have life, and that they might have it more abundantly. I am the good shepherd: the good shepherd giveth his life for the sheep. But he that is an hireling, and not the shepherd, whose own the sheep are not, seeth the wolf coming, and leaveth the sheep, and fleeth: and the wolf catcheth them, and scattereth the sheep. The hireling fleeth, because he is an hireling, and careth not for the sheep. I am the good shepherd, and know my sheep, and am known of mine. As the Father knoweth me, even so know I the Father: and I lay down my life for the sheep. And other sheep I have, which are not of this fold: them also I must bring, and they shall hear my voice; and there shall be one fold, and one shepherd. Therefore doth my Father love me, because I lay down my life, that I might take it again. No man taketh it from me, but I lay it down of myself. I have power to lay it down, and I have power to take it again. This commandment have I received of my Father. There was a division therefore again among the Jews for these sayings. And many of them said, He hath a devil, and is mad; why hear ye him?

Others said, These are not the words of him that hath a devil. Can a devil open the eyes of the blind? And it was at Jerusalem the feast of the dedication, and it was winter. And Jesus walked in the temple in Solomon's porch. Then came the Jews round about him, and said unto him, How long dost thou make us to doubt? If thou be the Christ, tell us plainly. Jesus answered them, I told you, and ye believed not: the works that I do in my Father's name, they bear witness of me. But ye believe not, because ye are not of my sheep, as I said unto you. My sheep hear my voice, and I know them, and they follow me: And I give unto them eternal life; and they shall never perish, neither shall any man pluck them out of my hand. My Father, which gave them me, is greater than all; and no man is able to pluck them out of my Father's hand. I and my Father are one. Then the Jews took up stones again to stone him. Jesus answered them, Many good works have I shewed you from my Father; for which of those works do ye stone me? The Jews answered him, saying, For a good work we stone thee not; but for blasphemy; and because that thou, being a man, makest thyself God. Jesus answered them, Is it not written in your law, I said, Ye are gods? If he called them gods, unto whom the word of God came, and the scripture cannot be broken; Say ye of him, whom the Father hath sanctified, and sent into the world, Thou blasphemest; because I said, I am the Son of God? If I do not the works of my Father, believe me not. But if I do, though ye believe not me, believe the works: that ye may know, and believe, that the Father is in me, and I in him. Therefore they sought again to take him: but he escaped out of their hand, And went away again beyond Jordan into the place where John at first baptized; and there he abode. And many resorted unto him, and said, John did no miracle: but all things that John spake of this man were true. And many believed on him there (John 10:1–42).

A sixth way that the Spirit of God brings about the salvation of the believer is that He dwells with the believer eternally. Since John 14:16 says that the Holy Spirit abides with the believer forever, there is no way for the believer to lose his salvation. An eternal Comforter secures salvation.

> And I will pray the Father, and he shall give you another Comforter, that he may abide with you for ever;

In the seventh place, the Spirit sanctifies the believer. This declaration of holiness of the believer by the Holy Spirit is an important part of our salvation. Our sanctification gives us a holy standing before a Holy God. Paul wrote, in I Corinthians 6:11, that we are sanctified by the Spirit of our God.

> And such were some of you: but ye are washed, but ye are sanctified, but ye are justified in the name of the Lord Jesus, and by the Spirit of our God.

Peter wrote that our salvation is only possible by the work of the Triune God. It was the Father's foreknowledge, the sprinkling of the blood of Jesus Christ, and the sanctification of the Spirit.

> Elect according to the foreknowledge of God the Father, through sanctification of the Spirit, unto obedience and sprinkling of the blood of Jesus Christ: Grace unto you, and peace, be multiplied (I Peter 1:2).

In Romans 15:16, Paul stated that the salvation of the Gentiles was through the ministry of the Gospel, and the sanctification by the Holy Spirit.

> That I should be the minister of Jesus Christ to the Gentiles, ministering the gospel of God, that the offering up of the Gentiles might be acceptable, being sanctified by the Holy Ghost.

The Spirit dwells in the church

I know that many Christians talk about the indwelling of the Holy Spirit only in the individual believer. While it is true that the Holy Spirit indwells each and every believer individually, has sealed him and is the earnest of his salvation, the verses that we are going to discuss here actually deal with the corporate body, rather than the individuals in that body.

Three times the Apostle Paul addressed the work of the Holy Spirit in the Church. In I Corinthians 6:19-20, he called the church by several different names. In verse 19 he called the church your (plural) body (singular). It is one body made up of a number of people. This is not my personal human body, but the Body of Christ with many members. In the same verse, he called it "... the temple of the Holy Ghost." The church is the Body of Christ and the temple of the Holy Spirit. Paul followed that saying, "... which is in you (plural)." Every use of the word "you," in I Corinthians 6:19-20, is in the plural, as is the word "ye."

> What? know ye not that your body is the temple of the Holy Ghost which is in you, which ye have of God, and ye are not your own? For ye are bought with a price: therefore glorify God in your body, and in your spirit, which are God's.

These verses are clearly talking about the church being the temple of the Holy Spirit. This is likewise true for I Corinthians 3:16-17, where "you" is again plural, not singular.

> Know ye not that ye are the temple of God, and that the Spirit of God dwelleth in you? If any man defile the temple of God, him shall God destroy; for the temple of God is holy, which temple ye are.

While addressing the doctrine of separation, the Apostle Paul specifically dealt with the necessity of ecclesiastical separation, by again calling the church the "temple of God" in II Corinthians 6:14-18. It is obvious that Paul is looking at this as the corporate body since he used "ye" and "you" (plural) throughout the passage. This particular passage is a call to the church to separate, and is viewed as one of the works of the Holy Spirit.

> Be ye not unequally yoked together with unbelievers: for what fellowship hath righteousness with unrighteousness? and what communion hath light with darkness? And what concord hath Christ with Belial? or what part hath he that believeth with an infidel? And what agreement hath the temple of God with idols? for ye are the temple of the living God; as God hath said, I will dwell in them, and walk in them; and I will be their God, and they shall be my people. Wherefore come out from among them, and be ye separate, saith the Lord, and touch not the unclean thing; and I will receive you, And will be a Father unto you, and ye shall be my sons and daughters, saith the Lord Almighty.

As Paul wrote to the church in Ephesus, he took time, in chapter 2, to address the manner in which God had brought Gentiles into the church. In verse 18, he stated that both Jews and Gentiles "... have access by one Spirit unto the Father." Because of the work of the Holy Spirit, Gentiles were no longer "... strangers and foreigners, but fellowcitizens with" the Jewish saints, and members "... of the household of God" (verse 19). He then says that the church is "... an holy temple in the Lord" (verse 21) which was "... built upon the foundation of the apostles and prophets, Jesus Christ himself being the chief corner stone" (verse 20). The individual here is not viewed as the temple, but rather Paul sees all the believers "... together for an habitation of God through the Spirit" (verse 22).

> For through him we both have access by one Spirit unto the Father. Now therefore ye are no more strangers and foreigners, but fellowcitizens with the saints, and of the household of God; And are built upon the foundation of the apostles and prophets, Jesus Christ himself being the chief corner stone; In whom all the building fitly framed

together groweth unto an holy temple in the Lord: In whom ye also are builded together for an habitation of God through the Spirit (Ephesians 2:18-22).

The Holy Spirit has a very special relationship with the church in the work of salvation. The church is the temple of the Holy Spirit and must be kept free of the contamination of sin and the contamination of compromise with the enemy of God.

The Spirit of God's work in the church in relationship to spiritual gifts, and the gifts of Christ, and the gifts of the Father

We will now look at the Spirit of God's relationship to spiritual gifts as well as the gifts of Christ and the gifts of God the Father. This will be a brief study on this, but a more thorough study can be found in my book, *Though I Speak*.

Let's begin this study by looking at I Corinthians 12:1-3. Here Paul addressed the Gentiles in the church at Corinth and explained to them that because of their ignorance in the matter of spiritual gifts, they needed to know how to judge whether or not someone was actually using a spiritual gift. What Paul told these Gentiles was that the first test of a spiritual gift is not having a gift such as that of discernment, wisdom or knowledge, but judging the gift on the basis of agreement with sound doctrine. What was the person saying who supposedly had some spiritual gift? If he was saying that Jesus is accursed, then this is not the Word of God. It is contrary to known doctrinal truth from the Bible, and is therefore, not a spiritual gift.

> Now concerning spiritual gifts, brethren, I would not have you ignorant. Ye know that ye were Gentiles, carried away unto these dumb idols, even as ye were led. Wherefore I give you to understand, that no man speaking by the Spirit of God calleth Jesus accursed: and that no man can say that Jesus is the Lord, but by the Holy Ghost (I Corinthians 12:1-3).

Since signs were given to the Jewish people, while Gentiles sought after wisdom (I Corinthians 1:22), Paul gave Gentiles the wisdom that they needed to be able to understand the use of spiritual gifts in the church. He then began to explain how the Trinity operates in the church in the exercise of spiritual gifts.

A. The Trinity operates in the church

In I Corinthians 12:4-7, Paul divided the work of God in the church into three different categories: first the work of the Spirit (verse 4), second the work of the Lord (verse 5), and third the work of the Father (verse 6).

> Now there are diversities of gifts, but the same Spirit. And there are differences of administrations, but the same Lord. And there are diversities of operations, but it is the same God which worketh all in all. But the manifestation of the Spirit is given to every man to profit withal (I Corinthians 12:4-7).

Paul said that the χαρισμάτων [*charismaton*] (gifts) were given by the the same Spirit (αὐτὸ Πνεῦμα [*auto Pneuma*]). The διακονιῶν [*diakonion*] (administrations), which literally means ministries or services, were given by the same Lord (αὐτὸς Κύριος [*autos Kurios*]), the Lord Jesus Christ. The Father gave the ἐνεργημάτων [*energematon*] (operations) and it says that they come from the same God (αὐτὸς Θεός [*autos theos*]). The word ἐνεργημάτων [*energematon*] is the word from which we get the word "energy." The word means an effect operation.

While there were spiritual gifts in the church, the Holy Spirit gave them. The Lord Jesus Christ chose the men who would be His servants and possess these spiritual gifts. God the Father gave them the energy, or made them effective in the operation of these gifts.

Today, the Holy Spirit gives the "manifestation of the Spirit ... to every man." The Son of God chooses the man who will minister, and the Father still gives the energy needed to serve God.

B. Considering the work of each Person of the Trinity

1. The work of the Holy Spirit in regards to spiritual gifts and the manifestation

Paul describes the work of the Holy Spirit in regards to spiritual gifts and the manifestation of the Spirit in I Corinthians 12:7-18. Spiritual gifts were divided into three categories by the use of two Greek words in verses 8-10. Those two words are ἕτερος [heteros] and ἄλλος [allos]. ἕτερος [heteros] means "another different" thing, while ἄλλος [allos] means "another which is the same." When Jesus spoke of "another Comforter" (John 14:16) He used the word ἄλλος [allos] since He is God, the same as Christ. But when Paul talked about "another gospel" in Galatians 1:6, it was ἕτερος [heteros], another different gospel.

As we read this passage in verses 8-10 we can see how Paul talked about three different categories of spiritual gifts using the words ἕτερος [heteros] and ἄλλος [allos].

> 8 For to one is given by the Spirit the word of wisdom; to another (ἄλλος [allos]) the word of knowledge by the same Spirit; 9 To another (ἕτερος [heteros]) faith by the same Spirit; to another (ἄλλος [allos]) the gifts of healing by the same Spirit; 10 To another (ἄλλος [allos]) the working of miracles; to another (ἄλλος [allos]) prophecy; to another (ἄλλος [allos]) discerning of spirits; to another (ἕτερος [heteros]) divers kinds of tongues; to another (ἄλλος [allos]) the interpretation of tongues:

Paul made the division clear: "Word of wisdom" and "word of knowledge" go together. Those two gifts are called "wonders" and were revelatory in nature. Those gifts were given to the apostles so that God could reveal truth to them. Then we have the gifts of "faith," "healing," "the working of miracles," "prophecy," and "the discerning of spirits." These gifts were all considered "miracles." Lastly, we have the two gifts that were put together of "tongues" and "interpretation of tongues." This category was called "signs."

Paul mentioned these three categories several times, such as in II Corinthians 12:12.

> Truly the signs of an apostle were wrought among you in all patience, in *signs*, and *wonders*, and *mighty deeds* (or miracles).

Back in I Corinthians 12, Paul goes on to say that, unlike the "manifestation of the Spirit" which was given to all believers (I Corinthians 12:7), spiritual gifts were divided by the Spirit "severally as He will" (verse 11). Though it is one body (verse 12), there are only a few eyes, ears, hands, feet, and noses.

> But all these worketh that one and the selfsame Spirit, dividing to every man severally as he will. For as the body is one, and hath many members, and all the members of that one body, being many, are one body: so also is Christ. For by one Spirit are we all baptized into one body, whether we be Jews or Gentiles, whether we be bond or free; and have been all made to drink into one Spirit. For the body is not one member, but many. If the foot shall say, Because I am not the hand, I am not of the body; is it therefore not of the body? And if the ear shall say, Because I am not the eye, I am not of the body; is it therefore not of the body? If the whole body were an eye, where were the hearing? If the whole were hearing, where were the smelling? But now hath God set the members every one of them in the body, as it hath pleased him (I Corinthians 12:11-18).

That was the work of the Holy Spirit with regard to spiritual gifts and the manifestation of the Spirit. Now let's look at the διακονιῶν [*diakonion*] (service) gifts of the Lord Jesus Christ in relationship to the work of the Holy Spirit.

2. The work of the Lord Jesus Christ (διακονιῶν [*diakonion*])

The work of the Lord Jesus Christ is described in Ephesians 4:7-13. Here the Lord chooses the men who will be given spiritual gifts or the manifestation of the Spirit. Paul wrote:

> But unto every one of us is given grace according to the measure of the gift of Christ. Wherefore he saith, When he ascended up on high, he led captivity captive, and gave gifts unto men. (Now that he ascended, what is it but that he also descended first into the lower parts of the earth? He that descended is the same also that ascended up far above all heavens, that he might fill all things.) And he gave *some, apostles*; and *some, prophets*; and *some, evangelists*; and *some, pastors and teachers*; For the perfecting of the saints, for the work of the ministry, for the edifying of the body of Christ: Till we all come in the unity of the faith, and of the knowledge of the Son of God, unto a perfect man, unto the measure of the stature of the fulness of Christ:

Only some were placed in these offices. The Lord Jesus Christ made that choice personally. He chose twelve apostles, and only twelve (Revelation 21:14). He alone chose prophets, evangelists, and pastor-teachers. Today, He chooses men for the perfecting of the saints and the edifying of the body of Christ (Ephesians 4:12). The Son chooses the man and the Holy Spirit gives him the manifestation of the Spirit. Now, what does the Father do?

3. The work of the Father (ἐνεργημάτων [*energematon*])

When Paul wrote Romans chapter 12, he detailed the way that God the Father works in the church in regards to the gifts of the Spirit and the men that the Son of God chooses to work in the church. The Father energizes, or makes effective the different men with different manifestations of the Spirit. There is perfect unity in the way that the Father and the Son work together with the Holy Spirit.

The Relationship of the Holy Spirit to the Works of God

Paul first addressed the Father's working with the gifts (χαρίσματα [*Charismata*]) of the Spirit (Romans 12:6). Next, Paul addressed the Father's work in making those servants (διακονίαν [*diakonian*]) that were chosen by Christ to be effective in their work (Romans 12:7). In Romans 12:6-16, Paul wrote how the different men with different manifestations were to function with the energy that would come from God the Father.

> I beseech you therefore, brethren, by the mercies of God, that ye present your bodies a living sacrifice, holy, acceptable unto God, which is your reasonable service. And be not conformed to this world: but be ye transformed by the renewing of your mind, that ye may prove what is that good, and acceptable, and perfect, will of God. For I say, through the grace given unto me, to every man that is among you, not to think of himself more highly than he ought to think; but to think soberly, according as God hath dealt to every man the measure of faith. For as we have many members in one body, and all members have not the same office: So we, being many, are one body in Christ, and every one members one of another. Having then gifts differing according to the grace that is given to us, whether prophecy, let us prophesy according to the proportion of faith; Or ministry, let us wait on our ministering: or he that teacheth, on teaching; Or he that exhorteth, on exhortation: he that giveth, let him do it with simplicity; he that ruleth, with diligence; he that sheweth mercy, with cheerfulness. Let love be without dissimulation. Abhor that which is evil; cleave to that which is good. Be kindly affectioned one to another with brotherly love; in honour preferring one another; Not slothful in business; fervent in spirit; serving the Lord; Rejoicing in hope; patient in tribulation; continuing instant in prayer; Distributing to the necessity of saints; given to hospitality. Bless them which persecute you: bless, and curse not. Rejoice with them that do rejoice,

and weep with them that weep. Be of the same mind one toward another. Mind not high things, but condescend to men of low estate. Be not wise in your own conceits.

We have considered the relationship of the Holy Spirit to the other Members of the Triune Godhead, and His relationship to some of the Works of God. In the next chapter, we will consider His names, and how those names tell us about His character and His wonderful Person.

Chapter Seven

THE NAMES AND THE SYMBOLS OF THE HOLY SPIRIT

The names and symbols of the Holy Spirit could be organized in many ways. Some people would rather have His names listed in alphabetical order. Others would list His names according to His ministry. I am going to list His names as they are related to His Person and His attributes, His relationship to God the Father, His relationship to the Son of God, and the names that are related to His ministry. Later, we will also look at the Biblical symbols that represent the Holy Spirit.

The names of the Holy Spirit

A. The names of the Holy Spirit that deal with His Person and His attributes

What do we mean when we say that some names deal with the Person of the Holy Spirit? These are names that directly tell us Who He is and speak about His personality or His personhood. These names also identify Him with the attributes of God, which then prove His deity.

The first name that we will consider is where He is simply called, *"the Spirit"* in I Corinthians 2:10. *"The Spirit"* is not only His name, but it also identifies Him with the attribute of Spirituality.

> But God hath revealed them unto us by his Spirit: for *the Spirit* searcheth all things, yea, the deep things of God.

The second name that we will consider is His name, "*the Holy Spirit*" or "*the Holy Ghost.*" This name is one of the most frequently used names for the Third Person of the Trinity and not only identifies Him with the attribute of Spirituality, but also with the attribute of holiness. We find this name in I Corinthians 6:19, as well as many other places in the Bible.

> What? know ye not that your body is the temple of *the Holy Ghost* which is in you, which ye have of God, and ye are not your own?

Jesus Christ Himself in Luke 11:13, referred to the Third Person of the Godhead as the *Holy Spirit.*

> If ye then, being evil, know how to give good gifts unto your children: how much more shall your heavenly Father give *the Holy Spirit* to them that ask him?

A third name, which is closely related to the name *the Holy Spirit*, is the name, "*the Spirit of Holiness.*" This name, just as the name *the Holy Spirit*, directly refers to Him with the attributes of spirituality and holiness. We find Him called "*the Spirit of Holiness*" in Romans 1:4.

> And declared to be the Son of God with power, according to *the spirit of holiness*, by the resurrection from the dead:

In Hebrews 9:14, Paul calls the Holy Spirit by the name, "*the Eternal Spirit.*" This not only identifies Him with His personality, but also with His attributes of spirituality and eternality.

> How much more shall the blood of Christ, who through *the eternal Spirit* offered himself without spot to God, purge your conscience from dead works to serve the living God?

In the fifth place, the attributes of personality and grace are found in His name "*the Spirit of Grace.*" Paul used this name in Hebrews 10:29.

> Of how much sorer punishment, suppose ye, shall he be thought worthy, who hath trodden under foot the Son of God, and hath counted the blood of the covenant, wherewith he was sanctified, an unholy thing, and hath done despite unto the *Spirit of grace?*

The sixth name that we will consider is found in Psalm 51:12, where the Holy Spirit is identified as the "Free Spirit." The Hebrew word translated "free" is נָדִיב [*nadiyb*] which the lexicon[1] defines as:

> 1 inclined, willing, noble, generous. 1A incited, inclined, willing. 1B noble, princely (in rank). 1C noble (in mind and character). 2 noble one.

In calling the Spirit the "inclined or willing" Spirit, David is not only giving the Holy Spirit the attribute of spirituality, but that of volition as well. The Spirit of God is the Free Spirit, that is a Person, who is capable of freely choosing what He wants to do, according to Psalm 51:12.

> Restore unto me the joy of thy salvation; and uphold me with thy free spirit.

In Nehemiah 9:20, we find the seventh name that we will examine. In this verse Nehemiah calls the Spirit of God, "*the Good Spirit.*" This name again identifies the Holy Spirit with the attributes of God. "Good" recognizes Him with the attributes of love and righteousness.

> Thou gavest also thy *good spirit* to instruct them, and withheldest not thy manna from their mouth, and gavest them water for their thirst.

David reaffirmed these attributes in Psalm 143:10, saying:

---

1 Strong, J. (1995). Enhanced Strong's Lexicon. Woodside Bible Fellowship, #5081.

> Teach me to do thy will; for thou art my God: *thy spirit is good*; lead me into the land of uprightness.

The eighth name of the Spirit of God is the "*Spirit of Truth.*" Jesus called Him the "*Spirit of Truth*" in John 14:17. This name not only attributes spirituality to Him but also truth, which is another attribute of God.

> Even *the Spirit of truth*; whom the world cannot receive, because it seeth him not, neither knoweth him: but ye know him; for he dwelleth with you, and shall be in you.

Christ again referred to the Holy Spirit as the "*Spirit of Truth*" in John 15:26.

> But when the Comforter is come, whom I will send unto you from the Father, even *the Spirit of truth*, which proceedeth from the Father, he shall testify of me:

In Romans 8:2, we find the ninth name of the Holy Spirit that identifies Him with the attribute of personality. Paul called the Third Person of the Trinity, the "*Spirit of Life.*" This identified Him with the attributes of life and self-existence.

> For the law of *the Spirit of life* in Christ Jesus hath made me free from the law of sin and death.

A few verses later, in Romans 8:10, Paul again identified the Holy Spirit with the attribute of life, saying that *the Spirit is life*.

> And if Christ be in you, the body is dead because of sin; but *the Spirit is life* because of righteousness.

In Revelation 11:11, the Apostle John called the Spirit of God, the "*Spirit of Life.*"

> And after three days and an half *the Spirit of life* from God entered into them, and they stood upon their feet; and great fear fell upon them which saw them.

In Isaiah 11:2, the prophet gave seven different names for the Holy Spirit. We will look at three of them here, since these three address His Person or His attributes.

The first of these three names is the name, the *"Spirit of Wisdom."* This name is the tenth name we have discovered in this section, and it speaks of His attribute of perfection. The Spirit always decides perfectly since He is the *"Spirit of Wisdom."*

Isaiah 11:2 also calls Him the *"Spirit of Knowledge,"* which is the eleventh name associating Him with personality, and then the attribute of omniscience. The Holy Spirit knows all things. He is God.

The twelfth name that we will consider in this section likewise comes from Isaiah 11:2. He was called the *"Spirit of Might."* This name of the Holy Spirit goes way beyond personality and attributes omnipotence to Him.

> And the spirit of the LORD shall rest upon him, *the spirit of wisdom* and understanding, *the spirit of* counsel and might, *the spirit of knowledge* and of the fear of the LORD;

B. The names of the Holy Spirit that deal with His relationship with God the Father

The second section of this chapter deals with the names of the Holy Spirit that speak of His relationship with God the Father. Some of these names may be interpreted to equally speak of His relationship to the Son of God as well.

The first name that we will consider that associates Him with God the Father is the name, the *"Spirit of God,"* which we find in I Corinthians 3:16.

> Know ye not that ye are the temple of God, and that the *Spirit of God* dwelleth in you?

In Isaiah 11:2, we find a second name that was used by the prophet Isaiah, who called Him the *Spirit of the LORD* (Jehovah).

> And the *spirit of the LORD* shall rest upon him, the spirit of wisdom and understanding, the spirit of counsel and might, the spirit of knowledge and of the fear of the LORD;

The third name that we will examine that associates the Holy Spirit with God the Father was also used by the prophet Isaiah. In Isaiah 61:1, He was called the *"Spirit of the Lord GOD"* (Jehovah Adonai).

> The *Spirit of the Lord GOD* is upon me; because the LORD hath anointed me to preach good tidings unto the meek; he hath sent me to bind up the brokenhearted, to proclaim liberty to the captives, and the opening of the prison to them that are bound;

A fourth name that associates the Holy Spirit with God the Father can be found in II Corinthians 3:3. Here the Apostle Paul calls Him the *"Spirit of the Living God."*

> Forasmuch as ye are manifestly declared to be the epistle of Christ ministered by us, written not with ink, but with the *Spirit of the living God*; not in tables of stone, but in fleshy tables of the heart.

Peter called the Spirit of God the *"Spirit of Glory and of God,"* in I Peter 4:14. This is the fifth name of the Holy Spirit that links Him to the Father.

> If ye be reproached for the name of Christ, happy are ye; for the *spirit of glory and of God* resteth upon you: on their part he is evil spoken of, but on your part he is glorified.

Peter, in Acts 5:3-4, after calling Him the Holy Ghost, directly called Him *"God."* This is the sixth name that we will consider.

> But Peter said, Ananias, why hath Satan filled thine heart to lie to the Holy Ghost, and to keep back part of the price of the land? Whiles it remained, was it not thine own?

and after it was sold, was it not in thine own power? why hast thou conceived this thing in thine heart? thou hast not lied unto men, but unto *God.*

The seventh name that we will consider in this section is found in Job 33:4. The Holy Spirit here is first called the Spirit of God, and then He is referred to as the *"Breath of the Almighty."*

The Spirit of God hath made me, and *the breath of the Almighty* hath given me life.

The eighth name that we will consider is where Jesus called the Holy Spirit, the *"Spirit of Your Father,"* in Matthew 10:20.

For it is not ye that speak, but the *Spirit of your Father* which speaketh in you.

Moses called the Spirit of God *"His Spirit,"* which is the ninth name that we will examine that links the Holy Spirit to God the Father.

And Moses said unto him, Enviest thou for my sake? would God that all the LORD'S people were prophets, and that the LORD would put *his spirit* upon them (Numbers 11:29)!

And the Apostle Paul, in I Corinthians 2:10, used this same designation for the Spirit of God.

But God hath revealed them unto us by *his Spirit*: for the Spirit searcheth all things, yea, the deep things of God.

We find the tenth name of the Holy Spirit in Isaiah 63:10–11. Here the prophet called the Spirit of God, *"His Holy Spirit."*

But they rebelled, and vexed *his holy Spirit*: therefore he was turned to be their enemy, and he fought against them. Then he remembered the days of old, Moses, and his people, saying, Where is he that brought them up out

of the sea with the shepherd of his flock? where is he
that put *his holy Spirit* within him?

The Apostle Paul likewise used the name, "*His Holy Spirit*" in I Thessalonians 4:8.

He therefore that despiseth, despiseth not man, but God, who hath also given unto us *his holy Spirit*.

The eleventh name that strongly associates the Holy Spirit with God the Father can be found, first of all, in Nehemiah 9:30. Here the Holy Spirit is called "*Thy Spirit*."

Yet many years didst thou forbear them, and testifiedst against them by *thy spirit* in thy prophets: yet would they not give ear: therefore gavest thou them into the hand of the people of the lands.

He is again called "*Thy Spirit*" in Psalm 143:10.

Teach me to do thy will; for thou art my God: *thy spirit* is good; lead me into the land of uprightness.

The twelfth and last way that we will look at where the Holy Spirit was named in His relationship with God the Father is found in John 15:26. Jesus called Him "the *Comforter ... Which Proceedeth from the Father.*"

But when the *Comforter* is come, whom I will send unto you from the Father, even the Spirit of truth, *which proceedeth from the Father*, he shall testify of me:

C. The names of the Holy Spirit that deal with His relationship with the Son of God

Some of the names of the Holy Spirit identify Him with the Son of God. In many verses where the Holy Spirit is named in relation to Jesus Christ it also mentions His relationship to the Father. The names that relate the Spirit to the Son of God are very important

The Names and Symbols of the Holy Spirit

to examine, since they give us insight into the workings of the relationships of the Godhead.

The first name that we will consider for the Third Person of the Triune God is found in Romans 8:9. The name that Paul uses for Him here is the *"Spirit of Christ."* Notice that Paul first calls Him *the Spirit*, then *the Spirit of God*, and then *the Spirit of Christ*.

> But ye are not in the flesh, but in the Spirit, if so be that the Spirit of God dwell in you. Now if any man have not the *Spirit of Christ*, he is none of his.

In Galatians 4:6, we find the second name that we will consider for the Spirit of God which relates Him to the Son of God. Here the Holy Spirit is called the *"Spirit of His Son."*

> And because ye are sons, God hath sent forth the *Spirit of his Son* into your hearts, crying, Abba, Father.

In the third place, Paul called the Holy Spirit *"the Spirit of the Lord"* in II Corinthians 3:18.

> But we all, with open face beholding as in a glass the glory of the Lord, are changed into the same image from glory to glory, even as by the *Spirit of the Lord*.

The fourth name that we will look at is found in Acts 16:6–10. Luke begins by saying that Paul and the others "... were forbidden of *the Holy Ghost* to preach" the Gospel in Asia (Acts 16:6). Then Luke called Him *"the Spirit"* in Acts 16:7 where it says that *"the Spirit suffered them not."* The Holy Spirit then led the group to Troas where Paul had a vision of "... a man of Macedonia" (Acts 16:9). At that point Luke calls the Holy Spirit *"the Lord"* (Acts 16:10).

> Now when they had gone throughout Phrygia and the region of Galatia, and were forbidden of the Holy Ghost to preach the word in Asia, After they were come to Mysia, they assayed to go into Bithynia: but the Spirit suffered them not. And they passing by Mysia came down to

Troas. And a vision appeared to Paul in the night; There stood a man of Macedonia, and prayed him, saying, Come over into Macedonia, and help us. And after he had seen the vision, immediately we endeavoured to go into Macedonia, assuredly gathering that the Lord had called us for to preach the gospel unto them.

The fifth name that we will look at that relates the Holy Spirit to the Son of God is found in Philippians 1:19. Here the Apostle Paul calls the Third Person of the Trinity the *"Spirit of Jesus Christ."*

> For I know that this shall turn to my salvation through your prayer, and the supply of *the Spirit of Jesus Christ*,

D. The names of the Holy Spirit that deal with His ministry

The last category of names for the Holy Spirit that we will consider are the names relating to His different ministries and works. While many of these names are unique, it should be noted that many of the names that we referenced above that speak of His Person and His attributes could also be listed here. For instance, calling the Holy Spirit the *"Spirit of Truth"* also deals with His ministry in the inspiration, preservation, and illumination of the Word of God. Calling Him the *"Spirit of Life"* also speaks of His work in the impartation of eternal life through the preaching of the Gospel. When we call Him the *"Holy Spirit"*, we are also talking about His work in the sanctification of the believer in Jesus Christ. Let us go back and look at those names again as we study the relationship of the Holy Spirit to His ministries or His works.

The first six names that we will consider are found in Isaiah 11:2. The Holy Spirit's ministries are listed in the following six names given to Him there: the *"Spirit of Wisdom,"* the *"Spirit of Understanding,"* the *"Spirit of Counsel,"* the *"Spirit of Might,"* the *"Spirit of Knowledge,"* and the *"Spirit of the Fear of the LORD."*

> And the spirit of the LORD shall rest upon him, the *spirit of wisdom* and *understanding*, the *spirit of counsel* and *might*, the *spirit of knowledge* and of the *fear of the LORD*;

The Names and Symbols of the Holy Spirit 239

Another ministry of the Holy Spirit was to anoint the Lord Jesus Christ. The seventh name that is given to Him directly relates to that ministry. In Hebrews 1:9, He is called the *"Oil of Gladness."*

> Thou hast loved righteousness, and hated iniquity; therefore God, even thy God, hath anointed thee with the *oil of gladness* above thy fellows.

In John's Gospel we find the eighth name of the Holy Spirit. The Lord Jesus Christ gave Him this name. It speaks of His ministry to come along side of, or beside the believer to defend him. Here, the Lord called the Holy Spirit the *"Comforter."*

> But the *Comforter*, which is the Holy Ghost, whom the Father will send in my name, he shall teach you all things, and bring all things to your remembrance, whatsoever I have said unto you (John 14:26). ... But when the *Comforter* is come, whom I will send unto you from the Father, even the Spirit of truth, which proceedeth from the Father, he shall testify of me (John 15:26). ... Nevertheless I tell you the truth; It is expedient for you that I go away: for if I go not away, the *Comforter* will not come unto you; but if I depart, I will send him unto you (John 16:7).

John spoke of the Lord Jesus Christ as the "Advocate" in I John 2:1. The word "Advocate" is the translation of the same Greek word that was translated "Comforter" in the passages quoted from John above.

> My little children, these things write I unto you, that ye sin not. And if any man sin, we have an *advocate* with the Father, Jesus Christ the righteous:

A ninth name that we find for the Holy Spirit is the *"Power of the Highest."* This name, which is found in Luke 1:35, relates Him to His work in relation to the conception of Jesus Christ in the womb of Mary.

And the angel answered and said unto her, The Holy Ghost shall come upon thee, and the power of the Highest shall overshadow thee: therefore also that holy thing which shall be born of thee shall be called the Son of God.

In Romans 8:15, the Apostle Paul calls Him the "*Spirit of Adoption.*" This relates to the ministry of making the one who has been "born" into God's family, an adult son of God, at the very moment he believes. The Jewish people call this Bar Mitzvah. This is not "adoption" in the typical Gentile understanding of "adoption." The Jewish people never "*adopted*" an orphaned child. The nearest kinsman had to *redeem* him. He was then kept as a member of the family. The Christian *was born* into God's family (John 1:12-13; 3:3). God brings in His children that are born into His family as adults and responsible for their actions at the time of the new birth. That is why Romans 8:15 calls the Third Person of the Godhead the "*Spirit of adoption.*"

> For ye have not received the spirit of bondage again to fear; but ye have received the *Spirit of adoption*, whereby we cry, Abba, Father.

In Isaiah 4:4, God gave another name to the Spirit. He called Him the "*Spirit of Judgment*," and this is the eleventh name in our list of names that relate to His ministries or works.

> When the Lord shall have washed away the filth of the daughters of Zion, and shall have purged the blood of Jerusalem from the midst thereof by the *spirit of judgment*, and by the spirit of burning.

Isaiah 28:6 again spoke of the Holy Spirit as the "*Spirit of Judgment*," when Israel was facing coming judgment.

> And for a *spirit of judgment* to him that sitteth in judgment, and for strength to them that turn the battle to the gate.

One of the ministries of the Holy Spirit is judgment. He is still the "*Spirit of Judgment*" today, as Jesus said in John 16:7-11.

> Nevertheless I tell you the truth; It is expedient for you that I go away: for if I go not away, the Comforter will not come unto you; but if I depart, I will send him unto you. And when he is come, he will reprove the world of sin, and of righteousness, and *of judgment*: Of sin, because they believe not on me; Of righteousness, because I go to my Father, and ye see me no more; *Of judgment*, because the prince of this world is judged.

The twelfth name that we will consider for the Spirit of Holiness in our list of names that deals with His ministries or works is the "*Spirit of Life*." Paul used this name for Him in Romans 8:2. This name identifies Him as the One Who gave life to the dust that the Son of God had formed in the Garden of Eden (Genesis 2:7). He is the One who gave us life the moment that we believed (Ephesians 2:5).

> For the law of the *Spirit of life* in Christ Jesus hath made me free from the law of sin and death (Romans 8:2).

He is also the One who raises the dead, as can be seen in Revelation 11:11.

> And after three days and an half the *Spirit of life* from God entered into them, and they stood upon their feet; and great fear fell upon them which saw them.

In Revelation 19:10, we find the thirteenth name that we will study that relates the Holy Spirit to one of His ministries; it is the "*Spirit of Prophecy*" This particular name relates Him to one aspect of His ministry which is the inspiration of the Scriptures.

> And I fell at his feet to worship him. And he said unto me, See thou do it not: I am thy fellowservant, and of thy brethren that have the testimony of Jesus: worship God: for the testimony of Jesus is the *spirit of prophecy*.

In His relationship to the inspiration of the Word of God, we also find the fourteenth name for the Spirit; He is called the "*Spirit of Revelation*" in Ephesians 1:17.

That the God of our Lord Jesus Christ, the Father of glory, may give unto you the *spirit of* wisdom and *revelation* in the knowledge of him:

The last name that we will consider for the Third Person of the Triune Godhead is the *"Holy Spirit of Promise."* This name is found in Ephesians 1:13 and relates Him to the Scriptures again. His promise is that which we must believe.

In whom ye also trusted, after that ye heard the word of truth, the gospel of your salvation: in whom also after that ye believed, ye were sealed with that *holy Spirit of promise,*

The symbols of the Holy Spirit

There are nine different symbols that represent the Holy Spirit. These symbols generally refer to some aspect of His ministry. Our usage of the word symbol has the meaning of the dictionary[2] definition:

1. a mark or character used as a conventional representation of an object, function, or process, e.g. the letter or letters standing for a chemical element or a character in musical notation.

1.1 a shape or sign used to represent something such as an organization, e.g. a red cross or a Star of David.

2. a thing that represents or stands for something else, especially a material object representing something abstract, e.g. "the limousine was another symbol of his wealth and authority"

---

2 https://www.lexico.com/en/definition/symbol

A. Clothing

The first symbol of the Holy Spirit that we will consider is found in Luke 24:49. That symbol, which speaks of the Holy Spirit, is that of clothing and is found in the word *"endued."*

> And, behold, I send the promise of my Father upon you: but tarry ye in the city of Jerusalem, until ye be *endued* with power from on high.

The lexicon[3] defines the Greek word (ἐνδύω [*enduo*]) which is translated "endued" as:

> 1 to sink into (clothing), put on, clothe one's self.

This word was used by Christ to speak of *"clothing"* the apostles with the power of God.

B. The Earnest[4] (the Down-payment)

The second symbol of the Holy Spirit is found in the reference to Him as the *"Earnest"* which means the *"down payment"* of our salvation. He is twice referred to as the Down Payment in II Corinthians

> Who hath also sealed us, and given *the earnest* of the Spirit in our hearts (II Corinthians 1:22). ... Now he that hath wrought us for the selfsame thing is God, who also hath given unto us *the earnest* of the Spirit (II Corinthians 5:5).

The Holy Spirit is specifically mentioned as the *"Earnest,"* or *"Down payment"* of our future guaranteed inheritance in Ephesians 1:14.

---

3 Strong, J., #1746.
4 ἀρραβών [*arrhabon*] n m. Of Hebrew origin. 1 an earnest. 1A money which in purchases is given as a pledge or down payment that the full amount will subsequently be paid (Strong, J. (1995). *Enhanced Strong's Lexicon*. Woodside Bible Fellowship, #728).

> Which is *the earnest* of our inheritance until the redemption of the purchased possession, unto the praise of his glory.

C. The Dove

All four Gospel accounts use the *"Dove"* as a symbol of the Holy Spirit. The *"Dove"* symbolized several things about the Holy Spirit. First of all, the Holy Spirit comes down from Heaven. Second, the *"Dove"* is white, which speaks of His purity and holiness. Third, the *"Dove"* is peaceful and is not a predator. Fourth, the *"Dove"* does not come swooping down, but rather is gentle and "lights" where it lands. And last, the *"Dove"* is a clean animal, which speaks of His righteousness.

In Matthew 3:16, the Holy Spirit is spoken of as being *"... like a dove."*

> And Jesus, when he was baptized, went up straightway out of the water: and, lo, the heavens were opened unto him, and he saw the Spirit of God descending *like a dove*, and lighting upon him:

Again, in Mark 1:10, He is referred to with the words, *"... like a dove."*

> And straightway coming up out of the water, he saw the heavens opened, and the Spirit *like a dove* descending upon him:

Luke 3:22 also refers to the Holy Spirit as descending *"... like a dove."*

> And the Holy Ghost descended in a bodily shape *like a dove* upon him, and a voice came from heaven, which said, Thou art my beloved Son; in thee I am well pleased.

It is no surprise that the three Synoptic Gospels all used similar language in describing something, but John often used more distinct language about the same event. That was not true though in his description of the Holy Spirit in John 1:32. He likewise described the Spirit as descending "... *like a dove.*"

> And John bare record, saying, I saw the Spirit descending from heaven *like a dove*, and it abode upon him.

D.   Fire

Symbolically, the Bible often refers to the Holy Spirit as fire. In Acts 2:3, the Spirit's gift of tongues, bestowed on the apostles on the day of Pentecost, was described as "... *like as of fire.*"

> And there appeared unto them cloven tongues *like as of fire*, and it sat upon each of them.

The promise and the oath that were made by the Spirit of God to Abraham describe God's Spirit as "... *a smoking furnace and a burning lamp*" in Genesis 15:17.

> And it came to pass, that, when the sun went down, and it was dark, behold *a smoking furnace, and a burning lamp* that passed between those pieces.

Fire was again used as a symbol of the Holy Spirit when God appeared to Moses as "... *a flame of fire out of the midst of a bush*" and as a "... *bush burned with fire.*" We read about it in Exodus 3:2–6.

> And the angel of the LORD appeared unto him in a *flame of fire out of the midst of a bush: and he looked, and, behold, the bush burned with fire, and the bush was not consumed.* And Moses said, I will now turn aside, and see this great sight, why the bush is not burnt. And when the LORD saw that he turned aside to see, God called unto him out of the midst of the bush, and said, Moses, Moses. And he said, Here am I. And he said, Draw not nigh hither: put off thy shoes from off thy feet, for the place whereon thou standest is holy ground. Moreover he said, I am the God of thy father, the God of Abraham, the God of Isaac,

and the God of Jacob. And Moses hid his face; for he was afraid to look upon God.

As the Holy Spirit led the Children of Israel through the desert, He used *a pillar of fire* to give them light, according to Exodus 13:21-22.

> And the LORD went before them by day in a pillar of a cloud, to lead them the way; and *by night in a pillar of fire, to give them light*; to go by day and night: He took not away the pillar of the cloud by day, nor the pillar of fire by night, from before the people.

When He descended upon Mount Sinai, He did that "*... in fire*" according to Exodus 19:18.

> And mount Sinai was altogether on a smoke, because *the LORD descended upon it in fire*: and the smoke thereof ascended as the smoke of a furnace, and the whole mount quaked greatly.

The symbol of "fire" to represent the Holy Spirit is also seen in Exodus 24:17 where it calls Him a "*... devouring fire on the top of the mount.*"

> And the sight of the glory of the LORD was like *devouring fire on the top of the mount* in the eyes of the children of Israel.

The abiding presence of the Spirit of the LORD can be seen in the tabernacle in Exodus 40:38, where it says that "*... fire was on it by night.*"

> For the cloud of the LORD was upon the tabernacle by day, and *fire was on it by night*, in the sight of all the house of Israel, throughout all their journeys.

E. Oil

Oil is another frequently used symbol of the Holy Spirit that is found in the Scriptures. In Israel, oil was used in anointing the prophet, the priest, the king, and the judge. Therefore, Messiah as prophet, priest, king and judge had to be anointed, not with simple oil, but with the Holy Spirit. Luke 4:18 uses this type of an illustration speaking of *the Holy Spirit's anointing of Christ*.

> The Spirit of the Lord is upon me, because he hath *anointed* me to preach the gospel to the poor; he hath sent me to heal the brokenhearted, to preach deliverance to the captives, and recovering of sight to the blind, to set at liberty them that are bruised,

When Peter preached the Gospel to Cornelius and his household, he told him how Jesus of Nazareth was *anointed with the Holy Ghost* in Acts 10:38.

> How God *anointed* Jesus of Nazareth with the Holy Ghost and with power: who went about doing good, and healing all that were oppressed of the devil; for God was with him.

In II Corinthians 1:21, Paul talked about being *anointed*.

> Now he which stablisheth us with you in Christ, and *hath anointed us*, is God;

In I John 2:20, the same Greek word that was twice translated "*anointing*" was translated as "*unction*," which means the same thing. The Holy Spirit is called the Holy One in this verse.

> But ye have an *unction* from the Holy One, and ye know all things.

F. The Seal

The next symbol of the Holy Spirit to consider is *the seal*. Paul used this symbol for the Holy Spirit in II Corinthians 1:22.

> Who hath also sealed us, and given the earnest of the Spirit in our hearts.

Paul also used the symbol of *the seal* representing the Holy Spirit twice in the Epistle to the Ephesians. He used it first in Ephesians 1:13, where he stated that this was done immediately "... after that ye believed."

> In whom ye also trusted, after that ye heard the word of truth, the gospel of your salvation: in whom also after that ye believed, ye were *sealed* with that holy Spirit of promise,

Paul then used it again, in Ephesians 4:30, when he stated that the Holy Spirit has *sealed* the believer "... unto the day of redemption".

> And grieve not the holy Spirit of God, whereby ye are *sealed* unto the day of redemption.

G. Water

Another symbol for the Holy Spirit is *water*. John 4:14 alluded to the Holy Spirit when Jesus told the woman at Jacob's well that the water that He would give would spring "... up into everlasting life."

> But whosoever drinketh of the *water* that I shall give him shall never thirst; but the *water* that I shall give him shall be in him a well of *water* springing up into everlasting life.

In John 7:38-39, the Lord was much more specific in His application of the symbolism of *water*. Here the Apostle John explained, "... this spake He of the Spirit."

> He that believeth on me, as the scripture hath said, out of his belly shall flow rivers of living *water*. (But this spake he of the Spirit, which they that believe on him should

receive: for the Holy Ghost was not yet given; because that Jesus was not yet glorified.)

H. The Wind

Another symbol for the Holy Spirit is *the wind*. Jesus used this as He was telling Nicodemus how to be born again in John 3:8.

> The *wind* bloweth where it listeth, and thou hearest the sound thereof, but canst not tell whence it cometh, and whither it goeth: so is every one that is born of the Spirit.

Luke described the coming of the Holy Spirit on the day of Pentecost as the "... sound from heaven as of *a rushing mighty wind*" according to Acts 2:2.

> And suddenly there came a sound from heaven as of *a rushing mighty wind*, and it filled all the house where they were sitting.

I. The Light

Light is the last symbol of the Holy Spirit that we will consider at this time. This particular symbol speaks of the Holy Spirit's ministry of calling the unbeliever out of spiritual darkness and into *the light*. This ministry is what we call illumination. In Luke chapter fifteen, the Lord Jesus Christ gave the parable of the three lost things and the three seekers. In Luke 15:4-7, Jesus told about one lost sheep, and the Seeking Good Shepherd, the Lord Jesus Christ. In Luke 15:11-39, He told about the one lost Son and the Seeking Father. Sandwiched between these passages, Luke 15:8-11 tells of the lost coin and the Seeking Holy Spirit, represented by the woman. What does the Holy Spirit do to find the lost coin? He *lights a candle* (illumination) and sweeps the house (sanctification) according to Luke 15:8

> Either what woman having ten pieces of silver, if she lose one piece, doth not *light a candle*, and sweep the house, and seek diligently till she find it?

That work of turning on the light in the heart of the unbeliever is absolutely necessary for his salvation. But the Holy Spirit does not stop the work of illumination in the life of that man once he is saved. According to Ephesians 5:8, He continues to give the believer light.

> For ye were sometimes darkness, but now *are ye light* in the Lord: walk as *children of light*:

As we come to the conclusion of this book on Pneumatology, we have only begun a study that every Christian must continue to learn and appreciate. We need to know Him and all the ways He ministers in our lives. We must be sensitive to His promptings and His leading, and obedient to His Word, which is the Sword of the Spirit. Let's not forget that good doctrine always leads to living a godly life.

CPSIA information can be obtained
at www.ICGtesting.com
Printed in the USA
BVHW091949300121
599169BV00002B/225

9 781630 733629